The Practical Guide to America

Entertaining American History for Curious People

Practical Guides
Book 3

Tom McHale

Practical Guides

Contents

Introduction   v

Part One
Foundations and Revolution

1. America: The Prequel   3
2. How to Start a Country (Without Getting Hanged)   13
3. The Mad Scientists of 1776   26
4. Washington: The Man Who Wouldn't Be King   39
5. The Constitution: America's Owners' Manual   45

Part Two
Growing Pains

6. Founding Frenemies: Hamilton vs. Jefferson   57
7. Napoleon's Fire Sale, Jefferson's Jackpot   68
8. The War of 1812: America's Forgotten Sequel   74
9. Trail of Tears: The Dark Cost of Expansion   82
10. Manifest Destiny and the Wild Westward Push   90

Part Three
The Civil War and Reconstruction

11. Compromise Fails   103
12. The Civil War   114
13. Time to Rebuild: The Reconstruction Era   128

Part Four
Industrializing and Immigrating

14. Steam, Steel & Strikes   139
15. Liberty... Imported!   151
16. Cowboys, Indians, and Hollywood Myths   162

Part Five

World Power and Progress

17. Teddy Time: Roosevelt Rewires the Presidency   173
18. World War I   182
19. The Roaring Twenties: Fast Cars, Fast Money, and a Crash   193

Part Six

Hard Times and Big Government

20. FDR and the Alphabet Soup of Salvation   207
21. World War II: When America Went All-In   217

Part Seven

The Cold War Era

22. Reds, Rockets, and Refrigerator Spies   239
23. Back to the Civil Rights Movement   249
24. Vietnam and the Limits of Power   259

Part Eight

Modern Times

25. From Hippies to Yuppies   273
26. Reagan, Gorbachev, and the End of the Cold War   287
27. 21st Century War   296
28. The Geeks Shall Inherit the Earth   309
29. Space, the Next Frontier. Again.   326
30. What's Next?   336

About the Author   339
Also by Tom McHale   341

Introduction

America.

Sigh. Right off the bat, you're thinking the guy who wrote this book doesn't even know the proper name of the United States. Well, the title of this book isn't technically correct. I suppose it should read, "The Practical Guide to the United States of America." But, as a career marketing guy, it hurt my soul to call it that. It lacks a harmonious ring, and the book's cover would look far too busy.

So, in the interest of "a more pleasant sounding title" and our collective visual comfort, I made a forced error right off the bat. Hopefully, my credibility remains intact as I readily admit to the faux pas and intend to correct it post haste.

So, before I get myself into more trouble, let's address the misnomer.

America technically refers to the entire landmass represented by the continents of North and South America. So, think of all the countries in South America, those kind of in the middle, like Mexico, the United States, Canada, and...Greenland. Yes, it is geographically part of North America, even though it's more politically aligned with Europe.

Perhaps you recall that old children's rhyme.

In fourteen hundred ninety-two,
  Columbus sailed the ocean blue.
  He had three ships and left from Spain;
  He sailed through sunshine, wind, and rain.

It continues, but you get the idea. It was Columbus who "discovered" the Americas, right?

Well, sort of, unless you enforce technicalities like the judges on Jeopardy.

Columbus made his famous voyages between the years of 1492 and 1502, landing at various times somewhere in the Bahamas, the "then" Caribbean Island of Hispaniola (now Haiti and the Dominican Republic), Trinidad, various parts of South America and Panama. So, while he did land in the "Americas," he never did make landfall anywhere in North America. But that's not the technicality.

The problem was that Columbus, at least initially, thought he had succeeded in his mission of finding a new route to Asia from Europe. Believing he had landed somewhere in Asia, he didn't understand he'd discovered a whole new continent in the middle.

That honor went to Amerigo Vespucci, who made his voyage between 1499 and 1502. Unlike Columbus, when he landed in Brazil, he realized it was not part of Asia, but a new continent altogether. Vespucci documented his journeys meticulously, and those journals were widely read throughout Europe, earning him the de facto naming rights.

Skip ahead to 1507 and we encounter German cartographer Martin Waldseemüller, who was undertaking an ambitious project to map the world. Quite an undertaking, as much of it hadn't been discovered yet. Anyway, he labeled the new area of Vespucci's *Novus Mundus* (Latin for 'New World') as "America" in honor of Vespucci's first name. It's a slight feminization of Amerigo's name, as countries were traditionally referred to as "she's" at the time.

So, there you have it. Technically speaking, if one refers to "America", they are really referring to the entire region known as North and South America.

As we'll see a couple of chapters from now, a bunch of cheeky colonists decided to call part of this new world the United States of America, often shortened to "America." Of course, other "Americans" to the north and south might take some offense.

At the risk of upsetting our friends in Canada and all those in South America, and for the sake of saving lots of letters in this book, we'll frequently use the term "America" to refer to the United States of America, or perhaps the U.S. or USA.

How to Read This Book...

I hope it's obvious that a 350-page book can't possibly cover every significant event and person in American history.

What it can do, however, is provide a "greatest hits" overview of the good, bad, the glorious, the shameful, the adventurous and the tragic events that shaped the Great American Experiment.

While the "greatest" part of my analogy doesn't always apply (the United States has plenty of blemishes in its history), I think the analogy still works.

I'm a music fanatic and love my hundreds of vinyl records, especially when played on my vintage audio gear. Sometimes I love Goodwill Stores as they've delivered a killer vintage sound system, far better than the one I had in High School. But I digress.

Sometimes, I do enjoy listening to the "greatest hits" compilations. Those give me a taste of the most popular songs by various artists. What they don't provide is the whole album experience. For that, you have to listen to the entire record. Side A first, followed by side B. That's the way the artist intended it to be heard.

And this book is similar in that regard. It touches on many of the big things (I still couldn't hit them all, so don't get too upset if you think I 'forgot' something), but I couldn't possibly fit them all in this book, so I had to make some tough calls.

As one of dozens of examples, I would have loved to spend time relating the story of the Tuskegee Airmen—their triumphs in the war and their subsequent mistreatment and struggles when they returned home. But, as with the dozens of other topics, much had to be left on the cutting-room floor. Perhaps I'll produce a future book diving into some of these wonderful and sometimes difficult stories.

So, enjoy the highlights, but don't stop there. I encourage you to bookmark sections that capture your interest, and continue to dig deeper on your own. Getting a taste of the "big picture" is a great way to start.

Ready? Let's get to the story of... America!

What about Martin Waldseemüller's map? It lived for nearly 400 years in a castle in Southern Germany. Then, in 2003, through a cooperative effort between United States and German officials, the Library of Congress purchased the map for the tidy sum of $10 million. It's currently on display there if you'd like to take a gander at it.

Part One

Foundations and Revolution

Chapter 1

America: The Prequel

Before the Europeans ever splashed ashore with their muskets, maps, and funny hats, the land was anything but empty. For thousands of years, North America was home to thriving societies: hunter-gatherers who became farmers, mound builders, traders, and empire-makers. From mammoth-chasing Clovis hunters to city-building Mississippians, Native peoples shaped the continent long before Jamestown or Plymouth were on the drawing board. By the time Europeans showed up, there were hundreds of nations, each with their own languages, customs, and politics.

Turns Out, America Had Tenants Before the Lease

"Americans" keep getting older.

For a long time, we believed "America" (referring to the entirety of the Western Hemisphere) was devoid of people until about 13,000 years ago, based on evidence of the Clovis Culture. You know, the Clovis people, prehistoric hunter-gatherers. These folks migrated across the then-exposed Bering Land Bridge connecting to what's now known as Alaska. Coming to North America, and being the first humans to set foot in any of the Americas, they originated from Siberia and other parts of northeast Asia and eventually worked their way south.

Then the timeline started to change. Excavations in Chile found evidence of human activity more than 14,000 years old. A dig in Idaho pushed things back to 16,000 years, and later, evidence surfaced in Oregon dating back 18,000 years. Footprints preserved in New Mexico radically wound the clock back even further, with dating of pollen and seeds smashed under the footprints dating back 23,000 years. Add to that evidence in Mexico of tools and other items dating back 33,000 years or so.

So, while we once were convinced that humans first walked into the Americas after the peak of the last ice age, it sure appears they got here before the glaciers covered everything up north and were already established in parts to the south.

It just goes to show that science is never really "settled," especially when it comes to studying old stuff.

Those 23,000-year-old footprints caused quite the uproar in the scientific community. Many didn't believe the dating of those seeds crushed underfoot was accurate. Apparently, something to do with how carbon dating can be thrown off if the host plants from those seeds grew underwater or from the dirt.

So scientists found the pollen traces from the same footprint indentations and dated those. Same results.

The Original Cutting Edge Technology

According to the "Clovis First" theory, discussed in the previous section, this is the point where the first North and South Americans started to reach permanent resident status.

Surviving, and arguably thriving, on a more advanced hunter-gatherer diet, these folks made breakthroughs with tools and methods supporting their "big game" hunting lifestyle. Think really big meat sources like Mammoths and Bison. Now think about taking them down with spears and sharp stones. Impressive, huh?

For trivia bonus points at your next social event, you can talk about Clovis points. While it's a bit strange to talk about chipped stones as a technological advance, that's exactly what it was.

Think of stones, carefully chipped into arrow or spearhead shapes, having the distinctive appearance resulting from the maker knocking small bits from the original stone until what was left was a sharp, knife-like rock. The Clovis points were distinctive in that they featured concave half-moon bases and long fluted sections at the base, either for impact and shock dissipation or perhaps easier mounting to arrow-like weapons or spears. The points were also used as knives and scraping tools to process hides and usable material from the game they took.

In addition to the advanced edged weapons and tools, many believe the Clovis folks used weapons like the atlatl (a pair of sticks where one supports the base of another outfitted with a point that is flung for increased leverage and resulting velocity). They're quite difficult to master. Ask me how I know.

The Clovis people were highly mobile, likely pursuing the megafauna (large game) they consumed as their primary food source. Archaeologists know this because Clovis points have been discovered at dig sites hundreds of miles from the sources of the stones used to produce them.

We recognize the Clovis culture as one of the earliest well-documented Paleo-Indian cultures in North America.

In 2007, archaeologists found a Clovis point lodged in the rib of a mammoth in a Wisconsin dig site. The wound had healed, meaning the mammoth survived the attack for some time before dying from some other cause. This seems to prove Clovis hunters were indeed hunting the continent's megafauna with their stone-tipped weapons. Normally, bones and tools are found near each other, but not actually stuck together!

Goodbye Mammoth Steaks, Hello Rabbit Stew

It would be inaccurate to say the Clovis culture ended. More likely, beginning about twelve and a half thousand years ago, it evolved into regional societies, which ultimately led to the Native American era. Possibly the shift was related to decreased availability of the primary large game food sources, maybe from overhunting, or perhaps a result of significant climate shifts (end of the ice age) during that era.

Whatever the actual cause, the changes involved an increased focus on smaller game and plant-based supplements in their diet. Along with this came more stability from the nomadic life, and the establishment of regional cultures like the Folsom tradition in central North America, Cumberland in the south, and Suwannee in the southeast.

With a less nomadic lifestyle, we start to see the development of communities. With that comes cultural advancement. You know, things like organization, power struggles, homeowners' associations, and the like. But seriously, this was what drove the development of society more like we know it today. Consider the next evolution, the

American Indian cultures. While still nomadic to a degree, the social structures were much like those we're accustomed to today.

As a closing fun fact, modern DNA testing shows direct linkage of the Clovis and post-Clovis cultures to the people of the American Indian era.

When mammoths disappeared, hunters didn't just chase rabbits. They evolved their hunting technology. Archaeologists studying Folsom-era sites in New Mexico discovered that hunters managed to bring down massive Ice Age bison, which were even larger than today's version. These beasts could weigh twice as much as a modern buffalo. To hunt these huge animals, Folsom hunters designed smaller and sharper spear points capable of penetrating tough hides.

Mounds, Maize, and Mississippians

Long before Europeans set foot on the North American continent, the land was alive with civilization. Millions of Native peoples had built thriving societies stretching from the Arctic tundra to the Everglades.

The process was slow, of course. During the Archaic period, say from 8,000 BC to about 1,000 BC, we saw the transition from nomadic to a community lifestyle. Shifts such as increased gathering and development, along with reliance on fishing, marked the transition to "towns," to oversimplify. From 1,000 BC to 1,000 AD, we started to see interaction and trade between communities, along with early forms of true agriculture as opposed to plant gathering.

During this time, we see evidence of what humans always seem to do: build stuff. Many population centers were characterized by "mounds" likely built and used for ritualistic activities. Later, mounds were used for residential purposes, with the wealthier citizens even building wooden homes on top of them while the less well-heeled made do with thatch huts on the outskirts. Some things never change, do they?

Oh, a quick side note. Along with the shift to urban life, we see the domestication of the dog. Now, back to the history.

By the Mississippian Culture window, from about 1,000 AD to the Europeans' arrival beginning about 1,500 AD, we were seeing intensive agricultural focus, larger "cities" and extensive trade.

From the Mississippian mound cities like Cahokia to the intricate irrigation systems of the Pueblo peoples, Native nations demonstrated complex political systems, trade networks, and spiritual traditions. They weren't one culture but rather hundreds.

By the time the Europeans began to enter the scene, there were somewhere over 500 diverse groups (or nations) across North America. Largely independent, they had unique languages and social customs. Lifestyles varied, including nomadic bison hunters on the Plains to settled farmers in the river valleys, and fishing communities along the coasts.

The City of Cahokia (located in the area we now know as Illinois) is a shining example of the establishment of real population centers. Its prime time was between about 650 and 1,350 AD, and like other cities of the time, it featured mounds. Lots of them. Somewhere over 100, including one enormous one, likely the ritualistic center.

Cahokia featured shops, fields for agriculture, a public solar calendar, high and low-rent residential districts and even fields for recreation. No, the NFL was not founded here.

Europeans Enter: Stage Right

Guess what happened starting around 1,500 and continuing until, well, now? A bunch of people barged into North America and set up shop, some with good intentions of being neighborly and many others who didn't give a hoot for those who already lived here. It was a predictable and oft-repeated scenario since the beginning of humanity.

I should mention, long before the massive influx of Europeans began, colonies had been established in Greenland and parts of Newfoundland by Norse seafarers. Dating to around 1,000 AD, some of these colonies remained viable until near 1,500. As far as we know, they never made it as far south as the areas defined by the United States.

Here's the quick summary.

As we learned earlier, Columbus really didn't land in the area now known as the United States, but his West Indies landfall did mark the beginning of the colonization of the Americas.

It didn't take long for settlers to follow the first explorers into the New World. Once people saw Martin Waldseemüller's map, they saw an opportunity for a new life, for one reason or another. Religious freedom. Free gold everywhere (according to the rumors). Or maybe just the opportunity to exit filthy European cities (nothing personal here, ALL cities were nasty back then) and live off the grid. Whatever the reason, the settling began.

In 1565, the first real, long-term settlement was established in St. Augustine, Florida, by the Spanish. While touristy attractions abound there, it's a fun place to visit, as many of the old buildings, walls, and even the fort remain.

The race between settlers from different countries began in earnest as everyone wanted a slice of what they saw as "free" territory. Never mind the millions of Native Americans already established there. The French, British, Dutch, and later Swedes all joined the race. Jamestown, Virginia, was established in 1607; Plymouth

Colony, Massachusetts, in 1620; the Dutch ended up in New York; and the French planted flags in Quebec in 1608. You get the idea. All this colonizing continued, especially along coasts, bays, and rivers in North America and the Caribbean, and there was no turning back.

Stop and think about the impacts of two completely isolated societies colliding. For hundreds of years, Europeans had been living in densely packed cities, sharing germs and, pardon the level of grossness, excrement in the streets. Now factor in the common close proximity of all manner of farm animals like cows, sheep, chickens, pigs and the like. Put all that together, and you have the world's largest germ factory. While Europe was plagued by occasional...plagues and such, people had, over time, developed lots of natural immunities to the everyday stuff.

However, the American Indians lived a completely different lifestyle. While they interacted with each other and animals, it was on a completely different level.

The bottom line? The Native Americans had virtually no natural immunity to threats like smallpox, typhus, influenza, diphtheria, measles and more. The result was shocking and tragic. While no one really knows for sure, historians believe somewhere over 10 million native Americans died as a result. Some believe the number could have been as high as 100 million.

Add to that reports of intentional spread of disease by settlers, and you are looking one an ugly situation.

Wars Continue

You might notice the use of wars "continue" rather than wars "begin." Again, back to human nature. Things certainly weren't all rosy during the Native American era before Europeans arrived. They fought, killed and enslaved each other in horrible ways, just like the Europeans continued to do once they arrived. Some things never change.

The reasons? The usual: territory grabs, displays of power and bravery. Long-standing feuds. Control over resources. The slavery element was mostly less institutional and more "tactical" as some tribes would capture the conquered to replenish their man (or woman) power, gain some workers and that sort of thing.

But the settlers took things to a new level with large, organized armies and gunpowder.

For example, the French and British fought over "their" new territory in the Seven Years' War until the British prevailed in that particular conflict and assumed control of the territory all the way to the Mississippi River. This became important later as both the French and British back home were competing for the loyalty of the colonists. When the French had significant clout, the British authorities had to at least pretend to play nice with colonists.

In parallel to the fighting and expansion race, another country-defining movement began between the first colonization and the American Revolution: slavery. Slavery itself didn't start here; that had been going on forever. What began was the mass importation of slaves to work the increasingly profitable agricultural endeavors. As it's an integral part of United States history, we'll get into that a lot more later in the book.

So, this is the overall situation that sets the stage for the beginning of the "America" we're talking about in this book: the United States of America. A handful of rarely cooperative European countries have all claimed territory in the New World. The British seem to hold the upper hand in managing the prime real estate along much of the Eastern seaboard. Colonies, towns and cities are growing. There's a thriving agricultural business and money to be made, in large part due to the practice of slavery to provide cheap labor.

Money, power and potential all enter the melting pot, setting conditions for a big argument over who is going to be in charge.

The Seven Years' War (1756–1763) is often called the first true world war. While colonists in America knew it as the French and Indian War, battles were raging simultaneously in Europe, West Africa, India, the Caribbean, and even the Philippines. At one point, Britain captured Manila from Spain. And here colonists thought the Ohio River Valley skirmishes were the main event.

Chapter 2

How to Start a Country (Without Getting Hanged)

A bunch of colonists, farmers, lawyers and businessmen, picked a fight with the biggest empire on Earth over taxes, tea, and tyranny. But this wasn't just about taxes and tariffs. Beginning with secret meetings in taverns and under oak trees, the movement progressed to armed rebellion at Lexington and Concord. Let's explore how these idealists turned colonial complaints into a full-blown revolution. It wasn't inevitable, and according to the British, it sure wasn't legal.

Molasses, Mobs, and a Missing Claret

Fresh off a pricey war, the English crown was broke and needed a refill, and they figured the colonists in America should help foot the bill.

The answer? Tax and policy acts.

In 1764, Parliament passed the Sugar Act, slapping a three-penny tax on molasses. That hit colonial merchants right in the rum supply. Later that year, they expanded the Currency Act, requiring colonists to send hard-earned legal tender back to England to pay debts. Also not cool.

Next came the Stamp Act of 1765, taxing pretty much anything made of paper—newspapers, legal documents, playing cards, and most everything else paper-related. This one wielded a double-edged sword as it was the first tax on business within the colonies. Before, taxes levied by the Crown applied to international business. This didn't sit well either.

Soon after, the Stamp Act Congress formed and sent King George a strongly worded letter about no taxation without representation. The colonists had a valid argument, for as English citizens, they had a right to their own local representation. The complaints fell on deaf ears, and more taxes came rolling in, as they always do.

By 1766, with protests spreading like wildfire, Parliament repealed the Stamp Act, but not before slipping in a clause saying, "We're still the boss." That would later come back to bite them.

In 1767, Parliament tried again with new taxes on imports. The colonists fought back with boycotts and increased local production, kicking off a chain of events that would eventually turn into a full-blown revolution.

People were mighty hacked off about all the onerous Acts. One night in August 1765, an angry mob of Stamp Act protesters crashed a dinner party hosted by Massachusetts Lieutenant

Governor and Chief Justice Thomas Hutchinson. The governor and his guests barely escaped before the ill-tempered crowd polished off what was left of a lovely claret.

The Sons Who Wouldn't Behave

All the "acting" tweaked a lot of folks in the colonies. Bully behavior tends to do that. Well, at least in their view, the King and all the rest of the British authorities were abusive overlords. But what to do? It's not like a ragtag bunch of farmers and townspeople had many options to resist the world's most powerful army.

Enter the Sons of Liberty, the OG tea party crashers.

As we see glamorized in lots of Hollywood productions, the Sons of Liberty were a secret society established to organize resistance to the English Crown. Loosely organized, the term "Sons of Liberty" seemed to gain traction in 1765 as part of the broad opposition to the Stamp Act. Gathering in pubs and identifying coded meeting places like "the Liberty Tree" or "Liberty Pole," the group intended to fire up the masses through communication and agitation. In other words, organize resistance.

You know some of the key players. Early members included John Hancock (I wonder if he signed his membership card first?), Paul Revere and Samuel Adams.

It didn't take long for things to get ugly. Under the "No taxation without representation" motto and rallying cry, members of the group inspired a mob to burn down the office of Stamp Act commissioner Andrew Oliver. Such threatening activities caused many officials and distributors of stamps to resign in fear for their well-being. Burning and hanging effigies sprinkled with some occasional tarring and feathering will cause one to reflect on their career choice.

Starting primarily in Boston and New York, the movement spread throughout the 13 colonies. By the fall and winter of 1765, the groups in various areas were forming alliances, strengthening the movement even more. The mission continued, and by 1769, the Sons of Liberty were well-known and powerful enough to stage large public gatherings and celebrations for their wins against onerous policies delivered from across the pond.

The most notable party hosted by the Sons of Liberty took place in Boston Harbor in December 1773.

Interestingly, the name "Sons of Liberty" came from an Irish member of British Parliament. During a debate on the Stamp Act, Isaac Barré stood up and spoke in favor of "these Sons of Liberty." Needless to say, the words of support weren't so popular on the floor, and Barré was roundly criticized. Of course, as an Irishman, he held many sympathetic views to the plight of the Colonists.

The Original Tea Party Crashers

In 1773, King George III conceived an arguably slimy government-funded corporate bailout. You see, the British East India Company was in dire straits. They'd overbought a pile of tea, were unable to sell it profitably, and were desperately seeking a solution. Recognizing the company's immense size and the potential consequences of its failure, King George and Parliament devised a plan to unload the excess tea on the colonists.

Politicians have been dreaming up shady schemes since the beginning of time, and this one was no different. The idea was to have the British East India Company unload the tea supply at a price well below market value. Of course, a tax would be attached! The goal was simple. Run the local distributors out of business and regain near-monopoly power in the tea industry. British East India would make lots of money, and the Crown would garner more tax revenue. Everybody wins! Except the colonists, of course.

Pop quiz... What happened next? You got it. The Boston Tea Party. Actually, it was more like a Boston Tea Riot as the Sons of Liberty-organized protesters dumped 342 crates of tea into Boston Harbor on December 16, 1773.

This didn't go over particularly well with the British. Although the harbor now smelled lovely, like a fine Earl Grey tea, Parliament had had enough of the disrespect shown by those cheeky farmers across the pond.

The British immediately closed the harbor, thereby shutting down business and trade almost entirely. No more exports to foreign countries meant no more income for local and regional businesses. The King intended to keep the harbor closed until the Colonists apologized and showed they meant it by paying full restitution for the destroyed tea.

Interestingly, it wasn't only the British who were upset. Many patriots weren't in favor of the move either. You see, one of the underlying principles they were protesting for was that of natural rights. For example, the right to own and possess property. That applies to everyone, even the British. So, even though the authorities were acting abusively, the British East India Tea Company owned that tea (remember, property rights), so no one else had a right to destroy it. Among others, George Washington himself wasn't happy about the event.

The aftermath was predictable. England got busy developing punishment policies.

The Massachusetts Government Act, at least in practical terms, ended the illusion of local authority by placing the Governor, Parliament, and King George in charge of government hiring.

The Administration of Justice Act effectively added a layer of immunity to government representatives in America. Another bit of devious rule-making, the act allowed the Governor to move any trials of British officials to England at his discretion. This had a chilling effect on anyone pursuing justice for acts of wrongdoing, as any trial would likely never happen if prosecutors and witnesses had to travel to England to plead their case. It was only a six-to-twelve-week travel nightmare, each way, to get to England. And if you think plane tickets are expensive now, imagine that fare.

Then there was the Quartering Act, requiring colonists to house British soldiers in unoccupied buildings if needed. This one was more of a slap in the face than a practical issue, but it helped fuel the fires of resentment even more.

The bottom line? The Colonists were largely British citizens, and, as such, they were accustomed to enjoying well-defined natural rights of representation, grievance address and such. They inherently believed they had, and were owed, a measure of general freedom. The more they asserted this traditional independence, the more the Crown tightened the screws of tyranny.

It was becoming clear this wasn't going to end well.

The Boston Tea Party was no small event. Those 342 crates of tea dumped into the harbor represent about 92,000 pounds, or 46 tons. Using some tea party doily math, one might be able to steep somewhere around 16 million cups of tea. And the value? A quick look online shows many retail teas selling for somewhere in the neighborhood of $20 per pound. That translates to roughly $1.8 million in today's money.

Give Me Liberty (Or at Least a Good Quote)

It's a big step to escalate from being disgruntled with an occasional protest to armed rebellion, but that's exactly what was happening.

The most famous example of someone stepping up and publicly

proclaiming it was time for armed rebellion left us with a timeless quote.

During the Second Virginia Convention held at St. John's Church in Richmond, Virginia, Patrick Henry delivered a speech calling for war. He argued that the time for compromise of peaceful resolution had long passed and that Virginia should commit its armed militia to the fight.

Oh, and guess who was in the audience? George Washington and Thomas Jefferson, among many others.

Anyway, the famous line comes from this segment of Henry's speech.

"Is life so dear, or peace so sweet, as to be purchased at the price of chains and slavery? Forbid it, Almighty God! I know not what course others may take; but as for me, give me liberty or give me death!"

As a side note, Henry later boycotted the Constitutional Convention, saying he "smelt a rat." Henry believed the Constitutional Convention to be a power grab by those advocating for a strong, and eventually, tyrannical federal government.

Lexington and Concord: Britain's Worst Road Trip

Before we get into the serious business of the war between the colonies and the British, we need to mention one violent encounter everyone has heard of—the Boston Massacre.

Amid growing frustration from everything we've discussed so far, on March 5, 1770, a group of Bostonians faced off with a garrison of British Redcoats. Insults were flung, then snowballs, ice, and rocks followed. As the crowd pushed into the British, they fired, killing five protesters, including Crispus Attucks, a man of African descent.

The soldiers involved were arrested and tried, but most were later acquitted. Interestingly, patriot John Adams defended them, believing that everyone is entitled to a fair trial. It's important to stick to your principles.

On April 19, 1775, all those years of name-calling, riots, protests, and passive-aggressive legislation finally exploded into musket fire. British generals, convinced the colonies were in open rebellion, decided it was time for a preemptive strike on the colonists' ability to mount armed resistance.

The plan was simple. March from Boston to seize or destroy suspected weapons stockpiles in the nearby towns of Lexington and Concord.

The key to success of such an operation usually involves not letting the target know it's happening. But word got out, and in part thanks to the famous rides of Paul Revere and William Dawes, the local militias got wind of the impending attack and organized their resistance. By the time British troops reached Lexington, they were greeted by about 80 armed and ready locals under the command of a serious manly man, Captain John Parker.

Parker wasn't necessarily there to start a shooting war. But he also wasn't keen on rolling over and letting the British soldiers have their way. He instructed his militiamen, "Stand your ground. Don't fire unless fired upon. But if they want a war, let it start right here."

Tensions were obviously high when large groups of people faced each other with loaded and primed guns. Someone fired a shot—no one really knows who—and the chaos began. When the smoke cleared, eight militiamen lay dead, ten were wounded, and one British soldier was wounded.

The Redcoats marched on to Concord, still intent on completing their mission. That wasn't going to happen as the advance warning had allowed the colonists to move their weapons cache. Colonel James Barrett led his men to a high ridge outside town and allowed the British to complete their search. Remember, there was nothing to find, so there was no real need to start shooting again. But, as you might expect, another shot rang out. The British forces had divided, so in this case, they were outnumbered by about 400 to 90. After some respectful shooting, the British withdrew and started the process of heading back to Boston.

Here's where things got ugly for the Redcoats.

Word had spread among the militiamen in the region, and as the British began their long march home, colonials joined the marching fight, picking off Redcoats along the way. Early on, the militiamen numbered about 2,000 and instituted leapfrog tactics to repeatedly harass, meaning shoot at, the British troops.

The influx of colonial fighters continued. By the end of the march, some 15,000 militiamen had shown up to fight and surround the British stronghold of Boston.

War had officially broken out. Oddly enough, no one had declared independence...yet. That would come later. But for now, the colonies were at war.

You may have heard the term, minuteman referring to a colonial militia member. Remember, there was no country in place at this time, and partially because of that, no standing army fighting on behalf of the colonies.

The "militia" was simply the collection of citizens who were expected to "be ready to fight at a minute's notice," using their own arms, powder, and ammunition. Hence, the term "minuteman."

The "Pre-Congresses." Now with Actual Shooting.

As the burning desire for freedom sparked into outright flames, the political process gradually made its way towards the actual founding of a new country based on the principles, rules and instructions defined by the three documents we know today: The Declaration of Independence, the Constitution, and the Bill of Rights. But to get to those final products, some early attempts and failures prepared the way.

The goal of the First Continental Congress in September 1774 was to coordinate among the colonies a formal protest against the Crown's policies. Most colonies (12 of 13) sent delegates to Philadelphia for the first Congress in September and October. Georgia declined to send a representative, but only because they were, at the time, reliant on British cooperation to help fight the Native Americans.

It was slow progress as opinions were split on how best to deal with the British. Conservatives, including John Jay and Edward Rutledge, desired a measured approach. Send a message, but nothing too hostile that risks moving the dialogue past the point of a graceful recovery. The more radical factions, led by Samuel Adams and others, thought the time was appropriate to get more aggressive.

What happens when a bunch of budding politicians meet for a Congress? Like now, nothing much, although the delegates did agree to a boycott of British goods. The thinking was that a boycott would send a message, but maintain the possibility of restoring civil relations with the British government.

When all was said and done, the seven weeks of work resulted in a sternly worded letter to the King. Interestingly, the letter apparently never made its way out of the House of Lords and House of Commons, and it's unclear whether the King ever saw it.

The last resolution from the First Continental Congress was an agreement to have another Congress in the future, should it be needed. Some things never change.

Once the shooting started, the marker on that previous agreement for a follow-up congress was called in. All 13 colonies made the trip for this one as the situation had become very real. The time for a hopeful return to normalcy had passed.

This time around, there was a greater sense of urgency because war had broken out, and the colonies were woefully unprepared for such things, which are normally run by established countries with proper leadership structures.

Job one was to create an army. And, of course, an army needs a General, so the second task was to hire George Washington as its commander. Fun trivia fact: he agreed to take the job, but only under the condition that he not be paid. It's nice to be independently wealthy.

This congress became the de facto governing body of the colonies, but make no mistake: the real power was still assumed to remain at the state level.

The results of the second Congress were more significant. Delegates delivered The Declaration of the Causes and Necessity of Taking Up Arms, the Olive Branch Petition, the Declaration of Independence, and the Articles of Confederation.

As we'll see, much changed later with the adoption of the Constitution and Bill of Rights, but this second Congress really was the start of the formal government of the United States. The Congress created the post office, a national currency, managed the war effort, designated foreign dignitaries to represent the colonies and seek allies and assistance, and more. However, there were some serious shortfalls in the design, leading to big changes later.

From Ragtag to Regulars

As we've seen, fighting was already happening, yet the collection of colonies calling for war didn't really have an army.

Up to this point, Colonial armed resistance relied mostly on local militias. These were the community residents, complete with privately owned arms. They drilled together occasionally and when trouble loomed, "mustered" to form a fighting unit. They were certainly motivated, as they were fighting quite literally around their homes, but disciplined and professional? Not so much. And in this case, they were picking a fight with the most powerful army the world had ever seen.

The Second Continental Congress, meeting in Philadelphia in May 1775, quickly figured out that scattered and largely disorganized militias would never be enough to confront the British Army.

On June 14, 1775, Congress took the bold step of creating the Continental Army. It was bold because one of the things they were fighting against was the whole idea of powerful governments backed by powerful standing armies. Regardless, this move created the first national military force for the American colonies. One day later, delegates unanimously chose George Washington as their commander-in-chief. Washington's selection was a clever strategic move. He had experience from the French and Indian War, but he was also a southerner. Placing him in charge helped bind the southern colonies to the New England colonies.

The early Continental Army was kind of a hot mess. It was a hodgepodge of volunteers, militias, and newly raised regiments. Supplies were usually scarce, with soldiers lacking uniforms, shoes and even gunpowder. Pay was unreliable, discipline was shaky, and desertion rates were high. Imagine the pressure for soldiers to keep paying the bills at home during their time in service.

Slowly but surely, this army began to coalesce, helping the often antagonistic colonies to unify against a common cause while fighting with a common army.

Foreign assistance, especially from France after 1778, helped immensely. Foreign expertise helped too. European officers like Baron von Steuben drilled troops at Valley Forge, teaching modern tactics and battlefield discipline. By the war's later years, the army was no longer a ragtag band but an increasingly effective fighting force capable of taking on the British.

The resistance to the new United States having a large and powerful standing army was fierce. In one debate, as the story goes, a delegate suggested that the standing army of the new United States be limited to 5,000 troops. According to the legend, George Washington offered a somewhat sarcastic response, agreeing with this proposal provided that the Constitution also limited the size of any future invading armies to 3,000 men.

Chapter 3

The Mad Scientists of 1776

It takes some serious nerve to stand up against the world's most powerful empire, whose will is enforced by the world's most powerful army.

But men like Thomas Jefferson, Ben Franklin, John Adams, and others signed their own death warrants by crafting not just the Declaration of Independence, but a new experiment in self-government. Let's unpack both the classical and new radical ideas they baked into America's founding documents and resulting structure. We'll also explore the implementation of these ideals, leading to the establishment of the great experiment of consent-based government.

Enlightenment Influence: Montesquieu Made Us Do It

The ideas that powered the American Revolution didn't all spring from the colonial rebels. Many were imported from Europe's Enlightenment thinkers. Philosophers like John Locke and Montesquieu had long challenged traditional ideas about government, authority, and human rights.

For example, John Locke's theory of natural rights, that life, liberty, and property are inherent and must be protected by governments, heavily influenced Jefferson's thinking. Locke also argued that people have a right to overthrow any government that violates those rights, a principle we'll see in the forthcoming Declaration of Independence.

Locke's work also elevated the importance of government being a social contract of a voluntary nature between citizens and the ruling body they create. Said government should only have power, limited power at that, for as long as the citizens choose to grant that power.

While Locke's thinking offered insight into the concept of natural rights and voluntary consent, Charles-Louis de Secondat, baron de la Brède et de Montesquieu, helped plant the seed of the wisdom behind the concept of separation of powers and checks and balances. Can we agree to just refer to him as "Montesquieu?" That's a really long name. Anyway, his 1748 work, *The Spirit of Laws*, was one of the most quoted references during the revolutionary debates.

While frustrating at times (OK, most of the time), the built-in conflict between groups and branches of government, think House and Senate, and the three branches' sharing of power between the Executive, Legislative and Judicial, is designed to prevent any individual or group from assuming too much authority. That leads to tyranny, something the architects of the founding documents were desperate to avoid at all costs.

These Enlightenment ideas provided the intellectual framework for revolution and the blueprint for what came next. They turned grievances into principles and rebellion into a cause worth fighting for.

When James Madison was studying political theory before drafting the Constitution, he basically binge-read Montesquieu. The Spirit of Laws was so widely read in colonial America that one historian found it was cited more often than any author except the Bible. The colonists weren't just skimming, either—they were copying Montesquieu's passages directly into pamphlets, sermons, and legislative debates. His idea that "power should be a check to power" became the heartbeat of the separation of powers we now take for granted.

Dear King George: It's Not Me, It's You

Most scientific endeavors of note begin with some false starts and failed efforts. While the Second Continental Congress accomplished much and took the big step of formally declaring revolution with the drafting and release of The Declaration of Independence, there were some growing pains.

The Olive Branch Petition

On July 5, 1775, the Second Continental Congress finished the Olive Branch Petition.

Members of the Second Congress were divided on the degree of their pursuit of independence versus reconciliation with Britain through agreements on trade, taxation, and representation. Civil discussion or virtual yelling and screaming?

John Dickinson, the primary author of the Olive Branch Petition, was clearly in favor of calm and collected reconciliation. There's always someone in the room who excels at maintaining a cool head, right? However, some, like John Adams, believed that war for complete independence was inevitable, but were willing to allow things to unfold before pushing for complete separation.

While the Olive Branch Petition expressed a desire for agreement, reconciliation, and continued loyalty to the crown, its sincerity was questionably passive-aggressive. The shooting had already begun, and the English were furious. When your army is the finest fighting force on planet Earth, respected and feared everywhere, you can't just let a bunch of ragtag farmers take potshots without serious reprimand. Just one day later, on July 6, 1775, the Second Congress approved the Declaration of the Causes and Necessity of Taking Up Arms. It's hard to believe that anyone placed much faith in a positive outcome from the Olive Branch Petition.

Nevertheless, it served an essential purpose. By writing the petition, the rebel government had expressed a "sincere" desire to reconcile with England, at least officially. We already know many in the resistance movement had no such desires. Now, when King George III rejected this plan, as everyone knew he would, the Americans would be united in their quest for total independence since the English would have dismissed the proffered olive branch.

The Declaration of the Causes

Even a literary and penmanship prodigy like Thomas Jefferson needed a practice run to craft the Declaration of Independence, and that practice run was the Declaration of the Causes and Necessity of Taking Up Arms. While John Dickinson (yes, the Dickinson College guy) penned the final draft of this document, Jefferson was the driving force behind the primary message and early draft. Dickinson also penned the earlier "stern letter" to George III, solidifying his reputation as a "troublemaker" across the pond.

Regardless of Dickinson's penmanship prowess, this Declaration of Causes was crucial because it articulated the colonists' grievances against the world's dominant superpower.

This declaration was somewhat analogous to a letter you might write to your cable company after months of frustrating customer service issues. You document and share their shortcomings, failures of their service, and their inability to resolve your problems. Then, you express your valiant efforts to assist them in resolving the problems, because all you want is resolution, not to be "one of those perpetual complainers." Next, you reiterate your patience and perseverance. Finally, you conclude with a threat to switch to satellite TV unless they rectify their situation.

The Declaration of Causes and Necessity of Taking Up Arms followed a similar pattern, albeit with a significantly reduced vocabulary.

While the threat to switch to a more accommodating government was unmistakable, the closing language of the Declaration still proposed an amicable resolution, but with plenty of teeth should things not end up as desired.

Consider this excerpt. "Our cause is just. Our union is perfect. Our internal resources are great, and, if necessary, foreign assistance is undoubtedly attainable."

And, "We shall lay them down when hostilities shall cease on the part of the aggressors, and all danger of their being renewed shall be removed, and not before."

In August 1775, King George issued a Royal Proclamation stating that the American colonists were "engaged in open and avowed rebellion."

King George III is often remembered for his stubborn refusal to compromise with the colonies, but he's equally famous for his quirks. Later in life, he suffered bouts of mental illness (likely caused by a blood disorder called porphyria) that sometimes left him ranting for hours, talking to trees, or writing 400-word sentences without punctuation. During one episode, he shook hands with an oak he believed was the King of Prussia.

While these troubles came after the Revolution, they cemented his reputation in American lore as "Mad King George." At the time of the Olive Branch Petition, though, he was perfectly lucid—just stubborn.

Franklin, Adams, Sherman... and the Forgotten Two

The Declaration of Independence was not a solo act; it was a team sport.

On June 2, Richard Henry Lee of Virginia proposed the following resolution.

"That these United Colonies are, and of right ought to be, free and independent States, that they are absolved from all allegiance to the British Crown, and that all political connection between them and the State of Great Britain is, and ought to be, totally dissolved."

While most of the delegates saw a severance with England in the cards, there was still much debate over the proper timing. As the Congress prepared to recess, five delegates were chosen to draft a formal declaration for public view.

So, Jefferson may have written the first draft as history remembers, but it was reviewed, edited, and refined by a committee that included Benjamin Franklin, John Adams, Roger Sherman, and Robert Livingston. Each man brought unique perspectives, political clout, and intellectual rigor to the process.

Franklin, the Renaissance man, elder statesman and international diplomat, helped soften Jefferson's sharpest language while preserving the document's spirit. Adams, a fiery advocate for independence, helped guide the document through Congress. Sherman and Livingston played quieter but crucial roles in gaining consensus. An "all-in" mentality would be key to success.

Their collaboration mattered because the Declaration needed more than great prose; it needed buy-in from thirteen colonies with different motivations and interests. The edits and discussions ensured the final draft was bold enough to ignite revolution, but broad enough to unite a fragile coalition. This collaboration helped create not just a document, but a new national identity.

Robert Livingston, one of the five on the drafting committee, never actually signed the Declaration of Independence. He thought the timing was premature and left Philadelphia before the final vote. Ironically, a few years later, he administered the oath of office to George Washington at the first presidential inauguration in 1789. Roger Sherman, the other "quiet member," went on to be the only man to sign all four of America's founding documents: the Declaration, the Articles of Association, the Articles of Confederation, and the Constitution. You might say he was the Forrest Gump of the Revolution—somehow always present for the big events.

Jefferson's Colonial Air B&B Draft

After delegates left the Second Continental Congress for recess, Jefferson remained behind to do the work.

He holed up in a second-story colonial Air B&B on the outskirts of Philadelphia to write the first draft. After making some edits based on feedback from Adams and Franklin, Jefferson sent the draft to the advisory committee of five and, after review, forwarded the draft to the entire Congress on June 28.

On July 2, 1776, the Second Continental Congress resolved to formally declare independence from England. Of the 13 colonies, 12 supported the declaration. New York abstained from the resolution. There is no real significance to the decision to abstain. At the time, each colony had to clarify, on its own, whether its delegates had the authority to vote for decisions of such significance. As of July 2, the

New York delegation hadn't yet received instructions from the New York Provincial Congress.

Once delivered, Jefferson's masterpiece was subjected to editing and criticism by a committee for two straight days.

Two sections were struck from the document. One was a complaint against the British people for allowing their King to become such a tyrannical weenie. The other was a blistering condemnation of slavery and the British slave trade, which was still active at the time.

On July 4, 1776, the Declaration of Independence was approved in the form we know today.

From a united front of the 13 colonies, it formally declared independence, laid out the philosophical justification for rebellion, and listed 27 offenses by the king.

The Declaration of Independence was, in a sense, a justification to other nations. As liberty and freedom were universally understood to be human rights, the world at large would understand why the Americans rebelled against the British government.

Jefferson didn't write the Declaration in a grand hall, but in a rented room on the second floor of a brick house owned by a bricklayer named Jacob Graff. The modest digs sat just a few blocks from Independence Hall. Legend says Jefferson liked to pace the floor while writing, his violin nearby for breaks when he needed to think. The house itself became a kind of shrine. Later, Jefferson reportedly downplayed the setting, saying the building was "of no particular interest." Still, tourists in Philadelphia today can visit a reconstructed version of Graff House and stand where some of the most famous words in American history first met paper.

The Odd Couple of Independence

Thomas Jefferson and John Adams were allies in the whole idea of revolution and freedom from British rule, but they were often mortal adversaries in terms of the specifics.

Adams was a Federalist who believed in a strong(er) central government. Jefferson was a Democratic-Republican who feared centralized power and championed agrarian independence. Keep in mind, if we're looking at things through today's lens of a massive federal government, both men were opposed to that idea. Their fierce debate was really more along the lines of "We need a stronger and more powerful, but still small, federal government" (Adams) versus "We need an even smaller and less powerful federal government subservient to state authority" (Jefferson).

Their debates, over decades in letters, speeches, and policies, shaped America's political culture. Adams feared mob rule; Jefferson feared tyranny. Their disagreements reflected the broader national tension between liberty and order, states' rights and federal power. Interestingly, most founders believed that built-in tension and debate like this was a good thing, leading to more debate and better overall decisions.

In fact, one of their battles, in 1801, as Jefferson was assuming Presidential duties as Adams was exiting the role, led to the famous Marbury Supreme Court case, which developed the precedent of the court being able to rule legislative actions as unconstitutional. The process gave the whole concept of separation of powers some teeth.

These debates were important because they established the foundational ideas for America's two-party system. They also demonstrated that disagreement could coexist with mutual respect in the political Octagon. After years of silence and rivalry, the two reconciled late in life, exchanging letters about philosophy and governance until they both died in 1826.

In a truly amazing display of patriotism, three different United States presidents died on July 4—Independence Day. Thomas Jefferson and John Adams died less than six hours apart on July 4, 1826, although we don't think they planned that maneuver. Jefferson was keen on making it to the 50th Anniversary of the Declaration of Independence. He did. James Monroe died on July 4, 1831.

Stripes Fixed, Stars on the Rise

The American flag is more than a design someone concocted when we became a country. Like the United States, it has grown and changed throughout American history.

The Continental Congress passed the Flag Resolution on June 14, 1777. They had things pretty well mapped out, declaring: "the flag of the United States be 13 stripes, alternate red and white; that the union be 13 stars, white in a blue field, representing a new constellation."

While it seems pretty clear, lots of variants popped up across the 13 colonies using different shades of blue and red and different patterns for those 13 stars.

But what about Betsy Ross? Didn't she invent it based on instructions from George Washington? Well, maybe. And maybe not. Here's the wrinkle in the flag fabric. The story wasn't really a story until her grandson began to promote the tale almost a century after the fact. We don't want to cause a ruckus here, so we'll just say there were others with a role in the process. It seems credible that multiple seamstresses and flag makers did some work on the early flags project, too. For example, Philadelphia's Rebecca Young and Francis Hopkinson. Hopkinson actually billed Congress for designing the flag, so that adds a bit of direct evidence.

As the nation grew, the flag had to evolve. The original 13-star and stripe design was great for the original 13 colonies, but it didn't account for the addition of more states. In 1795, Congress added two stars and two stripes for Vermont and Kentucky. In fact, this 15-star and stripe edition was the flag that inspired Francis Scott Key to write "The Star-Spangled Banner" after watching it fly over Fort McHenry during the War of 1812.

In 1818, Congress figured out we were going to run out of space for more Stars and Stripes, so they passed the Flag Act of 1818. This was a clever plan as it fixed the number of stripes at 13 to honor the original colonies, but allowed for the addition of new stars for new states. Much more manageable and visually appealing as the number of states grew.

Since then, the star field on the American flag has grown with the Union, from 20 stars in 1818 to 50 stars after Hawaii's admission to statehood in 1960. The current arrangement, designed by high school student Robert Heft in 1958 as part of a class project, was one of thousands of proposals. His teacher originally gave him a B– but raised it to an A after President Eisenhower selected the design. See? Having friends in high places can help your GPA.

As the story goes, Francis Hopkinson, the same man who signed the Declaration of Independence, really wanted credit for designing the first U.S. flag. In 1780, he submitted a bill to Congress asking for compensation, suggesting they pay him in "a quarter cask of public wine" along with some cash. Congress denied the request, arguing that many people had contributed to the design. Hopkinson was annoyed but pressed on, even filing multiple versions of his claim. He never got a dime or even the wine.

Democracy in America: The Outsider's Report

When Alexis de Tocqueville arrived in the United States in 1831, he was just 25 years old. Then again, many of the Founders of the country were young guys, too.

His trip to the United States was to study the American prison system, but in his nine months of traveling across the country, he greatly expanded his findings.

He returned to France and began writing his book, *Democracy in America*. This two-volume work became one of the most influential studies of the United States and its great democratic experiment ever produced.

Tocqueville was struck by the way Americans combined real liberty with civic engagement. He saw the proliferation of voluntary associations, where citizens banded together for everything from religious work to local infrastructure projects. In his view, this concept of self-government was America's true genius. He contrasted it with Europe's rigid class hierarchies, noting that while American democracy was plenty messy at times, it still managed to foster a remarkable sense of equality among (white) men. And yes, following on to that statement, he did see serious contradictions over slavery and the plight of American Indians, and the second-class citizenship of women.

The phrase "American exceptionalism" arrived on the scene later, but Tocqueville's analysis set the stage. In a time when monarchies dominated Europe, he suggested that the United States had a unique role in pioneering a democratic model.

Over the years, American leaders from Abraham Lincoln to Ronald Reagan would invoke this idea of American Exceptionalism to frame America's mission at home and abroad. Critics counter that such rhetoric might be used to justify "undemocratic" activity. Still, the Tocquevillian vision of America as an experiment with global significance endures.

Like this book, Alexis de Tocqueville's writing wasn't all serious and weighty stuff. He also shared experiences of the oddities he encountered. In Michigan, he marveled at how fast forests were being cleared, remarking that the sound of the ax seemed to echo everywhere. In Boston, he was surprised that ordinary citizens could walk right up and criticize their leaders without fear. Remember, this was unthinkable in the monarchies of Europe. He even commented on America's obsession with money, noting that while equality flourished, so did a restless drive to get rich.

Chapter 4

Washington: The Man Who Wouldn't Be King

By historical accounts, George Washington was a guy with pretty noble political principles. At a time when the country's architects were primarily worried about things like individuals, politicians, and governments as a whole gaining too much power (you know, that whole human tendency thing), he took the opposite approach and voluntarily ceded authority.

Washington didn't want the job of the new nation's first president. Once forced by overwhelming public pressure to accept it, he didn't want to keep it. And that may have saved the republic. In an age when power usually led to crowns and dynasties, George Washington shocked the world by giving it up.

Washington's Greatest Victory: Giving Up Power

After leading the Continental Army to victory in the Revolutionary War, George Washington did something unprecedented. Remember, while the beginning of the war with him at the helm started rough, it ended with a stunning victory over the British, so he had attained hero status.

In December 1783, Washington appeared before the Continental Congress and formally resigned his military commission. To a world accustomed to victorious generals becoming dictators or kings, this was shocking.

Washington's resignation was more than symbolic; it was a statement of principle. He believed in civilian control of the military and that no one person should hold too much power in a republic. His action reassured a nervous nation that the new government would not become a monarchy in disguise.

This moment was so profound that King George III reportedly said, "If he does that, he will be the greatest man in the world." True? It's hard to tell; the report stems from a story related by an American painter, Benjamin West, who frequented the King's court at the time.

You know the saying. It's not what you say; it's what you do. In this case, one might argue that Washington's resignation laid the foundation for the American tradition of peaceful transitions of power.

When George Washington resigned his commission in Annapolis in December 1783, he was only 51 years old. He bowed, handed in his commission, and quietly went back to Mount Vernon to become, in his words, a "private citizen on the banks of the Potomac." The stunned spectators wept openly. Thomas Jefferson later wrote that this act was "the most sublime moment in the history of mankind." Napoleon Bonaparte called him "the only man in history who ever voluntarily gave up absolute power."

When Walking Away Made History (Again)

After serving two terms as president, Washington voluntarily stepped down in 1797, declining to run for a third term. At the time, this wasn't a constitutional requirement. In fact, Presidential term limits didn't become a thing until ratification of the 22nd Amendment in 1951, right after FDR's 4-0 Presidential Election victory streak.

So, the "two-term limit" idea that Washington began was really a custom, not a requirement. There were no Presidents prior to FDR who were elected more than two times.

Washington believed that leadership in government should be temporary and that new voices should have a chance to serve. Remember, the whole idea of government for the people by the people is the "people" part. Career politicians weren't a thing during the formation of the country. By stepping aside, he reinforced the idea that the presidency was not a lifetime appointment or a path to dynastic rule. That's for kings.

His choice wasn't necessarily popular, as many wanted him to stay. But it became a defining act of American democracy.

After resigning his military commission and returning to Mount Vernon, Washington threw himself into farming with the same intensity he once reserved for war. He experimented with crop rotation, built one of the largest whiskey distilleries in the young nation, and obsessively bred mules, believing they were the future of American agriculture. He inspected his fields daily, notebook in hand, tracking soil conditions and livestock like a 1790s data analyst. The man who could have been king instead spent his days fussing over compost piles and mule breeding charts.

Washington's Blueprint for a Republic

In 1796, Washington delivered his farewell address, ending his second term as the first president of the United States. Actually, it wasn't really a speech per se, but rather a blueprint or instruction document delivered to the newly minted citizens of the United States of America. In this prescient masterpiece, Washington shared his ideas, many of which were written by Alexander Hamilton, on how to best proceed as a fledgling country.

For example, Washington warned against the dangers of forming and giving loyalty to political parties and factions. Such alliances had created the opportunity for improper and imbalanced motivations. Rather than concern for the well-being of the country as a whole, it might just tempt political players to demonstrate loyalty to their party over the country. Sound familiar?

Washington also warned about the possibility of slipping away from a central core of morality. Washington's personal opinion was that morality must be maintained through prioritization of religion, and he warned against the dangers of attempting to maintain a moral state without religion being a key component.

Among many other topics, he relayed the importance of maintaining a sound financial picture for the country as a whole. He warned specifically against accumulating national debt and indicated that taxes should be very carefully and responsibly levied for absolute necessities, as any tax would be a burden on the taxpayer by definition. The country should avoid expensive wars, projects, and undertakings in the interest of maintaining a healthy balance sheet and should make all efforts to pay off all debts as quickly as possible. Reading between the lines, it's pretty clear that Washington desired a business model for the United States of America that carried zero debt on a regular basis. Boy, how things have changed.

The Farewell Address wasn't just a goodbye; it was a blueprint for national stability.

Washington's Farewell Address became a revered document. Starting in 1862, at the height of the Civil War, the U.S. Senate began a tradition of reading the entire address aloud on Washington's birthday. Senators would take turns reciting it, a ritual meant to remind the country of unity and principle in times of turmoil. The tradition continues today, with a different senator chosen each year, alternating parties, to read Washington's words into the record. The reading Senator records their name and reflections in a special leather-bound book. Few presidential documents have enjoyed that kind of ceremonial afterlife, which says something about how seriously Americans took the general's warnings, even if they didn't always follow them.

When a General Refused a Crown

Throughout the Revolutionary War and its aftermath, there were whispers and even sometimes serious suggestions that Washington should become king of the new United States. Some believed a strong central figure was necessary to hold the new nation together. Because having a king completely defeated the underlying point of the entire revolutionary undertaking, Washington consistently rejected these overtures.

He understood that becoming a monarch would betray the very principles of the revolution. His commitment to republican (the ideological system where people hold the power, not the political party) values over personal ambition earned him the nickname "the American Cincinnatus," after the Roman general Lucius Quinctius Cincinnatus, who returned to his plow after saving the republic.

In fairness, this movement to make George Washington an American king was very limited. In fact, some of it arose during the tough years of the Articles of Confederation, arising from frustration with Revolutionary War soldiers not being able to be paid by the new and struggling government.

Washington's refusal helped define the American presidency not as a throne, but as a temporary public trust. That single decision helped ensure the U.S. would remain a republic, and that no one, no matter how popular, was above the people.

The Roman statesman Lucius Quinctius Cincinnatus was a farmer when Rome called on him in 458 BCE to deal with a military crisis. He was granted near-absolute power as dictator in a role meant to last six months. Cincinnatus took command, defeated Rome's enemies in just 15 days, then shocked everyone by resigning and returning to his plow. No victory parade, no palace, just back to the fields. Romans held him up as the ideal of civic virtue: power used only when necessary, and surrendered willingly. Washington's contemporaries loved the comparison so much that they founded the Society of the Cincinnati in his honor, celebrating the general who, like his Roman counterpart, chose his farm over a throne.

Chapter 5

The Constitution: America's Owners' Manual

After the first attempt at a blueprint for building a new type of country, the Articles of Confederation, flopped harder than some NBA players whose names we won't mention here, the Founders went back to the drawing board. The Constitution didn't just rearrange the furniture; it created a whole new house. This chapter explains the debates, behind-the-scenes deals, and last-minute compromises that gave us checks, balances, and a system that still (mostly) functions.

America's First Rough Draft

One of the outputs of the Second Continental Congress was the Articles of Confederation. It was a complete failure in national government design.

Here's the problem.

Intended to create a national government with limited authority, it only succeeded in making government by 13 unrelated bodies even worse than if there were no national governmental structure.

Remember, the states were chock-full of fear about a too-powerful, tyrannical government (England) and were leery of creating the same problem all over again with a new government of their own design, so the Articles of Confederation intentionally limited powers. And by "limited," think more like neutered.

The Articles of Confederation didn't do much more than document a voluntary friendship between states. A direct quote from the Articles illustrates the problems succinctly.

"The said states hereby severally enter into a firm league of friendship with each other...."

The Articles of Confederation offered no provision for an executive leader (think in terms of today's President, Vice President, and associated staff) or government agencies to handle the chores associated with running nation. And there was no concept of a judiciary to even mediate, much less rule, on disagreements between states.

One of the bigger flaws was the lack of a provision to raise money. Forgetting about any costs related to national priorities like establishing currencies, making and honoring treaties with foreign countries, and addressing international trade, think about the elephant in the room—national security. No funding for wars. You know, like the Revolutionary War.

The situation of voluntary contribution from states was arguably no different than that of the voluntary "splitting of the check" at Happy Hour. You know how it works. Ten or twelve people gather for drinks and snacks. When the check comes, everyone kicks in "more than their fair share," but the pile of money on the table is inevitably 30% less than the bill, not even counting the tip. It's a miracle of human nature.

With no central organization or authority, the economic situation was dire. One Daniel Shays, a Revolutionary War veteran, was so ticked off by the economic disaster that he organized 4,000 ill-tempered farmers to take over the Springfield Armory and try to overthrow the government.

I could go on, but you get the idea.

There's a road to hell paved with good intentions, but I think it really leads straight to the Articles of Confederation. On the positive side, the Articles brought to light lots of flaws in government design that would later be rectified with the Constitution.

There was one benefit to the Articles of Confederation. It gave the new country its name.

Article I. The Stile of this confederacy shall be, "The United States of America."

Stacking the Deck: Madison's Virginia Plan

James Madison arrived at the Constitutional Convention with more than luggage; he brought a plan. Think of how much smoother committee meetings go when someone has done their homework and offers up a starting point for the group.

It also suggested a two-part legislature with representation based on population. Rather than starting the Constitutional Convention with a bunch of guys staring at each other, asking who had any good ideas, they had a well-thought-out document to guide them. It's a lot easier to edit, change and delete than start from scratch.

The Virginia Plan was a radical departure from the Articles of

Confederation and laid the groundwork for what would become the U.S. Constitution. The Virginia Plan, which he co-authored with Edmund Randolph, proposed a strong federal government with three branches: legislative, executive, and judicial. It emphasized checks and balances, separation of powers, and the concept of federalism.

Federalism is a structure of divided government, where authority is enumerated and shared between a national governing body and regional (states in this case) authority. Madison believed the national government needed to be strong enough to function but restrained enough to prevent tyranny. That's where the enumeration of power comes in. States are assumed to have all the power except that specifically and voluntarily ceded to the national government. At least, that's how it's supposed to work.

Madison's contributions earned him the title "Father of the Constitution." He was also instrumental in the drafting of the original 12 amendments in the Bill of Rights, 10 of which were ultimately ratified. His detailed note-taking at the Convention provides historians with much of what we know about the debates and compromises that occurred behind closed doors.

James Madison was seriously productive during the Constitutional Convention. Not only did he come prepared with a starting point for the eventual Constitution, but he also took copious notes during the convention. After his death, the government purchased his journal for the sum of $30,000. That was a lot of money in 1837.

How the House and Senate Were Born

One of the biggest stumbling blocks at the Constitutional

Convention was how states would be represented in the new legislature.

Even with just 13 states, all along the Eastern seaboard at the time, there were early population centers, and some states were more densely packed than others. Think bigger and more economically powerful. Large states wanted proportional representation (more people, so more votes). Small states wanted equal representation to avoid being steamrolled by the agendas of the larger players. This was an interesting precursor to the forthcoming Constitutional debates over minority representation in general, a thorny question. You know the classic quote.

"Democracy is two wolves and a lamb voting on what to have for lunch. Liberty is a well-armed lamb contesting the vote."

— Often attributed to Ben Franklin, but it doesn't appear in any of his writings.

The solution? The Great Compromise. Also known as the Connecticut Compromise, it established a bicameral legislature. The House of Representatives would have representation based on population, satisfying larger states. The Senate would have equal representation with two senators per state, pleasing the smaller states. Everyone wins. Sort of.

The Great Compromise almost didn't happen. In July 1787, the Constitutional Convention was deadlocked. Enter Roger Sherman of Connecticut, a man so plainspoken that one colleague called him "no orator" but "a man of good sense." Sherman proposed the middle ground: population-based representation in one chamber, equal votes in the other. His compromise broke the stalemate and saved the Convention. Ironically, Sherman wasn't a flashy founder like Madison or Hamilton, but he ended up shaping one of the most enduring features of American government.

From Three-Fifths to Reconstruction

The issue of slavery nearly derailed the whole Constitutional Convention. At the time, Southern states were reliant on slave labor to support their agrarian economy. More industrial Northern states were not.

The bottom line was predictable. Southern states wanted enslaved people counted for purposes of representation in the new national government. Of course, they did not want those people counted for taxation purposes, so there was some desire to have the cake and eat it too. Obviously, the Northern states were opposed to this concept.

Enter another compromise, and this one was a doozie.

Slaves would be counted as three-fifths of a person for both purposes—representation and taxation. I'm pretty sure no one asked the slaves of the time for their opinions on the matter.

This compromise remained in effect until two of the Reconstruction amendments, the 13th and 14th, were ratified in 1865 and 1868.

The Three-Fifths Compromise skewed representation and shaped politics for decades. Because slaves boosted Southern population counts without having any political voice, the South gained extra seats in Congress and, by extension, extra votes in the Electoral College. Historians argue this skew helped elect at least five pro-slavery presidents, including Thomas Jefferson in 1800. Without the "slave bonus," Jefferson might have lost to John Adams. The Three-Fifths Compromise tipped the scales of power.

Ratification: Federalists vs. Anti-Federalists

"We want small government!"
    The Federalists
    "No! We want an even smaller government!"
    The Anti-Federalists

Once the Constitution was written, the real fight began. Ratification required approval from nine of the thirteen states, and not everyone was on board.

Delegates, voters, and state Constitutional Convention party-goers had pledged allegiance to two rival gangs: the Federalists and the Anti-Federalists. The Federalists were supportive of a more powerful central government. The Anti-Federalists were concerned about preserving individual and states' rights against the onslaught of a powerful federal government.

The bottom line was this: the Federalists believed the Constitution on its own was good to go "as is," and adequately defined the power structure and balance. The Anti-Federalists were concerned about the erosion of individual liberty under a national government and believed there should be an addition of a "Bill of Rights" that clearly addressed the rights of citizens.

The Federalist & Anti-Federalist Papers

At the time, the only way to reach broad swaths of the public was via the printed word, so debates raged in newspapers and pamphlets. The Federalist Papers defended the Constitution and explained its mechanisms. Anti-Federalists, including Patrick Henry and George Mason, warned of tyranny and demanded the inclusion of a specific Bill of Rights in the new Constitution.

The Federalist Papers were a series of 85 essays published under the pseudonym "Publius" to convince the public and skeptical state ratifying conventions to support the new Constitution. Written by Alexander Hamilton, James Madison, and John Jay in 1787 and 1788, these essays explained the philosophy and mechanics behind the proposed system of government.

They tackled topics like checks and balances, the need for a strong central authority, and the dangers of factionalism.

For example, Federalist No. 10 (written by Madison) warned about the dangers of political factions. Federalist No. 51 explained how the separation of powers would prevent tyranny. In Federalist 84, Publius (in this case, Alexander Hamilton) made arguments that the Constitution already protected individual rights. He states, *"the Constitution proposed by the convention contains, as well as the Constitution of this state, a number of such provisions."*

Under the pen names of Brutus, Centinel, and Federal Farmer, other equally patriotic colonists argued for a Bill of Rights. They were nervous about handing too much power to the new government.

The arguments between Federalists and Anti-Federalists (they all believed in Federalism) were largely one of degree. A government should be powerful enough to provide national security, enforce laws related to commerce and contracts, and provide a system for dealing with those who interfere with the natural rights of their fellow citizens. However, a government should be small enough to defend against man's natural tendency to exert power over others when in positions of influence. Governments are, by definition, staffed with imperfect humans. If the government had too much power, then bad behavior could lead to tyranny.

These essays weren't just arguments; they became a foundational text in American political thought. Today, they're still cited in legal arguments and constitutional interpretation. The Federalist Papers were crucial in winning public support and are essential reading for understanding the founding principles of the United States.

The end result? Federalists agreed to add a Bill of Rights once the Constitution was ratified. This promise helped secure the support needed, and the Constitution was officially adopted. New President

George Washington sent copies of the 12 proposed amendments to the states on October 2, 1789. By December 15, 1791, three-fourths of the states had ratified the ten amendments, and the Bill of Rights became official.

The Constitutional Convention proceedings of 1787 were secret, and few outside knew the direction that the new Constitution would take. On completion, a local woman, identified as Mrs. Powel, asked Benjamin Franklin, "Well, Doctor, what have we got, a republic or a monarchy?" Franklin's response? "A republic, if you can keep it."

Part Two

Growing Pains

Chapter 6

Founding Frenemies: Hamilton vs. Jefferson

Before television talk shows and social media, there were scathing newspaper essays and not-so-civil cabinet meetings behind closed doors. Alexander Hamilton and Thomas Jefferson loathed (OK, let's say vigorously opposed) each other's visions for the country. Hamilton wanted banks and big government; Jefferson wanted farms and individual liberty. Their feud shaped America's first political parties and nearly broke the Cabinet.

The Presidency Before Campaigns

George Washington was elected president in 1789 and again for his second term in 1792.

Fun Fact: He was the only United States president to ever receive every single electoral vote in two different elections. Another fun fact: There was no real campaign at the time. He was the only person under serious consideration, due to his national reputation as Commander of the Continental Army and President of the Constitutional Convention. That's a pretty good resume. His vice president? That would be John Adams, who was elected both times to that position.

Yes, modern presidents live under incredible pressure each and every day as the scale of their role has grown exponentially. However, Washington was keenly aware that he was the very first caretaker of the position for a new and hopefully enduring country. Every action he took, every decision he made, every process, procedure, or organization that he formed was likely to have a lasting impact on the future. So he was exceedingly cautious about everything he did, knowing that future generations would look back on those decisions with a critical eye.

The first cabinet included Thomas Jefferson as Secretary of State, Alexander Hamilton as Secretary of the Treasury, Henry Knox as Secretary of War and Edmund Randolph as Attorney General.

George Washington's cabinet was small, but the ideological divide between two of its members was oceanic. As Secretary of the Treasury, Alexander Hamilton envisioned a strong central government, an industrial economy, and close ties with Britain, the country they'd just defeated in a shooting war. As Secretary of State, Thomas Jefferson wanted a decentralized government, an agrarian society, and support for revolutionary France. Can you say awkward?

As you might imagine, this led to some interesting cabinet meetings, or maybe battlegrounds. Jefferson saw Hamilton's banking and debt schemes as aristocratic and dangerous. Hamilton saw Jefferson's views as dangerously naïve and rooted in utopian fantasy.

Political bickering is nothing new and certainly not unique to us in modern times; the founders were masters at it.

Washington, ever the unifier, tried to balance their views but often sided with Hamilton's pragmatic approach. Their rivalry laid the groundwork for America's first political parties (remember Washington's view on that?) and helped shape the broader ideological debates that still define American politics.

Only 10 of the 13 states participated in the first presidential election because only 11 of them had ratified the Constitution by that time and were able to vote. New York failed to create and present electors for that election and also did not participate.

The 1st National Bank of... America?

National Bank? Could the new government even do that? This became one of the first tests of the new Constitution and how it was to be interpreted as future ambiguities arose.

The Constitution was written, giving a limited list of enumerated powers to the federal government, as documented in Article 1, Section 8. This is the section that defines the role of the decision-making body—the legislature. Among the federal powers listed are all sorts of things like taxation, borrowing money, regulating commerce and trade, printing money, creating post offices, declaring war, and hiring armies and navies, just to name a few.

But it doesn't precisely spell out whether it's OK to create a national bank. Clearly, it dances all around the issue by including federal borrowing and money printing.

One of Hamilton's boldest proposals was the creation of a national bank—a central institution to hold federal funds, issue currency, and manage government debt. He believed it was essential for stabilizing the fledgling economy and asserting national credit-worthiness.

Jefferson and his political allies objected, arguing that the Constitution didn't authorize such a bank. They feared it concentrated too much power in the hands of the federal government and wealthy elites. The battle culminated in a showdown in Washington's administration.

The result?

Hamilton won. Washington signed the bank bill into law in 1791, and the First Bank of the United States became a cornerstone of Hamilton's financial system. The fight over the bank became a defining conflict over constitutional interpretation (broad vs. strict) and set the tone for future clashes over federal authority.

The idea remained controversial, and when the bank's charter expired in 1811, Congress voted not to renew it, although the margin was close, and the bank ended up closing.

But wait.

After the War of 1812 and its related financial challenges and difficulties without said bank, a new charter was granted by Congress to create the Second Bank of the United States, which operated into the 1930s.

Ordinary Americans were deeply suspicious of the First Bank, viewing it as a plaything for the rich elites and not something to benefit "regular folks." When the bank opened for business in Philadelphia in 1791, the very first thing it sold were shares of stock. But people went crazy buying them up, and prices doubled the first week. Jeffersonians sneered, calling it the first "bubble" in American history.

Thanks, Guys... The Birth of Political Parties

If you're paying attention, you're already seeing the development of political factions. On one side are the Federalists, as evidenced by people like Alexander Hamilton, and on the opposing side are the Democratic-Republicans represented by people like Thomas Jefferson and his allies. These two movements ultimately became America's first political parties. Thanks, guys...

Trying to look on the bright side, I guess it was at least somewhat of a good thing that the early disagreements were based on tangible political beliefs. Like the Federalists, who favored a strong central government, a commercial economy, and a pro-British foreign policy, while the Democratic-Republicans championed the rights of states, an agrarian economy, and better alliances with France. Whatever one's stance on those positions, at least they were clearly defined.

But just like today, the clear political positions were diluted with personal attacks and venomous diatribes flung in all directions by individuals, politicians, and newspapers, the primary media of the time. Sound familiar?

So, love or hate the idea of political parties from almost day one, the concept became a key feature of the American democratic society. I suppose it was inevitable because the system itself, as outlined in the Constitution, was designed to favor vigorous political debate over positions rather than blind acceptance of a prevailing viewpoint. Just think about how the legislature is formed with two opposing bodies elected differently and for different term durations. The conflict is designed into the system, so, at least in the ideal sense, the best outcome must be a result of "enthusiastic" debate based on the challenge and defense of positions.

The birth of America's first political parties got ugly fast. Newspapers became the 18th-century equivalent of Twitter flame wars. Jefferson's Democratic-Republicans secretly funded papers that accused President John Adams of being a wannabe monarch. One even claimed he planned to marry his son off to a European princess to start an American dynasty. Meanwhile, Federalist editors blasted Jefferson as a "cowardly atheist" who would unleash French-style guillotines in the streets. The venom went beyond print, too: in 1804, Federalist Alexander Hamilton and Democratic-Republican Aaron Burr literally settled their feud with a duel, ending Hamilton's life. So if today's political shenanigans feel vicious, remember: the very first parties set the tone with scandal, slander, and pistol shots at dawn. Maybe if our present-day politicians had to settle their differences that way, they'd find ways to get along?

Media at War: Hamilton's Gazette vs. Jefferson's Gazette

Given its importance throughout American history, one would think the media was an entity designed and created by the Constitution itself as a foundation of our political system. Of course it wasn't, but it sure was given plenty of teeth by the First Amendment in the Bill of Rights. The idea was to empower both citizens and the press alike to continuously challenge the government. Remember, by definition, governments were not to be trusted, even this new Constitutional Republic.

Just like now, in the 1790s, newspapers weren't just sources of information; they were political weapons. Editors like Philip Freneau, of the "National Gazette," supported by Jefferson, published scathing critiques of the Federalists and Hamilton's policies. As an interesting sidebar, Jefferson drove the creation of this particular branch of the media by actively seeking a counter to the predominant Federalist-oriented media of the day. He went so far as to get Freneau a job at the State Department to help support his budding editorial career.

In response, Federalist papers like John Fenno's "Gazette of the United States" struck back with equal ferocity. Likewise, Alexander Hamilton helped directly launch the Gazette by providing financial and editorial support. Modern politicians didn't invent the idea of leveraging (or creating) allies in the media either!

These newspapers helped shape public opinion and were essential to building party loyalty. In addition to reporting on events of the day, they spread rumors, exaggerated claims, and published pseudonymous attacks. Readers weren't just consuming bland and neutral reporting of the news—they were joining sides and augmenting their positions using the commercially printed word for added credibility.

Just like today, although the means have changed from printed papers and pamphlets to television and social media, the press demonstrated powerful abilities to sway public opinion.

As King Solomon said in the Book of Ecclesiastes, "There is nothing new under the sun."

The newspaper battles of the 1790s got "soap opera" personal. Hamilton himself, writing under pen names like "Phocion" and "Pacificus," churned out essays defending his policies and torching Jefferson. Jefferson's ally Philip Freneau fired back with biting satire in the National Gazette, calling Hamilton a monarchist who wanted to shackle Americans to British bankers. The mudslinging escalated so far that George Washington, who hated public brawls, fumed privately that Jefferson had turned the press into a "diabolical" weapon.

Paranoia in Action: From Liberty to Lockup

Lofty ideals always sound great on paper. Then reality strikes, and the waters get a bit muddier.

Just seven years after ratifying the Bill of Rights, Congress passed the Sedition Act of 1798. Federalists, led by President John Adams, were nervous about possible French influence during the "troubles" with France. They were also concerned about bad treatment in the press.

So these guys, the ones who had just fought a shooting war with the British for individual rights and against big governments acting like bullies, made "false, scandalous, and malicious writing" against the government illegal. Dozens of newspaper editors and political opponents were arrested.

Sometimes the jokes just write themselves. This was slightly hypocritical to say the least.

The backlash was fierce. Thomas Jefferson and James Madison denounced the act as unconstitutional overreach, and voters agreed. They elected Jefferson in 1800, effectively squashing the new law.

If it can happen once, it can happen twice.

In the 20th century, similar fears resurfaced, this time during World War I. The Espionage Act of 1917 and its 1918 Sedition Act amendment criminalized interference with the draft, support for enemy powers, and even "disloyal" speech about the government, Constitution, or the military. In other words, "we will not tolerate 'wrongspeak' under penalty of law."

More than 2,000 people were prosecuted, among them union organizers, pacifists, and Socialist leader Eugene V. Debs, who received a ten-year prison sentence simply for delivering an anti-war speech. Didn't we have that whole Freedom of Speech thing in place by then? Yes, I'm being cynical, that was made quite clear in the Bill of Rights!

Interestingly, the Supreme Court, in cases like Schenck v. United States, upheld these laws, introducing the famous but dangerous "clear and present danger" standard for limiting speech. Critics pointed out the irony: a nation founded on dissent and rebellion against the government was jailing citizens for...well, you get the idea.

As you'll see, this wasn't the end of bending the rules and principles during times of great fear. Just ask the Japanese-American citizens who were living here when the United States got involved in World War II.

One of the most outrageous Sedition Act prosecutions was against Congressman Matthew Lyon of Vermont. In 1798, he was fined $1,000 and sentenced to four months in jail for writing that President John Adams had "an unbounded thirst for ridiculous pomp, foolish adulation, and selfish avarice." Instead of destroying his political career, Lyon campaigned for re-election from his jail cell. And he won. His constituents even paraded through the streets carrying a liberty pole in his honor. The episode made him an instant folk hero and turned Adams into the butt of jokes. Nothing quite says "free country" like tossing your critics in prison, only to watch voters send them right back to Congress. Isn't American history great?

Electoral Quirks: How to Elect Frenemies

Since we're talking about how similar things have always been in the political arena, we ought to mention the post-George Washington elections. Again, while from our modern perspective, we think all these shenanigans began in recent history, they've really been going on forever.

The election of 1796 marked the first real test of America's new political system—and an early look at the masters of political division in action. John Adams, a Federalist, narrowly defeated Thomas Jefferson, the Democratic-Republican. As a result, Adams became president and Jefferson became vice president.

As originally outlined by the Constitution, the process of picking the president and vice president was not like the elections we have today. Each elector from a given state wrote down their vote for two individuals they thought would make the best president. The votes were tallied for that particular state's electors, and the sealed list was sent to the President of the Senate. In the presence of the Senate and House of Representatives members, the Senate President opened the sealed ballot counts from each state, then named the majority vote winner president.

The second-highest vote count designated the vice president. Did you get that? The top two people running against each other were named to the same team as President and Vice President. Try to imagine any two Presidential contenders from opposing parties going to work together in the White House every day. That sounds like a recipe for major dysfunction.

With all that said, the election of 1800 was even more significant. Dubbed the "Revolution of 1800," it was the first peaceful transfer of power between rival political parties in American history. Adams won when Washington bowed out as promised after two terms, but they shared similar political views. In 1800, Jefferson defeated Adams, and despite intense bitterness, the handoff occurred without violence or upheaval, although dirty looks were almost certainly at play.

These elections helped underscore the resilience of the new Constitutional Republic. The electoral system was still evolving (and would undergo changes later), but the idea that power could pass peacefully between political enemies became a proud American tradition.

The election of 1796 gave America a president and vice president who couldn't stand each other. John Adams and Thomas Jefferson had once been close allies during the Revolution, but by the late 1790s they were political arch-enemies. Adams called Jefferson "weak" and too sympathetic to the French Revolution; Jefferson thought Adams was a would-be monarch.

Their four years together were so frosty that Jefferson skipped cabinet meetings and used his vice presidency to quietly undermine Adams from the Senate chair. The dysfunction was so obvious that Congress eventually rewrote the rules with the 12th Amendment (1804), which created separate ballots for president and vice president.

Chapter 7

Napoleon's Fire Sale, Jefferson's Jackpot

Napoleon had a bit of a cash and resource problem. Jefferson had an open mind for some serious expansion. Put these factors together, and the stage was set for some serious bargaining. The Louisiana Purchase was a 530-million-acre real estate deal that doubled the size of the U.S. with no war, no bloodshed, and hardly any paperwork. Let's explore the geopolitical grand prize of 1803 and how it redefined the geography and future of "America."

How Jefferson Doubled the Country Overnight

Back and forth, back and forth...

Let's condense a long and complicated story to a perhaps overly simplified version, but still reasonably accurate.

As you already know, the land that eventually became known as the United States of America was populated and settled by everyone under the sun. The British, the Spanish, the French, the Dutch, and so on. And of course, the Native Americans. Up until the French and Indian War, France maintained control of large chunks of land, including New Orleans and Louisiana west of the Mississippi River. After the French and Indian War, those territories were transferred to Spain and the northern parts of that to Britain.

A few decades later, enter Napoleon with his grand plans. He aimed to reassert France and reclaim territory now held by Spain. Spain had been cooperating with the fledgling United States and allowing access to the Mississippi River and the port at New Orleans for the export of colonial goods, so things were relatively hunky dory from the Americans' perspective.

But while Napoleon Bonaparte had dreams, he had even bigger problems. In the early 1800s, he envisioned a French empire in the Americas, anchored by the Louisiana Territory and supported by sugar-rich colonies in the Caribbean, especially Saint-Domingue (now Haiti).

However, a brutal slave revolt led by Toussaint Louverture and others devastated French control in Haiti. Facing massive casualties, military personnel decimation resulting from a bout with yellow fever, logistical nightmares, and a looming war with Britain, Napoleon abandoned his New World ambitions. He needed funds and focus for his European campaigns.

American leadership didn't fully appreciate France's dire straits, so their reentry into this scene caused no small amount of consternation. Jefferson and Secretary of State James Madison worked to resolve the issue with France diplomatically. And Jefferson dispatched James Monroe to Paris to act as Minister Extraordinary to help resolve the situation. That's quite a job title, isn't it?

As things turned out, the French had a surprise solution in mind. Bottom line: They were interested in an outright sale of most of what's now known as part of the flyover country of the United States to the Americans for dirt cheap. While the lines don't exactly match up, think of 15 states as we know them today, including western Louisiana, Arkansas, Missouri, Iowa, Oklahoma, Kansas, Nebraska and sizable portions of North Dakota, South Dakota, Montana, Wyoming, Colorado, Minnesota, New Mexico and northern Texas.

In 1803, Jefferson, under a handshake deal made by U.S. Minister to France Robert Livingston and James Madison, made one of the boldest and most consequential executive decisions in American history: the Louisiana Purchase.

When the dust settled, Jefferson had purchased 827,000 square miles of land, immediately doubling the size of the United States. The price? A cool $15 million, or about four cents per acre. That's the equivalent of about $426 million today—still a bargain under any definition.

Nearly everyone involved in this epic real estate transaction exceeded their technical authority. Livingston and Madison were authorized to spend up to $10 million for New Orleans and some territory in the Floridas. Jefferson wasn't sure he had the Constitutional authority to buy all this property. Napoleon reclaimed the territory from Spain, but we're not necessarily sure the Spanish were prepared to give it up. Then again, they didn't have the military clout to do much about it.

Lewis & Clark: America's First Road Trip

When you buy a new home, the first thing you want to do is explore every room, nook and cranny to see what you've got. When you buy a new country, you do the same thing, although you call it an expedition and send a bunch of brave, or perhaps crazy, explorers to go forth and map it out.

Jefferson quickly commissioned a military-led expedition, to be commanded by Captain Meriwether Lewis and Lieutenant William Clark, to head westward to map the land, establish trade with Native tribes, and find a route to the Pacific Ocean.

Also known as the Corps of Discovery, the team spent two years, 1804 to 1806, traveling over 8,000 miles into territories largely unknown, starting from St. Louis and heading northwest up the Missouri River and then across the top border of the current United States all the way to the Pacific Ocean.

The big prize would be to find and map a water-based route to the Pacific. That didn't happen, but the team of just under 50 did make lots of important discoveries.

They cataloged hundreds of new plant and animal species (Prairie Dogs and Grizzly Bears, for example), documented the geography, took soil samples and established claims to the Pacific Northwest.

Another element of the expedition aimed to establish relations with Native Americans. Most encounters appeared to be peaceable and included trade, sharing of provisions, food and entertainment. The reception by the Lakota in South Dakota was a bit cooler, owing to their existing agreements with the British, but the expedition and that tribe managed to part ways without bloodshed. The relatively unopposed passage was due in part to Native American guides. You might remember Sacagawea from her recent appearance on a dollar coin.

Perhaps the best evidence of success in establishing relationships with Native Americans was the fact that even after the teams split into relatively small groups, only one of the original participants died during the mission. From most accounts, the Native Americans they encountered often helped with food, supplies and shelter.

The expedition never did find a continuous water route to the Pacific, but it fulfilled its larger mission: proving the vastness and richness of the new territory. Lewis and Clark's journey fired the imagination of the nation and laid the groundwork for westward expansion. As we'll see, the rest of the westward expansion wasn't as friendly as the Lewis and Clark Expedition.

Sacagawea made the 8,000-mile trek while carrying her infant son, Jean Baptiste, on her back. The presence of a woman with a baby instantly signaled to tribes that the Corps of Discovery was not a war party. Who would march into battle with a baby? Clark was so impressed with the child that he nick-named him "Pomp" and later invited him to live with him in St. Louis, where he paid for the boy's education. Sacagawea's quiet strength and the image of her carrying an infant through the wilderness did as much to secure the expedition's safety as any musket.

When Expansion Meant Displacement

While the Louisiana Purchase was a triumph for the Eastern areas of the United States, it marked the beginning of a prolonged and painful chapter for Native American tribes. The U.S. government claimed vast new lands without consulting or recognizing the Indigenous peoples who lived there. As we learned earlier in this story, those cultures began tens of thousands of years earlier with the migration of eastern Asian and Siberian nomads into North and South America.

As settlers pushed westward, Native tribes were displaced,

forced into new conflicts, and subjected to increasing pressure from the federal government. The aftermath of the purchase ignited a cycle of broken treaties, forced removals, and violent confrontations that would define much of the 19th century.

In 1832, Sauk leader Black Hawk led a band of Native Americans back across the Mississippi River into Illinois to reclaim their homeland after being pushed west. The U.S. government considered it an "invasion," sparking the Black Hawk War. Though his group included mostly women, children, and elderly, U.S. militias and regular troops pursued them relentlessly. The conflict ended in tragedy at the Battle of Bad Axe, where hundreds of Native people were killed while trying to flee across the river. Among the Illinois militiamen was a young Abraham Lincoln. This was his only military service before becoming president. Lincoln later joked that the closest he came to combat was "fighting mosquitoes," but the war left a grim legacy of how even small acts of Native resistance were crushed.

Chapter 8

The War of 1812: America's Forgotten Sequel

While the Revolutionary War didn't officially end until the signing of the Treaty of Paris on September 3, 1783, the major fighting ended back in 1781 when the British surrendered during the Siege of Yorktown.

It didn't take long for a rematch. Round two of the British—American bout kicked off in 1812.

The British weren't done with us. We weren't quite done with them. The War of 1812 saw invasions, embarrassing defeats, and a possible do-over with the whole American independence thing. Also, the White House got fried, Andrew Jackson became a national hero, and Francis Scott Key had a front-row seat to history in the making and the greatest song-writing opportunity ever.

The War of 1812: Pride, Trade, and a Dash of Canada

Did anyone really think the world's most powerful army would quietly slink back into the corner after getting whooped in the Revolutionary War by a bunch of farmers? No.

Some level of bad blood festered between the Americans and British over issues like trade. For example, the British were at war with the French, and were mighty hacked off about the Americans' trading with France, so they applied pressure to stop it, including attempts at blockades. At the time, the British Navy far surpassed the capability of its American counterpart.

Then there were the puffed-up Americans, chock full of confidence and making forays into British-held Canada, perhaps seeking to claim some additional territory in the north. The British weren't going to stand for much of that.

And, as settlers continued westward to the Pacific coast, the British decided to facilitate a bit of guerrilla warfare by arming, supplying and training indigenous tribes in the Pacific Northwest who already had a proclivity to fighting American forces.

And then there was the impressment issue. The British Royal Navy had a habit of stopping American ships and forcibly drafting (impressing) sailors, many of whom were U.S. citizens, into British Navy service. To Americans, this was a national insult and a direct assault on their sovereignty.

Let's add yet another cause: simple pride. Whether in response to an attack on American honor via incidents like the Chesapeake Affair, where a British ship pursued and boarded the American USS Chesapeake seeking "deserters," or just a puffed-up sense of exceptionalism by the new Americans, wars have certainly kicked off for lesser reasons.

The pressure built as American "War Hawks" in Congress demanded action. They saw the conflict not only as retaliation against British abuse, but as an opportunity to defend national honor and possibly seize Canada. The War of 1812 became a messy mix of tempers, economic frustration, and territorial ambition.

Early in the War of 1812, the USS Constitution squared off against the British frigate Guerriere. As cannonballs slammed into her sides, American sailors were astonished to see them bounce off the Constitution's thick live-oak hull. One shouted, "Huzzah! Her sides are made of iron!" That sounds like a great nickname in the making, and it was: "Old Ironsides" was born. The victory electrified the young nation, proving that the U.S. Navy could go toe-to-toe with the world's most powerful fleet. Old Ironsides became such a legend that when the Navy tried to scrap her in the 1830s, public outrage and a poem from Oliver Wendell Holmes saved the ship. Today, Old Ironsides is still afloat as the world's oldest commissioned warship.

The British Burn the Americans

One of the most humiliating moments of the War of 1812 (or arguably, all of American history) came in August 1814, when British troops casually strolled into Washington, D.C., and set about torching the place.

In fairness, there was an element of "what comes around, goes around," as the Americans had done a similar thing in the British colony of York (now Toronto) not long before.

Back to Washington. These weren't rogue arsonists; they were elite British soldiers under orders. British forces numbering about

4,500 were led by Major General Robert Ross and Rear Admiral George Cockburn. As the Americans had just been defeated at the Battle of Bladensburg, there was little hope of stopping the oncoming British forces. Most of the leadership evacuated, and the Americans even burned the Washington Navy Yard to prevent the British from gaining hold of supplies and ships.

So, there was little, if any, opposition to the Redcoats' raid on the capital. In fact, rumor has it that British officers enjoyed a fine meal in the White House (before setting the place on fire) that had been prepared for President Madison before he and Dolly rushed out the door.

When all was said and done, the British burned the Capitol building, the Treasury, and yes, the White House.

This wrapped up quickly, except for the big bruise on the new nation's pride. British forces were in and out of Washington, D.C. in about 26 hours total. No invasion inland. No occupation. Just a quick hit and run with one heck of a dinner followed by a campfire.

The British saw their actions as fair play, considering the York incident. Americans, on the other hand, were horrified. The capital city had been violated, and the young nation's pride was singed along with its government buildings.

That old story about Dolly Madison refusing to leave and flee from the British until she saved a portrait of George Washington? True. She had the frame broken and rolled up the canvas for easier transport.

Oh, and the White House wasn't really "The White House" until well after it was rebuilt from the fire damage. "Well after" meaning not until Teddy Roosevelt officially named it in 1901. Prior to that time, people referred to it as either the "President's House," "President's Palace," or "Executive Mansion."

From Drinking Song to National Anthem

At risk of a terrible oxymoron, war was so civilized back then.

During the British bombardment of Fort McHenry in Baltimore in September 1814, Francis Scott Key found himself in an awkward position onboard a British warship. Key, a Washington, D.C. lawyer and amateur poet, had come under a flag of truce to negotiate the release of a captured American civilian.

He was successful, but there was a catch. Just like in the bad guy thriller shows and movies, he and his companions had "seen too much." The British were about to launch a major attack on the city of Baltimore, and they couldn't have Key and company sharing their secret plans with the enemy. So, they simply detained them on a ship until the battle concluded. As a result, Key became an accidental eyewitness to one of the most dramatic moments of the war.

For 25 straight hours, British warships pounded the protective bastion of Baltimore harbor, Fort McHenry, with everything they had, including rockets, mortar shells, and cannon fire. From his vantage point aboard ship, Key could only watch helplessly through the smoky chaos, wondering if the fort and the city behind it would survive. The night sky lit up with fiery trails and explosions, and the outcome was uncertain until the following morning. In the dawn's first light, Key saw something that fired up his national pride: the giant American flag still waving defiantly.

Overcome with emotion, he began scribbling lines of verse on the back of an envelope. The result was "Defence of Fort M'Henry," a four-stanza poem that captured both the destruction and the hope of what he had witnessed. It was quickly printed and set to the tune of "To Anacreon in Heaven," a popular British drinking song, even in the new United States.

The song struck a chord, literally and figuratively, in part because so many people already knew the tune from the drinking song, with different words, of course. It spread rapidly, especially among soldiers and veterans, who saw in it a reflection of their own grit and determination. Though it would take more than a century, until 1931, for Congress to officially designate it as the national anthem.

Key's words did more than commemorate a single night of battle, as if that wasn't enough. They captured the spirit of a nation that refused to crumble under fire, quite literally. "The Star-Spangled Banner" remains a powerful reminder of a young republic that, despite being outgunned, outmanned, and under siege, still stood tall when the sun came up.

That famous flag Francis Scott Key saw at dawn was enormous. Commissioned by Fort McHenry's commander, Major George Armistead, it measured 30 by 42 feet. He wanted it to be so large that "the British will have no trouble seeing it from a distance." Baltimore seamstress Mary Pickersgill and her 13-year-old daughter stitched it together in just six weeks, working late into the nights. They had to spread the fabric across a nearby brewery floor to assemble it. The giant banner took 400 yards of wool bunting and weighed over 80 pounds. Today, it rests in the Smithsonian, carefully preserved under dim lights. It's a little ragged, but still larger than life.

The War That Changed Almost Nothing

Some wars end with a bang; others with a whimper.

The War of 1812 ended with the result of...not much. The underlying issues that started the war were largely unresolved.

The Americans didn't seize Canada. The British support of the guerrilla war effort in the Pacific Northwest didn't stop American expansion into the area. Sailors were still impressing each other into servitude. And pride still remained on both sides of the pond.

The Treaty of Ghent (modern Belgium) was signed on December 24, 1814. Both parties agreed to restore pre-war territorial boundaries, more or less. Both agreed to give back prisoners they'd taken. Both agreed to return to business as usual regarding trade and such. And both agreed it would be a good idea to try to end the slave trade. Obviously, that one took quite a bit longer to resolve.

If you count intangibles, the War of 1812 did bolster America's confidence as a real country, capable of entering world affairs as a power and defending itself. Once again, the country had gone toe-to-toe with the most powerful military in the world and come out in one piece with its head held high.

The anticlimactic end of the War of 1812 gave way to one of the strangest chapters in U.S. politics: the so-called "Era of Good Feelings." With the Federalist Party collapsing after opposing the war (and looking unpatriotic in the process), President James Monroe enjoyed a period where serious political opposition nearly vanished. Newspapers even joked that campaign speeches were basically just "Monroe being congratulated for being Monroe." Of course, beneath the surface, tensions over slavery, regional rivalries, and economic policy simmered. But for a brief stretch in the 1810s and 1820s, Americans liked to imagine that partisanship had melted away. As we'll see, that didn't last long.

The War Was Over, but the Shooting Wasn't

Oops. No one got the mail. While the treaty in Ghent was signed on December 24, 1814, many on the battlefields didn't get the memo until much later.

On January 8, 1815, American and British forces clashed near Chalmette Plantation, just outside New Orleans.

The Americans, really a collection of mixed forces including US Army regulars, local militia, free men of color, Choctaw Indians, and even some pirates (really) set up defensive positions against the British, who were trying to seize control of New Orleans and of the Mississippi River. The British mounted a full frontal attack, and the results were disastrous. Over 2,000 British were killed, wounded or captured, while just 100 on the American side suffered the same result.

A popular hero emerged from this battle "after the war's end." Major General Andrew Jackson led the American side and was hailed as the conquering hero based on the battle's results. As we'll soon see, that later gave him quite a bit of political clout in Washington.

So, while the battle had no impact on the outcome of the War of 1812 (it was already over), it did contribute mightily to growing national confidence and pride.

Those "pirates" who fought alongside Jackson at New Orleans weren't your average rum-soaked rogues. They were led by one Jean Lafitte, a French privateer who ran a smuggling empire out of the bayous. When the British tried to recruit him, Lafitte offered his services to the Americans instead, under one condition: his captured men must be pardoned. Jackson initially called him a "hellish banditti" but changed his tune when he saw Lafitte's men bring cannons, gunpowder, and invaluable knowledge of Louisiana's swamps. Their contribution was so vital that the Louisiana legislature later thanked Lafitte for his "courage and fidelity."

Chapter 9

Trail of Tears: The Dark Cost of Expansion

Manifest Destiny, combined with explosive population growth, had a dark side. As America's eastern population exploded and more people spread west, Native American nations were forced to move, sometimes via "negotiation," but often violently. The Trail of Tears wasn't just one event but a symbol of systemic betrayal. Let's explore the policies, people, and precedents that left lasting impacts.

Jackson's "Voluntary" Evictions

In 1800, the population of the new United States of America was a bit over five million. Largely due to natural activity (lots more births as opposed to just immigration), it exploded to over 12 million by 1830. Add to that inherent beliefs by many that it was America's moral obligation to grow and spread democracy to the world (primarily westward for now), and conditions were ripe for some serious rationalization justifying bad behavior.

Lots of underlying factors were at play, driving the upcoming forced relocation of many tens of thousands of Native Americans representing numerous well-established tribes. They lived on developed land, much of it in the southeast. White settlers had little interest in trying to co-exist with Indian residents, so one has to believe a healthy dose of simple racism was at play. Lands west of the Mississippi were seen by white settlers as less desirable, and therefore, in their mind, just fine for Indian populations.

Add all sorts of reasons and justifications like those together, and pressure mounted for a "solution."

The Indian Removal Act, advocated for and signed by Andrew Jackson in 1830, outlined a "voluntary" process that would help resident Native Americans primarily in the southeastern United States move to new and permanently titled land, mostly in Oklahoma. This was a very bold move. By this time, Native Americans were living in developed settlements and towns with prepared farmlands, trade, and representative government, non-agrarian occupations, educational systems, and so on. We're not talking about a nomadic "hunting and gathering" existence where folks could just "keep moving" to a new place.

Anyway, one might think of the "voluntary" nature of this program kind of like "voluntary" federal taxes. Sure, you can choose not to pay, but the IRS will seize your property, handcuff you and "voluntarily" relocate you to a federal prison. So, while framed as a "voluntary" relocation, in practice, it often involved coercion, deception, and force. All the while, the program was painted as benevolent.

The Indian Removal Act paved the way for the forced relocations that became known as the Trail of Tears. As we'll see, the marches of 60,000 to perhaps as many as 100,000 residents ended in death for as many as 25 percent of those impacted. Disease, starvation and outright violence all took their toll.

It also marked a low point in the U.S. government's treatment of Native nations, legitimizing land grabs and breaking plenty of treaties. Jackson's role in this process remains deeply divisive, with some seeing him as a nation-builder and others as a violator of human rights.

A Cherokee survivor named Tsali left behind one of the most haunting accounts of the Trail of Tears. He described soldiers driving families from their homes at gunpoint, giving them no time to gather belongings before being herded into stockades. During the march west, people collapsed from hunger, cold, and exhaustion. Tsali recalled mothers laying their blankets over sick children while they themselves froze to death. Contemporary witnesses also described the Little Tennessee River running red with blood from those who had no shoes in the snow. Roughly 4,000 Cherokees died along the 1,200-mile march. That was nearly a quarter of the entire group.

Cherokee vs. Georgia: Stacked Deck Justice

With a new court system in place, some tribes took to the legal system to protect their homelands. For example, in 1831, the Cherokee Nation sought to stop Georgia from enforcing state laws that stripped them of their rights and land.

In conjunction with the federal Indian Removal Act, the state of

Georgia had passed its own laws directing the division and reassignment to white settlers of Indian lands within the state. In this case, the dispute was pursued by the Cherokee Nation, which claimed it was not subject to Georgia state law because it was an independent, sovereign nation. For example, along similar argument lines, France wouldn't be subject to Georgia state law either.

The case made its way to the Supreme Court with this argument, but it was eventually shot down. The Court, led by Chief Justice John Marshall, ruled that the Cherokee tribe was not a foreign nation but a "domestic dependent nation." This technical classification denied them standing to sue and left them vulnerable to the actions of the state.

This represented the birth of a new can of worms, as the "domestic dependent nation" idea presented the notion that the tribes had limited sovereignty but were also under federal authority. It was kind of like saying, "Yes, you are free and in charge of your destiny, but you have to do what we say." The idea seems somewhat contradictory in nature.

Though the case didn't result in a definitive legal victory for the Cherokee, it was the beginning of legal battles over tribal sovereignty. It also highlighted the challenges Native nations faced when seeking protection through American courts. The Native Americans might have argued the deck was stacked against them.

The Cherokee weren't just fighting in courtrooms; they were also fighting with the power of the pen. Around the same time as their Supreme Court case, they published the "Cherokee Phoenix" in both English and Cherokee syllabary. It was the first Native American newspaper. Its editor, Elias Boudinot, used the paper to rally support for sovereignty and to publicize injustices like Georgia's land seizures. The very existence of the Phoenix undermined stereotypes of Native people as "uncivilized" and proved the Cherokee were every bit as literate, organized, and politically savvy as their white neighbors.

The Symbolic Triumph of Worcester v. Georgia

Battles ebb and flow, even courtroom dramas. Just one year later, as the Cherokee continued to pursue a remedy through the legal system, things took a turn in their favor. Like many landmark decisions, this one arose from a seemingly inconsequential detail.

First, some quick background. Georgia had laws on the books to restrict white presence and influence on native lands. In fact, one needed a license from the state to reside in Cherokee territory.

Missionary Samuel Worcester (and others) were arrested for living on Cherokee tribal lands. The case made its way to court and eventually to the Supreme Court.

In a stunning apparent reversal of position, the court held that Cherokee lands were a "distinct, independent political community" not subject to state laws. Rather, it was the federal government that had authority over regulation, treaties and such. Therefore, all the laws related to the regulation and relocation of the Cherokee established by the state of Georgia were null and void. Chalk up some points in favor of tribal sovereignty.

Court rulings are fine and dandy, but the Supreme Court has no police force or army to enforce its decision. Those things reside in the Executive Branch, and Andrew Jackson was not of a mind to enforce the ruling, nor was the state of Georgia.

The case showed the limits of judicial authority when the executive branch refuses to comply. It also underscored how legal victories for Native Americans were often symbolic rather than practical.

Samuel Worcester, the missionary at the heart of the case, didn't just fight for Cherokee rights from afar. He lived among them, learned their language, and even helped publish the "Cherokee Phoenix." After the Supreme Court ruled in his favor, Worcester remained in jail for over a year because Georgia refused to release him. He was only freed when the state quietly pardoned him to defuse tensions. Rather than retreat, Worcester moved with the Cherokee people westward after the Trail of Tears, continuing his work as a translator and advocate. His life story shows that Worcester v. Georgia wasn't just a legal footnote; it was also the story of a man who literally put his life on the line for tribal sovereignty.

John Ross and Cherokee Resistance

John Ross (1790–1866) was born to a Scottish father and a Cherokee mother. Growing up bilingual in a dual-cultural environment, he steadily rose through the ranks of the Cherokee Nation leadership until he eventually became Principal Chief in 1828. He held that position for 40 years, longer than any other leader in Cherokee history.

Ross emerged as a tireless fighter for the cause of the Cherokee people, fighting legal and diplomatic battles in the legislatures and courts. When faced with the demoralizing lack of enforcement of the Worcester v. Georgia (1832) decision, he led the Cherokee people on the forced march, better known as the Trail of Tears, to their new assigned lands in Oklahoma. Along the way, the nation lost about a quarter of its population from the harsh treatment and conditions. In fact, Ross's wife Quatie perished on the journey.

Once in the new land, Ross continued to serve the Cherokee people, struggling to implement a new representative government and unify the various factions heading into the Civil War. In the brother against brother conflict, even the Cherokee Nation was divided, with some factions supporting the Confederacy and others the Union.

During the Trail of Tears, John Ross's wife, Quatie, reportedly gave her only blanket to a sick child during a freezing night on the march and later died of pneumonia. Her death became a symbol of the suffering endured by thousands of Cherokee families. Despite his personal loss, Ross stayed with his people throughout the ordeal, helping organize food, shelter, and burials along the way. Later, when the Cherokee split during the Civil War, Ross tried desperately to keep unity, even traveling to Washington, D.C., to negotiate with Lincoln himself.

Stockades, Starvation, and Sorrow

While the "Trail of Tears" is often used to refer to the forced migration of Native Americans from their ancestral homes to new lands in the West, it really refers specifically to the removal of the Cherokee during 1838 and 1839. Just this part of the displacement affected about 15,000 Cherokee people.

This program primarily affected five eastern tribes, including the Cherokee, Chickasaw, Choctaw, Creek (Muscogee), and Seminole from 1830 through about 1850. Under the guise of the 1830 Indian Removal Act, both federal troops and state militias rounded up Indian peoples and relocated them to stockades prior to the march westward. Many died even during the early stage, owing to the unsanitary and crowded conditions.

Once things got moving, the 800 to 1,200-mile journey claimed the lives of thousands. Estimates are inexact, but most historians believe at least 60,000 Native Americans were forcibly relocated during the program. Other estimates range as high as 100,000.

Today, the Trail of Tears serves as a sobering reminder of the darker chapters in American history, where progress for some came at great cost to others.

Not all of the "Trail of Tears" was a march by land. Some groups of Cherokee and Creek were transported part of the way by steamboat and flatboat. Conditions on those vessels were just as deadly as the forced marches. One account tells of a group of Creeks crammed aboard boats on the Mississippi River in winter. Disease spread easily in the crowded conditions, and the riverbanks became makeshift graveyards as bodies were buried along the journey. Eyewitnesses described long lines of shallow graves marking the trail and river routes west. The U.S. government called the process "removal." Survivors remembered it somewhat differently.

Chapter 10

Manifest Destiny and the Wild Westward Push

I want that.

Is it on sale? No? Well, we can just take it. As the Blues Brothers would say, "We're on a mission from God."

The great democratic experiment, among other things, led to a societal belief that it was a mission, or perhaps moral obligation, to spread the ideals of this new country and its "power to the people" form of government. Add a pinch of the attitude, "We're going to 'civilize' this place!" and you begin to understand the concept of Manifest Destiny.

The term was coined by journalist John L. O'Sullivan in 1845 to describe the justification (and even obligation) underlying territorial expansion in the new United States. Remember, at this time, the country was defined mostly by the East Coast and a bunch of territory surrounding the Gulf down south.

It was a grand and noble idea, until one started to consider the details. To those fervently believing it was their mission to spread liberty, democracy, and civilization for the betterment of the world at large, the concept was chock full of purpose. To those already living in the lands subject to this Manifest Destiny, it must have seemed hypocritical at the very least, for they would have to be displaced, conquered, or whatever you want to call it, for the mission to succeed.

As we'll see, this underlying mission goal led to policies and events including the annexation of Texas, the Oregon Trail migration, the Mexican-American War, and the eventual acquisition of the Southwest and California. It even had a little something to do with the Gold Rush.

Texas: Independent-ish Since 1836

To understand how Texas became a state, you really have to go to Mexico.

Back in the day, prior to 1821, Spain owned the territories now known as Mexico, Texas and much of the current southwestern United States. I suppose if you go back even further, Spain took it from the Aztecs and others in the early 1500s, and they either morphed into or took it from the Siberians who crossed the land bridge 10 or 30,000 years ago. It gets complicated depending on how far back you choose to go.

Anyway, the folks who lived in what we now know as Mexico, Texas and the Southwest United States decided to fight for independence from 1810 to about 1821, and ultimately broke away from the Viceroyalty of New Spain, establishing the Mexican empire.

The area now known as Texas was wild and free, but don't tell that to the Comanche and Apache peoples who lived there. To grow this territory into something valuable to Mexico, the government essentially opened the borders to American settlers through the empresario system in return for their conversion to Catholicism and pledging loyalty to Mexico. That sounded great on paper until many Americans ignored the whole religious conversion bit, refused to speak the language and kinda did as they pleased.

You can probably guess where this is going, right?

The Mexican government started to crack down, reduce immigration and tried to limit what slavery practices had crept in. The Texans had gotten used to a certain degree of freedom and rebelled. Also sound familiar?

Battles ensued. Then there was the Alamo, where a small group of Texans held out for almost two weeks before being overrun by Santa Anna's vastly larger army.

But the Texans got their revenge a month and a half later, catching Santa Anna's army literally napping and in the 18-minute Battle of San Jacinto, routing them, and capturing Santa Anna in the process. The Texans, led by Sam Houston, forced Santa Anna to sign a treaty recognizing Texas as independent. He didn't have the authority to do that on behalf of Mexico, and Mexico never accepted the treaty signed under duress, but who was reading the fine print?

So, while not legal in the eyes of the Mexican government, there wasn't much they could do about it since the Texans had just whooped them. Ipso facto e pluribus unum, the Republic of Texas was born.

So from 1836 until 1845, Texas was its own thing and not part of the new United States. They had a president (Sam Houston), an army, their own money and currency and a truckload of past-due bills. It's expensive to run a country.

In the United States, talk of the annexation of Texas grew, and in 1844, it reached a vote in Congress. It was contentious, as you can imagine, with people fervently for or against this move. Texas was enjoying independence, but was potentially under threat from

Mexico. Then there was the slavery issue. Many didn't want slavery to expand with Texas becoming an official state. And annexation would drive up tensions between the United States and Mexico, possibly leading to war.

Regardless, through some rule-changing shenanigans in Congress, the measure was passed by a simple majority vote on March 1, 1845. The Texans called their own convention in July 1845 and ultimately accepted the deal to become a state.

By the end of that same year, Texas officially became the 28th state.

Oh, and as kind of expected, the annexation ticked off Mexico big time, and war started about a year later.

There were some weird conditions in the Texas statehood deal. For example, it included a provision that Texas could divide itself into as many as five states in the future. Let's see... Texas, Texas Jr., Texas the Third? Oh, and Texas maintained owner-ship of its public lands instead of ceding them to the federal government. In part, this was to help the new state with paying off its debt, which the United States refused to assume in the deal.

How the West Was Walked

Not to slight I-10, I-40 and I-80, but these days, I-90 might be considered the iconic main artery connecting the east and west coasts of the United States. It stretches just over 3,000 miles, connecting Seattle, Washington, to Boston, Massachusetts. However, when Seattle-ites need fresh lobster, they don't use this highway, as it takes at least 50 hours of non-stop driving to make the trip.

Back in the "almost mid-1800s," the road to travel was the Oregon Trail, stretching some 2,000 miles from Missouri to the

Oregon Territory. It's important to think of the "Oregon Trail" as more than a road. It was the essence of the American westward expansion spirit of opportunity; a symbol, so to speak.

If you think a 50-hour non-stop drive in an air-conditioned car is a tough trip, consider a wagon train journey lasting months, complete with river crossings, mountain range transits, disease, attacks from the previous residents, starvation, and who knows what other threats to life and limb. Let's just say the mortality rate was somewhat higher than that of an interstate road trip in today's world.

Land was getting scarce in the East. Remember, this is a relative observation, simply meaning it wasn't infinite and free for the taking anymore. Word came back from the west (Oregon Country) about fertile valleys, rich farmland, and the opportunity to make many acres one's own if they were inclined to put in the work and take the risks of not only the journey, but life in the Wild West.

The actual route varied as we're not talking about a singular road, but rather a network of trails from areas surrounding Independence, Missouri, to the Willamette Valley. And, by trails, remember we're talking dirt, not defined roads per se.

You might think four to six-month trips sound a bit on the long side, but consider this. Most people walked, even though they traveled via wagon train. The number one priority was to keep the animals healthy while pulling the supplies. People wouldn't last long without those two things, so travelers usually walked beside their wagons, limiting progress to ten or 15 miles per day.

The first "deal" was between the British and American governments, as both wanted to claim the "Oregon" territory. Without slipping into yet another war, the parties agreed to share via the Treaty of 1846, with the U.S. taking control of what we now know as Washington, Oregon and parts of Idaho and Montana.

While the English and Americans negotiated amicably, the same wasn't true for the Indian tribes already present. The expansion, under the Manifest Destiny flag, often resulted in claimed lands and settlements without the consent of the current residents.

By the end of 1869, the Transcontinental Railroad was in operation, dramatically reducing all that walking and dying from disease and exhaustion. The journey by rail still took about a week, but compared to months of hiking, it was a win for everyone involved.

The Union Pacific Railroad company started in Omaha and built west using mostly Irish immigrant labor. Crews from the Central Pacific Railroad, using mostly Chinese immigrant labor, started in Sacramento, California and headed east. The two met at Promontory Summit, Utah, on May 10, 1860, and both halves of the country were connected by steam locomotives rather than really long walks. All those cartoons you've seen over the years about the railroad work crews meeting in the middle are essentially true, although they did manage to line up the tracks!

When these two projects were complete, the distance covered was just over 1,900 miles. Quite a feat for the time.

The migration helped populate the West and strengthen U.S. claims to contested regions like Oregon. It also brought settlers into conflict with Native tribes, accelerating displacement and frontier violence. The Oregon Trail was both a journey of hope and a trail of unintended consequences.

There weren't exactly toll booths or traffic cameras along the Oregon Trail(s), so estimates vary, but by most accounts, somewhere in the neighborhood of 300,000 to 400,000 intrepid souls made the journey west that way. And that's just in the time period before the transcontinental railroad was open for business.

The $15 Million Half-Mexico Sale

Remember when I mentioned increased tensions resulted from the official annexation of Texas by the United States? Well, when tensions are created between countries instead of individuals, a frequent result is a breakdown of diplomatic relations, otherwise known as war.

Before we get into details of the "little talked about" war that resulted in the largest territory expansion of this country, it's important to remember that the brief, nine-year existence of Texas as an independent nation was never officially recognized by Mexico. So, when the United States completed the annexation process, the Mexicans saw that as a direct seizure of their territory by the United States.

The United States' 11th President, James K. Polk, followed in the footsteps of Andrew Jackson by most accounts. A firm believer in the Manifest Destiny concept, Polk pledged (in advance) to serve one term only, from 1845 to 1849. Whether you agree or disagree with the results and methods, he arguably accomplished more than most any other one-term president, overseeing the biggest geographic expansion of the United States, ever.

From the start, Polk aimed to get his (our) hands on what's now known as New Mexico and large parts of California. His first move was to buy the land from Mexico. He authorized John Slidell to head to Mexico City with the U.S. checkbook and an available balance of $40 million. That's about $1.7 billion in today's dollars.

Mexico refused the offers.

While Mexico was still bent about the overall Texas situation, there was a particular strip of contested land, which both the U.S. (via Texas) and Mexico claimed as their own. The simple version is that each side recognized a different border, and those two lines were 150 miles apart.

Polk sent troops into the disputed region, who were attacked in April 1846. So, he then used the "aggression by Mexico" argument to declare war. You might consider the whole sequence of events a setup and an excuse for a fight.

Anyway, the U.S. Army entered the fray in strength and eventually marched all the way to Mexico City, seizing it in September 1847.

To end the conflict, Mexico ended up ceding lots and lots of land, including California, Arizona, New Mexico, Nevada, Utah, and parts of Colorado and Wyoming. In return, the U.S. paid Mexico $15 million and assumed some amount of debt incurred by the Mexican government.

So, everyone was happy, if by "everyone" you mean the United States government and not necessarily Mexico. That land transaction represented about half the territory Mexico had previously claimed as its own.

Now, keep in mind the background situation. At this time, some states, primarily in the north, were anti-slavery states. Others, primarily in the southern plantation/agrarian economy regions, were pro-slavery.

Every time a new state was added to the Union, there was an opportunity to tip the scales of power in Congress as each state brings two new Senators and a number of House Representatives based on its population. So, whether a new state was a "free" or "slave" state mattered a great deal to the politicians in Washington, who, then, like now, only really care about maintaining power.

There was a lot of debate over how to handle the situation. Should Congress decide whether new states would be free from slavery? Should the new state decide? Who was going to end up in charge, pro slavery or anti slavery states and their representatives? You can begin to imagine the heat rising in the halls of Washington, D.C., as all this new territory brought the possibility of a number of newly minted states.

So, in summary, this land acquisition completed the continental shape of the nation, but it also deepened internal divisions over slavery in the new territories.

One of the most famous military units to fight for Mexico during the war wasn't Mexican at all. It was the San Patricio Battalion, made up mostly of Irish immigrants who had deserted from the U.S. Army. Many of them were Catholic and felt more kinship with Mexico's Catholic population than with the often anti-Catholic sentiment in the U.S. ranks. They fought fiercely at battles like Churubusco in 1847, where many were captured and later executed by the Americans. In Mexico, however, the San Patricios are remembered as heroes, with memorials and a special commemoration held each year on St. Patrick's Day. Their story is a reminder that the war wasn't just about land, but also about divided loyalties.

Gold! Gold! Gold!

It all started with some flakes spotted by one John Sutter while working at Sutter's Mill near Coloma, California. He tried to keep the finding a secret for fear of losing all his workers to a gold-seeking frenzy, but the news spread like, well, a gold rush. Eventually, head-lines of East Coast papers featured stories like, "Gold! Gold! Gold!"

Think about the chaos resulting from heavy discounts on TV sets during Black Friday sales, and you can imagine the frenzy of free money for the taking, albeit in the form of gold nuggets with some assembly required. Hundreds of thousands flocked by land and sea to California.

A quick sidebar... Ever wondered what the "49ers" are all about? A simple reference to gold seekers heading west, primarily during 1849.

During the gold rush years, it's estimated that miners pulled in some 12 million Troy ounces of gold. That's about 750 tons, worth over $400 million in 1850s dollars. By the time all was said and done, historians estimate perhaps $2 billion worth of gold (again in 1850s dollars) was unearthed. That would be worth some $75 billion today.

As is often the case, the people who made much of the real money weren't the prospectors, but those who supplied, fed, housed, and even clothed them. Whether one would find any gold was up to chance, and a slim one at that. Whether one could make money selling (for cash, not credit) items the prospectors needed was a sure thing. At least two major enterprises we know today began by selling the proverbial "picks and shovels" to the prospectors in training: Wells Fargo and Levi Strauss.

Arguably, it was the gold rush that propelled the California territory into statehood eligibility. While there was no fixed population number requirement, the state in waiting must demonstrate a republican (representative, not the party) form of government compatible with the Constitution, have a workable government, and support of its population.

While not directly enforced, there was a de facto population target of at least 60,000 per the 1787 Northwest Ordinance. By 1850, California's population exceeded 100,000, including many immigrants, making it the melting pot of the time.

The lure of free money brought nothing but tragedy to the Native Americans living in California and Oregon. Their population, estimated at 100,000 to 130,000 prior to the Gold Rush influx, fell to an estimated 30,000.

Most of the deaths resulted from diseases brought by prospectors, while the remainder were a result of widespread violence, even including government-sponsored genocide in some cases. The greed-crazed prospectors and supporting communities brought all manner of terrible human behavior, including murder, displacement, human trafficking and even slavery. The environmental devastation from mining without regard to long-term consequences left a lasting impact.

Speaking of gold... Fort Knox, the most interesting safe deposit box ever, houses most of the United States' gold reserve, although conspiracy theories abound as to whether all that gold is still in there.

How much is stashed behind its 21-ton, 21-inch thick vault door? How about 147 million Troy ounces? That's about 10 million pounds, worth an estimated $470 billion. Don't waste your time thinking of how to steal it. Barring the layers of security, you'd have to move 367,500 gold bars, each weighing about 27 pounds. You'd need somewhere over 200 semi-trucks to complete the job.

Part Three

The Civil War and Reconstruction

Chapter 11

Compromise Fails

Slavery didn't just divide the country—it defined it.

As far back as the Constitutional Convention, the slavery issue had been irreconcilable and subject to the strategy of "kicking the can down the road." Every time tensions flared, a "compromise" was reached, with all parties knowing full well it was nothing but a temporary abatement of symptoms, not leaving a dent in the underlying causes.

Cotton was king, abolitionism was rising, and no number of Senate speeches could hold back the storm.

Missouri and Maine: A Package Deal

We have to take a step backward in time to set the stage for the looming civil war. Back in 1820, Congress made an effort to maintain relations between the North and South via the Missouri Compromise.

In the late 18-teens, Missouri was ready to file for statehood and wanted to do so as a state where slavery was legal. At the time, there was a detente in Congress between slave and free states. If my counting is correct, the Senate was split evenly, with 11 states on each side. The problem was that Missouri's admission to the round-table in D.C. would tilt the scales in favor of the pro-slavery crowd, which was unacceptable to the northern states.

Think back to the constitutional debates, when everyone kicked the slavery can down the road in order to create the union in the first place. Now, the issue had come to a head yet again in the form of irreconcilable differences.

Enter Kentucky Senator Henry Clay, born with the silver spoon of compromise.

What we now know as Maine had historically been part of Mass-achusetts, but with a growing population and infrastructure, it was prepared to assert its independence and become a state, but Congress wasn't ready.

In the face of the Missouri application, Clay, along with Senator Jesse B. Thomas, positioned Maine's desire for statehood as a bargaining chip. What if we admitted both Missouri (slave state) and Maine (free state) to the union simultaneously? While the United States would grow, the slave/free state ratio would simply move from 11 to 12. No change in the balance of power.

An additional part of the deal, which was inked into law by President James Monroe on March 6, 1820, was the ban on slavery north of the 36°30' latitude line. For those who haven't committed the United States survey to memory, that's the line defined by Missouri's southern border.

Notice this line includes Missouri, which had just been admitted as a slave state. It was an exception to this new law, of course.

Like similar compromises before, this didn't provide any resolution at all to the overall slavery debate. Questions and fights continued. Did the federal government have the power to regulate slavery policy within individual states? What about new states that either wanted to embrace or reject slavery? How would the shifting balance of power shake out? Remember, westward expansion was happening at the time, and many emerging states were headed into the statehood pipeline.

Though celebrated at the time as a great act of statesmanship, the Missouri Compromise revealed the deepening fault lines. It formalized the division of the country along geographic lines and set the precedent that slavery's expansion could be "managed" by political deals. As we all know, political solutions were taken off the table just a few decades later.

The Missouri Compromise debate was so heated that one congressman literally collapsed from exhaustion after giving a marathon speech against slavery's expansion. Outside the halls of Congress, ordinary citizens were following the drama like a sporting event. Newspapers printed blow-by-blow updates, and in Boston, a minister declared the crisis "the greatest question ever submitted to Congress, except that of independence in 1776." Henry Clay's ability to hammer out the deal earned him the nickname "The Great Compromiser," though not everyone was impressed. Former president Thomas Jefferson privately called the compromise "a fire bell in the night," warning it was just a temporary patch on a deep fracture that threatened the Union's survival.

The Duct Tape Compromise

While the Missouri Compromise didn't end debate, insults and infighting, it did, for the most part, prevent bullets from flying for a few decades.

It's a bit inaccurate to say the issue surfaced again in 1850, as it had never really gone away. That's expected when you repeatedly kick the can down the road for someone else to solve the problem at some vague future date.

The Mexican War had just ended with the United States claiming a lot, and I mean a lot of new land. It was only a matter of time before the never-ending westward migration would set up these new territories for statehood.

In fact, by 1850, California was ready to go, thanks to its insta-population from the Gold Rush, and it wanted to enter the Union as a free state. This caused a panic among the Southern state Senators and Representatives, as it would shift the balance of power towards the Northern States. So, same old story. Rewind, replay.

Add to this the existing festering problems. Texas was still in flux over its borders and the slavery issue. Southerners were not at all pleased with their slave labor escaping to the North for sanctuary. And the slave trade was alive and well in the nation's capital, Washington, D.C.

It was the same Henry Clay of Missouri Compromise fame who stepped up to help work out a compromise with the help of Stephen Douglas of Illinois.

After lots of wheeling and dealing, a new deal was struck with the following key provisions.

California was to be admitted as a free state.

For the Utah and New Mexico territories, the slavery question was left to popular sovereignty (local decision-making). One might think of this as an Olive Branch of sorts to the Southern States, who could plead their case directly to those emerging states.

In Washington, D.C., the slave trade itself was banned, but

slavery remained legal. Sound a bit familiar from the Constitutional Convention? Remember, in that case, slavery remained legal, but Congress could consider banning the slave trade anytime after 1808.

Last, harsh penalties were enacted in the North for harboring escaped slaves from the South. Obviously, this was not at all popular in Northern states, and it was a big political win for the South.

Far from settling the issue, the compromise heightened tensions. Northerners were enraged by the new fugitive slave provisions, while Southerners grew more anxious about maintaining parity. Like plugging a leak with duct tape, the Compromise of 1850 delayed but did not prevent the coming reckoning.

The Fugitive Slave Act of 1850, one of the most controversial parts of the compromise, backfired spectacularly in the North. Federal marshals could now drag accused fugitives before special commissioners, who earned $10 for ruling someone a slave but only $5 for setting them free. The law also compelled ordinary citizens to help capture escapees, meaning a Boston shopkeeper or a Pennsylvania farmer could suddenly be deputized into hunting down their neighbors. Instead of quelling tensions, the act radicalized many Northerners.

No Safe Haven

Part of the Compromise of 1850, the Fugitive Slave Act mandated that escaped enslaved people be returned to their enslavers, even once they had reached the haven of free states. It also penalized officials and citizens who did not cooperate with the enforcement of the Act.

This law enraged abolitionists and many in the North, who saw it as a gross overreach of federal authority and a moral abomination. Remember, in this new nation, the power of the people resided mostly at the state level over that of the federal government. In their view, it criminalized compassion and made every citizen a potential supporter of slavery.

While this seemed like a compromise of sorts, resentment and outright resistance grew quickly. Some states passed "personal liberty laws" to counteract it, and the Underground Railroad intensified its efforts. Violent confrontations erupted when bounty hunters tried to capture escapees.

Far from calming the nation, the Fugitive Slave Act turned the slavery issue into a national crisis.

You know where this is leading...

The Fugitive Slave Act produced dramatic standoffs that sometimes looked like mini–civil wars. In 1854, the case of Anthony Burns, an escaped slave captured in Boston, drew thousands of angry citizens into the streets. Federal troops had to march Burns, in chains, past a jeering, weeping crowd to the harbor for his return to Virginia. The U.S. government spent an estimated $40,000 (about $1.5 million in today's dollars) on soldiers, guards, and ships to send a single man back into bondage. The spectacle enraged Bostonians and galvanized anti-slavery sentiment. A local minister declared it "the funeral procession of Liberty."

Bleeding Kansas: Prelude to War

While the underlying sentiment was already there, it festered even more as a result of the Fugitive Slave Act, in part due to the perceived overreach by the federal government. Many asked the question, "Who gave the federal government authority to decide the slavery issue in our state?"

In 1854, Illinois Senator Stephen Douglas introduced the

Kansas-Nebraska Act, which repealed the Missouri Compromise line (stating that post-Missouri, only free states could exist north of it) and allowed settlers in those territories to decide the slavery question for themselves through local decision-making processes.

Remember all that new land from the Louisiana Purchase? This act established two new territories, Kansas and Nebraska, which would reignite the long-standing balance of power between pro- and anti-slavery powers.

The proposal in the Douglas legislation called for two major things. First, the Missouri Compromise of 1820, along with its line in the sand, would be repealed. And, once again, the concept of popular sovereignty would be brought into play. Residents of those new territories would decide whether or not to allow slavery.

You can guess the result. The North was ticked while the South was largely ecstatic over the opportunity to grow its influence.

The law was passed at the end of May 1854, and quite literally, set Kansas on fire.

Here's a clue as to how deep the sentiments over the slavery debate ran. People on both sides (pro- and anti-slavery) flocked to Kansas, not for a meeting or convention, but to permanently relocate there, as in "move." These folks felt so strongly about their respective sides of the issue that they wanted to relocate to Kansas so they could influence its future by swaying the vote.

Consider the vitriol evident in disagreements on social media today, then amp that up by a factor of a hundred, and you get the idea. When someone is willing to move their family over a political position, they are dug in to their side of the argument!

The result was chaos and bloodshed, known as "Bleeding Kansas," as armed militias clashed, towns were burned, and political murders took place.

The resulting violence shocked the nation and made it clear that the slavery issue was not going to be solved by peaceful legislation. The Kansas-Nebraska Act destroyed the Whig Party, gave birth to the Republican Party, and proved that compromise was no longer a viable path.

The violence in Kansas turned so personal that it spilled into the halls of Congress. In 1856, after Senator Charles Sumner of Massachusetts delivered a fiery speech denouncing "Bleeding Kansas" and mocking pro-slavery Senator Andrew Butler, Butler's cousin, Representative Preston Brooks of South Carolina, stormed into the Senate chamber and beat Sumner nearly to death with a cane. Sumner collapsed, bleeding on the chamber floor, and it took him years to recover.

Dred Scott: Property, Not Person

How can one discuss the good, the bad, and the ugly of the American story without mention of the Dred Scott case? To say this Supreme Court case and subsequent ruling was controversial might be an understatement. Maybe try, "powder keg."

Dred Scott was born into slavery in Virginia but spent much of his life in Missouri. His owner was an Army doctor who was frequently transferred around the country. This is important because the two lived, at various times, in both slave and free states.

Fast forward. The Army doctor eventually died, and Scott sued for freedom, arguing that living in free states had made him a free man. As these things go in the legal system, even then, the case wound through the courts for years before ending up in Washington to be heard by the Supreme Court.

Ready for the controversial ruling? Hold onto your shorts.

According to the 7-2 decision...

1. Scott had no legal right to sue. The Court declared that African Americans, whether enslaved or free, were not citizens and therefore had no legal standing in federal court.

2.The Court ruled that Scott's "living on free soil" argument was invalid because he was "property." And, as "property," it didn't matter where he lived, he was still "property."

3.Last, but not least, the Court ruled that the Missouri Compromise was unconstitutional and that Congress never had the authority to ban slavery in the territories in the first place. So, all the preceding decades of compromise were deemed invalid.

Nothing like putting out a fire with Bacardi 151. Under this ruling, one could interpret slavery as being legal pretty much everywhere. Southern state supporters certainly saw the ruling as such. In the North, anti-slavery advocates feared that if this ruling and interpretation held, they could be forced to accept slavery.

The bottom line? Any middle ground was destroyed, and the two sides were in a direct, winner-take-all, life-or-death standoff with no possible resolution or compromise in sight.

As for Dred Scott, he didn't win his freedom in the courts, but his supporters purchased and emancipated him in 1857. He was finally a free man, but the experience must have been more bitter than sweet. Sadly, he died just two years later. He was free at last, but only after his case had helped push the country toward its bloodiest conflict.

Chief Justice Roger Taney, who wrote the Dred Scott decision, believed he was solving the slavery question once and for all by removing Congress from the debate. Instead, he ignited the firestorm that made Civil War inevitable. His sweeping opinion went so far that even some Southern leaders worried it would provoke Northern backlash. Abraham Lincoln seized on the ruling in his debates with Stephen Douglas, calling it proof that slavery's defenders wanted to nationalize bondage.

Uncle Tom's Cabin and The North Star

History's tectonic shifts always result from passionate individuals.

Two of the most powerful voices in the fight against slavery came from very different backgrounds.

Harriet Beecher Stowe, a white preacher's daughter, grew up in New England and was the product of a family no strangers to political activism.

When the Fugitive Slave Act of 1850 passed, putting her and other Northern residents in the de facto position of supporting slavery in an indirect and involuntary sense, she became outraged. In 1852, she published *Uncle Tom's Cabin*. The book, a novel, attempted to shed light on the personal impacts of slavery on individuals and families for those who never had, and never would set foot on a plantation.

The book quickly became a runaway bestseller, selling some 300,000 copies in its first year. Consider the population at the time was about 23 million, including about three million slaves. So, the sales figures represented a very large number, sure to bring giddiness to any publishing house. Across the pond, the book sold another million-plus copies, making it second only to the Bible in overall sales. As for the book's impact on the country, President Lincoln allegedly called her "the little lady who started this great war."

Frederick Douglass (1818–1895) was born into slavery on Maryland's Eastern Shore. While growing up, he secretly learned to read and write. This was a big deal as he would have been severely punished for violating rules against his self-education.

At age 20, he escaped into free New England, where he began his lifelong mission of powerful oration and writing, all in support of emancipation and civil rights advocacy.

His work and success took him to the White House, where he advised President Lincoln on emancipation and black rights. He wrote three autobiographies personalizing the slavery issue, founded the abolitionist newspaper, The North Star, and drove recruitment of black soldiers to fight for the Union.

Together, these two individuals stirred the moral conscience of the North. Their advocacy changed and moved hearts, inspired activists, and helped shift public opinion.

Frederick Douglass used photography as activism. At a time when most depictions of African Americans were racist caricatures, Douglass sat for more portraits than almost anyone else in the 19th century. He deliberately posed in dignified clothing and with serious expressions, challenging stereotypes and presenting himself as the embodiment of freedom and intellect. Douglass believed images could change minds as powerfully as words.

Chapter 12

The Civil War

By the time Kansas was bleeding, the nation was long overdue for an ultimate resolution.

While limited violence had broken out, the tensions and emotions simply ran too high for any foreseeable peaceful conclusion.

From the Kansas-Nebraska Act onward, it was a brief, slippery slope leading the nation to war—with itself.

Douglas vs. Lincoln: Popular Sovereignty on Trial

In 1858, Abraham Lincoln and Senator Stephen A. Douglas squared off in a series of seven debates while vying for a U.S. Senate seat in Illinois. On the heels of the Kansas-Nebraska Act and Dred Scott court decision, these weren't casual town halls. They were multi-hour marathons focused largely on the future of slavery in America.

Lincoln took the moral position, claiming the spread of slavery threatened the new nation's democratic ideals, like natural rights. Douglas argued for popular sovereignty, claiming decisions like the legality of slavery should be decided by the people of each state.

Lincoln lost this Senate election but gained national prominence for his positions and arguments. The transcripts of the debate series were widely read nationally, setting Lincoln up to win the presidential election nomination in 1860.

According to history, Lincoln's speeches around this time were the origin of his famous quip, which later became a rallying cry, "A house divided against itself cannot stand."

The Lincoln–Douglas debates drew serious crowds. In Ottawa, Illinois, an estimated 10,000 people gathered with many traveling miles by horse, wagon, or even on foot. With no microphones, the candidates spoke for hours, their voices carrying over the prairie air as listeners picnicked, cheered, and jeered. Newspapers reprinted the debates word-for-word, though sometimes with partisan spin. Republican papers "polished" Lincoln's speeches, while Democratic presses did the same for Douglas. One reporter even joked that if readers compared both versions, they might think two entirely different debates had taken place.

Lincoln Wins, the South Bolts

The Republican Party, formed from the fire of the slavery debate over the previous six years, gained widespread support quickly enough to impact the 1856 election and earn victory in 1860.

The 1860 presidential election was one of the most consequential in U.S. history. Lincoln, running as the Republican candidate, opposed the expansion of slavery.

When the votes were counted, he claimed 180 out of 303 electoral votes and about 40% of the popular vote. In this election, four candidates were on the ballot, hence the unusual percentages.

His victory, including zero electoral votes from the Southern states, triggered the secession of South Carolina and six additional states before he was even inaugurated.

Lincoln's election was a tipping point. Though he promised not to interfere with slavery where it already existed, Southern leaders saw his presidency as a threat to their way of life. If it wasn't fractured enough already, the break compounded before he even took office.

Lincoln wasn't even on the ballot in ten Southern states during the 1860 election. Voters there literally had no way to choose him. That detail fueled Southern outrage when he still won the presidency. It was proof in their eyes that a "Northern" party could now control the nation without Southern support. Secessionists pounced, calling Lincoln's election illegitimate. The irony? Lincoln had been the most moderate Republican candidate, chosen because party leaders thought he could hold the Union together.

Shots Fired: The Day America Turned on Itself

The American Civil War (1861–1865) was anything but civil. It was the deadliest conflict in U.S. history, leaving over 600,000 dead and reshaping the nation forever. It pitted North against South, brother against brother, quite literally tearing the country apart until it began its long and painful healing process after the cessation of hostilities.

Slavery was the central issue, as it was central to the southern economy. Secondary factors included disagreements over power, money, states' rights, and the country's identity.

The fuse was lit in 1860 when Abraham Lincoln, tall, lanky, and not exactly a favorite in the South, won the presidency. Clearly, there were no hidden agendas in this election. Southern states believed they knew exactly where Lincoln stood on the slavery issue. They feared Lincoln would end slavery, the economic engine of the South's agrarian economy.

Before he'd even moved into the White House, seven Southern states seceded. These states soon formed the Confederate States of America and chose Jefferson Davis, a Mississippi senator, to be president.

It didn't take long for things to turn really ugly. And violent.

On April 12, 1861, the Civil War officially kicked off when Confederate forces opened fire on Fort Sumter in the middle of Charleston Harbor, South Carolina. After 34 hours of shelling, Union Major Robert Anderson surrendered the fort to Confederate Brigadier General P.G.T. Beauregard.

Escalation was near instantaneous, with President Lincoln calling for 75,000 reinforcement volunteers. More states, including Virginia, joined the Confederacy, and America was at war with itself.

While the ideological beliefs were entrenched, it wasn't like both sides had been building up war machines for the past decade. Southern forces had started seizing armories and stockpiles right after the secession acts, but both sides were generally unprepared for large-scale military campaigns. As one example, the South was caught a bit off guard with large stockpiles of cotton, which, with the benefit of hindsight, could have been sold for cash to fuel the war machine.

Once the wheels started turning, the North had the advantage in logistics, with more factories and transportation infrastructure, while the South arguably held an edge on experienced military leadership.

The first significant clash was at the First Battle of Bull Run (or the First Manassas Battle as named by the Confederates) on July 21, 1861, about 30 miles south of Washington, D.C.

The Union Army intended to make a bold statement that this war would be a short affair and headed South with the intention of taking Richmond. Early on, things looked good for the Blues. However, as Confederate reinforcements arrived, a soon-to-become-famous General, Thomas J. Jackson, rallied his gray forces by stubbornly holding his ground. The tide turned, and the Union forces panicked and began fleeing back to Washington.

An interesting side note... Confederate Brigadier General Bernard Bee declares that Jackson was standing like a "stone wall" resisting Union forces. And the name we know today, Stonewall Jackson, was born. The historical quip was costly as Bee was killed in the battle.

This first major fight demonstrated two things: this would not be a quick war, and picnic baskets are poor battle gear. You see, large numbers of spectators from Washington and outlying areas had come to watch the spectacle. It's no surprise they ended up fleeing in sheer panic as the battle ensued. All-out war isn't a safe spectator sport.

Recovering from the chaos of Bull Run, the Union Army launched an array of offensives, well, nearly everywhere.

In the Western regions, the Union quickly gained the upper hand in February, with victories in Tennessee. General Ulysses S. Grant captured Forts Henry and Donelson in Tennessee, demanding "unconditional surrender." At Shiloh, one of the war's bloodiest battles, Grant held the field after brutal fighting and heavy losses on both sides. It was becoming clear that this was going to be a costly war.

With victory in Memphis a few months later, the Union Army ended up controlling large parts of the Mississippi River, a vital move as that effectively split the Confederate territory in half and nearly stopped Confederate logistical use of the river. As part of this Western offensive, the Union also seized control of Missouri, Arkansas and New Mexico, largely securing the Southwest.

In the east, things weren't quite smooth for the Union Army. As the calendar rolled over from May to June during the Battle of Seven Pines, Confederate General Joseph E. Johnston was wounded, and a new Confederate hero, Robert E. Lee, took the stage along with command of Southern forces.

Lee had much more success on the battlefield than his counterparts in the West, pushing the Union Army back from Richmond a few weeks later, preventing Union General McClellan's Army from taking the city.

Taking the initiative back, Lee launched attacks into Maryland and Kentucky, but his Maryland objectives were thwarted at the bloodiest conflict of the Civil War, the Battle of Antietam in September 1862. When the smoke cleared after a long day of fighting, combined casualties of both sides numbered about 23,000. The battle ended in somewhat of a draw, but Lee withdrew his forces back to Virginia, so Lincoln was able to claim a victory of sorts.

When Confederate cannons opened fire on Fort Sumter in April 1861, no one was killed in the 34-hour bombardment. The only fatalities came after the surrender, during a ceremonial 100-gun salute as Union troops lowered their flag. A misfired cannon exploded, killing one soldier instantly and mortally wounding another.

The Duel That Sank Wooden Navies

The first full year of all-out civil war marked something else in history: the beginning of the end of wooden ships. Those mighty sailing vessels of old saw their obsolescence in 1862, when, during the Battle of Hampton Roads on March 9, the CSS Virginia, a Confederate ironclad ship, laid waste to a number of Union naval vessels of the wooden variety.

The Union's own USS Monitor arrived on the scene and commenced the world's first iron vs. iron naval duel. Both ships survived the fight, and the writing was now on the wall. Wooden ships were toast from this day forward.

Throughout the remainder of the war, both sides built dozens of iron warships in an effort to gain supremacy of the oceans and waterways.

The Union's USS Monitor was so unusual in design that sailors nicknamed it "the cheese box on a raft." Its revolving turret looked absurdly small compared to towering wooden warships, but it proved revolutionary. During the famous clash at Hampton Roads, curious civilians even rowed out in boats to watch the duel from a "safe" distance, treating it like a sporting event. One newspaper marveled that the battle "ended in a draw, but decided the future of navies."

The War Becomes a Crusade: The Emancipation Proclamation

Part of war is the messaging, and the side with the momentum generally gets to control, or at least influence, the narrative.

In September of 1862, on the heels of the claimed victory at

Antietam, Lincoln issued the Emancipation Proclamation, marking a turning point in the war.

If there was any ambiguity about the underlying causes of this civil war, that was put to rest when Lincoln proclaimed all slaves in the Confederate States to be free. Of course, that was not enforceable at the time as the Confederate government remained in control of the Confederate States, but it did "call the shot" in effect by publicly stating, "When we win this war, there will be no more slavery."

Interestingly, the Emancipation Proclamation didn't apply to Union-controlled areas or border states; it was aimed squarely at the Confederate States.

The result was predictable. The war was no longer just a fight to preserve the Union (of all states); it became a crusade for freedom and the end of slavery in the United States. The proclamation also allowed black men to serve in the Union Army, adding nearly 200,000 troops to Union forces.

When Lincoln first floated the idea of emancipation to his cabinet, he was persuaded to wait for a Union "victory" so it wouldn't look like a desperate move. The Proclamation was also aimed at Britain and France, both of which were considering recognition of the Confederacy. And both had already abolished slavery. By making the war explicitly about emancipation, Lincoln made it politically unpleasant for European powers to side with the South.

1863: Battles of the Burgs

The peak fighting of the Civil War took place on July 1 through July 3, 1863, around Gettysburg, Pennsylvania.

Lee's forces started strong on day one of the battle, driving the Union Army back to the outskirts of town. The second day was more of a stalemate with both sides enduring heavy losses and inconclusive movement.

On the third day, Lee ordered a bold but risky move to break the deadlock. You may have heard of Pickett's Charge, a tragic move that sent 12,000 to 15,000 Confederate soldiers across open fields straight towards the center of the Union lines, defended by heavy cannon and rifle fire. Let's just say it didn't end well for Lee's Army. The failed attack marked the end of the battle, and really, the high-water mark of the entire war for the Confederate Army. From that point on, the writing was on the wall.

As the Battle of Gettysburg wound down, the event at Vicksburg, Mississippi, wrapped up as well. For over a month, Union forces had been trying to seize control of the town overlooking the Mississippi River. The two sides were still fighting for complete control of the area.

After weeks of fighting, Grant's forces had driven the Confederates under General John Pemberton into the town. The Union side then commenced a 40-day-long siege, bombarding and starving the Confederate defenders. On July 4, Pemberton surrendered his 30,000 men along with complete control of the Mississippi. Oh, and Grant earned a fat promotion to the leader of all Union forces.

If it wasn't already clear from the results of Gettysburg, this victory sealed the fate of the South. The Confederacy was split in half and would never recover.

The outcomes of prolonged wars sometimes hinge on the acts of one or perhaps a few individuals. Although we'll never know the "What if?" answers related to the following story, it makes one wonder.

On the second day of battle at Gettysburg, Confederate forces were pounding the far left flank of Union lines, attacking the very edge positioned on Little Round Top hill. One Colonel Joshua Chamberlain, a college professor from

Maine, was given strict orders to hold the line at all costs. Had Confederate forces taken that hill, they would have held a significant advantage over the Union defenders along the entire line. After repulsing multiple Confederate charges, Chamberlain's men were weary and nearly out of ammunition. That's when the professor made a bold decision that may have changed the outcome of the war. He ordered his defenders to fix bayonets and charge the Confederate positions. Screaming and fighting their way down the hill, they broke the Gray lines, took many prisoners, and secured the overall Union position at Gettysburg. While fighting in the area would continue into the following day, the Confederate back was broken.

The Gettysburg Address: 272 Words That Shaped a Nation

During a time when it was fashionable to deliver speeches by the hour, President Lincoln delivered one of the highest "impact per minute" orations ever.

On November 19, 1863, at the dedication of a cemetery at Gettysburg, Pennsylvania, Lincoln reaffirmed the ideals he believed the nation was fighting for. In just over two minutes, using only 272 carefully-chosen words, he reframed the Civil War as a test of whether a nation "conceived in Liberty, and dedicated to the proposition that all men are created equal" could endure.

He took the Founding Fathers at their word, as the designers of a country that would ultimately make the phrase, "all men are created equal," a practical reality, not an abstract philosophical observation. Lincoln declared that the Union was not just fighting to survive, but to live up to the highest ideals underpinning the nation's founding.

The Gettysburg Address became one of the most enduring expressions of American purpose. It's hard to imagine a political statement with more clarity of vision.

The Gettysburg Address

Four score and seven years ago, our fathers brought forth on this continent a new nation, conceived in liberty, and dedicated to the proposition that all men are created equal.

Now we are engaged in a great civil war, testing whether that nation, or any nation so conceived and so dedicated, can long endure. We are met on a great battlefield of that war. We have come to dedicate a portion of that field as a final resting place for those who here gave their lives that that nation might live. It is altogether fitting and proper that we should do this.

But in a larger sense, we cannot dedicate, we cannot consecrate, we cannot hallow this ground. The brave men, living and dead, who struggled here have consecrated it, far above our poor power to add or detract. The world will little note, nor long remember, what we say here, but it can never forget what they did here.

It is for us the living, rather, to be dedicated here to the unfinished work which they who fought here have thus far so nobly advanced. It is rather for us to be here dedicated to the great task remaining before us, that from these honored dead we take increased devotion to that cause for which they gave the last full measure of devotion, that we here highly resolve that these dead shall not have died in vain, that this nation, under God, shall have a new birth of freedom, and that government of the people, by the people, for the people, shall not perish from the earth.

When Lincoln finished speaking at Gettysburg, the audience wasn't sure what to make of it. He had spoken for barely two minutes after following a two-hour-long speech by Edward Everett. There was a stunned silence before the crowd politely applauded. Lincoln himself thought he'd failed, reportedly telling a friend, "That speech won't scour," using a farm phrase for a plow that doesn't work. Everett, however, knew better: the next day he wrote to Lincoln, "I should be glad if I could flatter myself that I came as near to the central idea of the occasion, in two hours, as you did in two minutes." History obviously sided with Everett.

The Beginning and End... of the End

The year 1864 was marked by near constant fighting, and as Grant had now been promoted to the top leadership position, Grant vs. Lee.

As Grant moved towards Richmond to take on Lee's Army of Northern Virginia, he held a near two-to-one numbers advantage, but Lee's forces fought hard and inflicted massive casualties on the Union forces at the battles of The Wilderness and Spotsylvania, and Cold Harbor, among others. But Grant persevered, likely because he knew he was better able to replenish lost soldiers and supplies with the North's population and industrial advantages.

At the same time, other Union Army units under Sherman moved toward and through Atlanta on his "March to the Sea." Marking a shift in strategy aimed at breaking civilian support of the Confederate cause, Sherman set about destroying anything of possible military value, including facilities, agriculture and civilian infrastructure. The official policy was still not to kill civilians directly, but to break their will. Cutting a 50-mile-wide swath of destruction from Atlanta to Savannah, Sherman's forces then turned into the Carolinas with a similar, and even more aggressive, strategy of destruction in early 1865.

Meanwhile, a little further north, Grant's Armies had been pressuring Lee's forces in the Petersburg and Richmond areas, effectively creating siege conditions. In early April 1865, the Union broke through Lee's defenses, and Lee and his army fled Richmond with the Blues in hot pursuit. On April 9th, Lee surrendered to Grant at the Appomattox Courthouse. About a week and a half later, Confederate forces in North Carolina surrendered to Sherman. Then, in late

May and early June, Confederate soldiers surrendered in Louisiana and Texas, officially ending the war.

The Civil War left a battered country, with destroyed infrastructure in the South and catastrophic human losses everywhere, not to mention deep scars and hard feelings remaining between North and South.

When Lee surrendered to Grant at Appomattox on April 9, 1865, the moment was far less dramatic than Hollywood might suggest. Grant showed up in a mud-spattered private's uniform, apologizing that he didn't have proper dress clothes, while Lee appeared immaculate in full gray dress, sword polished and shining. Instead of demanding humiliation, Grant offered generous terms: Confederate soldiers could go home with their horses for spring planting, and officers could keep their sidearms. As Lee rode away, Union troops began to cheer, but Grant stopped them, reminding his men that the Confederates were now "our countrymen again."

The Shot That Shook the Nation

On April 14, 1865, just days after General Robert E. Lee surrendered at Appomattox, but before the end of the fighting in other areas, like the western regions, Lincoln was shot while attending a play in Ford's Theater by Confederate sympathizer John Wilkes Booth. He died the following day, shocking the nation.

As we know today, Lincoln's legacy only grew after his murder. Presiding over the most turbulent events in American history, he literally had a driver's seat influence on the shaping of the future United States of America.

As we'll see, there was a lot of heartache ahead, and the slavery issue was by no means resolved, but a big first step had been taken.

Abraham Lincoln was the first United States President to be assassinated, but he wasn't the first to endure similar attempts. In January 1835, Richard Lawrence tried to fire two pistols at Andrew Jackson right in the Capitol Building. Both misfired, and as we know, Jackson escaped that assassination attempt unscathed. But Lincoln's Ford Theater killing wasn't the only attempt on his life. Back in 1861, there was a plot to kill him in Baltimore, and in 1864, someone shot at him while he was riding his horse at night. The bullet pierced his trademark hat.

Chapter 13

Time to Rebuild: The Reconstruction Era

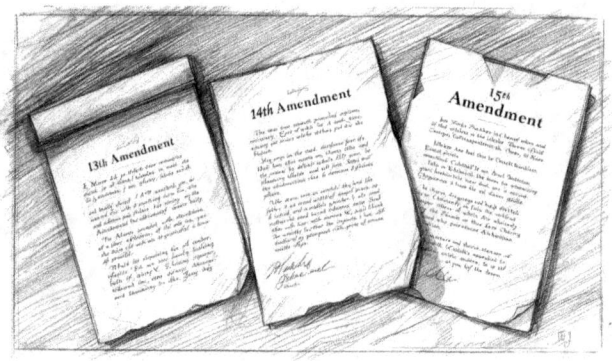

The Civil War ended, slavery was abolished, and the country was rebuilt. And everyone lived happily ever after.

Not so fast...

Slavery's roots ran deep, and it took many years, and a lot of fighting, both the physical kind and in the courts and legislatures, to finish the process.

Let's explore the Reconstruction Era to see how things progressed.

Lincoln's 10% Forgiveness Plan

Believing that of two possible approaches to reconciliation between states and the people residing in them, healing was more productive than punishment, Lincoln envisioned a reunification path that included a fair level of grace, so to speak. However, that led to its own problems.

Launched at the end of 1863, right in the middle of the war, Lincoln's Proclamation of Amnesty and Reconstruction (10% Plan) was intended to shorten the war by adding some carrot-like incentive to stop the fighting and move forward towards a slavery-free society.

The plan was something like this:

- If 10% of the voting citizens of a Confederate State agreed to certain terms, the state could be readmitted to the Union. Remember, they had officially seceded, so they were no longer technically part of the United States of America.
- Conditions included abolishing slavery, creating education programs for former slaves, electing delegates and forming new state constitutions. In return, most Confederate soldiers and citizens alike would be granted a pardon of sorts, and property would be given back to the original owners.

The idea was to make it as easy as possible to get back to a unified country, without slavery, and move forward with the American ideal.

Even before Lincoln was assassinated, the idea wasn't without controversy. Radical Republicans wanted far more accountability and punishment in the reunification plan. And after the assassination, Lincoln's successor, Andrew Johnson, intended to follow Lincoln's forgiveness strategy, keeping the disagreement in play.

Lincoln's 10% Plan was so lenient that some Northerners mocked it as "the 10% swindle." Radical Republicans like Thaddeus Stevens fumed that letting just a fraction of Southern voters pledge loyalty could restore their states to the Union with almost no consequences for rebellion. Lincoln, though, saw pragmatism: he hoped Southern states might "flip early" and speed the war's end. Louisiana actually tried it. By 1864, it had written a new constitution abolishing slavery and elected Unionist representatives. But when those representatives showed up in Washington, Congress refused to seat them, insisting Lincoln's plan was too soft.

No More Mr. Nice Reconstruction

As you can probably guess, the more lenient approach led to abuse by some in the former Confederate States. Technically, abolishing slavery did not necessarily equate to equality of civil rights. In fact, in much of the South, it quickly became clear that many white leaders intended to keep the old system in place, at least in practical, if not legal terms.

President Andrew Johnson's "more forgiving" Reconstruction strategy was, by design, generous and somewhat gracious for ex-Confederates and their supporters. His plan granted pardons liberally, restored property, and allowed many former Confederate officials to reclaim the power they held before the war. That softer approach enraged the Radical Republicans in Congress, a group of lawmakers who believed the Union hadn't spent four years and 600,000 lives just to return to business as usual.

Leaders like Thaddeus Stevens in the House and Charles Sumner in the Senate were not interested in reconciliation for reconciliation's sake. They wanted a reconstruction in a more meaningful sense. Specifically, they wanted to see the South rebuilt on new and revised foundations of equality and complete democracy for all citizens, and "citizens" should include former slaves and their children. Stevens, not one known for his subtle approach, wanted the plantation class and culture to be broken and rebuilt from the ground up.

The Radicals' distrust of Johnson's leniency wasn't just "what if" paranoia. Almost immediately after the war, Southern states began passing "Black Codes," laws that looked suspiciously like a new, slightly more subtle version of slavery. These codes restricted where former slaves could live, what jobs they could hold, and even allowed authorities to arrest them for vague crimes like "vagrancy."

And when laws weren't enough, vigilante violence picked up the slack. The Ku Klux Klan emerged during this time. The KKK was determined to restore white supremacy through fear and intimidation of everyone associated with the equal rights movement: former slaves, their families, and the whites supporting their cause. Night rides, lynchings, beatings, and arson were parts of coordinated campaigns to intimidate black voters and keep the old power structure in place. Newspaper reports and congressional testimony documented horror stories: teachers who tried to educate freedmen were whipped or murdered, churches were burned, and entire communities lived under constant threat from the Klansmen.

The reality on the ground fueled the fires of the already heated debates in Congress. The Radical Republicans used these realities to argue that Johnson's "trust the South to behave" policy was failing. In their view, only strong federal intervention could protect the rights of freedmen.

This led the Radical Republicans to assume more power in Congress from the Executive Branch, which had been leading the Reconstruction policies by passage of the Reconstruction Acts of 1867.

Ten of the eleven Confederate states were placed under direct military rule. They were divided into five districts, each commanded by a Union general. A direct penalty for bad behavior was loss of representation. Only once a state rewrote its constitution to guarantee black men the right to vote and ratified the 14th Amendment could it send representatives back to Congress.

The Radical Republicans then attempted to further codify these civil rights corrections constitutionally via the three Reconstruction Amendments. We'll touch on that in a minute.

Things improved—for a while. Former slaves registered to vote. They were elected to political office at the state and federal levels. In some cases, black legislators comprised the majority of state assemblies.

New state constitutions established the first public school systems in the South, expanded rights for women in some areas, and even opened the door to more democratic participation.

The Radicals weren't just focused on punishing the South, but they genuinely tried to create new opportunities for freedmen. Freedmen's Bureau agents built schools, distributed food, and offered legal help. Northern reformers (derisively called "carpetbaggers" by Southerners) headed south to help steer the rebuilding effort, often working alongside "scalawags"—Southern whites who cooperated with Reconstruction governments.

But progress came at a price. To many white Southerners, Radical Reconstruction felt like more of an occupation with a side helping of humiliation. Groups like the Klan and other organizations doubled down, violently resisting both federal troops and local black political activity. When elections approached, intimidation campaigns made it dangerous, and even deadly, for black citizens to cast a ballot.

It wasn't just the South that eventually tired of the Reconstruction fight. Voters and politicians in the North saw the effort as a Southern problem and grew weary of the cost and effort.

By the 1870s, the movement began to wane. The Compromise of 1877, which resolved a contested presidential election, effectively ended the federal campaign. Troops were withdrawn, and many Southern governments began to undo the new reforms.

In the end, Radical Reconstruction was a bold, messy, imperfect and ultimately, unsuccessful experiment in remaking a society and economy that had been built on slavery. It did establish some lasting foundations that would come into play down the road, like the Reconstruction Amendments. But it also revealed the limits of how much change could be forced from the top down, especially when political commitment at that top wavered. The Radicals won important battles, but when the North lost interest, the South quickly reclaimed at least part of the status quo.

During Reconstruction, black political participation wasn't just symbolic; it was unprecedented. In South Carolina, for example, the legislature became majority black by 1868, something unimaginable before the war. Among the new officeholders was Robert Smalls, a former slave who had stolen a Confederate steamboat in Charleston Harbor in 1862 and delivered it to Union forces, earning his freedom. Smalls went on to serve five terms in the U.S. House of Representatives. Yet even as men like Smalls rose, violent backlash tried to drag them down. Congressional hearings in the early 1870s recorded testimony of Klan attacks so brutal that one witness described the South as living under "a reign of terror."

Reconstruction's Constitutional Makeover

These three Reconstruction Amendments represented the most profound legal changes since the Bill of Rights.

The 13th Amendment unambiguously ended slavery. Congress actually passed the 13th Amendment before the Civil War even ended, and it didn't take long after the end of the war to ratify the 13th. On December 6, 1865, it was officially part of the United States Constitution.

The 14th, the second of the Reconstruction Amendments,

tackled problems of citizenship and equal treatment under the law for all citizens, along with a few other items. Passed by Congress on June 13, 1866, the 14th Amendment was ratified on July 9, 1868.

The 14th, at a high level, pushed natural rights protections to the state level. You might notice these principles were already well-established at the federal level under the Constitution and Bill of Rights.

For example, it addresses the citizenship status of former slaves and their children by clarifying that everyone born or naturalized in the United States is a citizen of both the country and the state in which they live and has the privileges and immunities of a full citizen. It prevents states from making any laws that infringe on the natural rights of citizens. It prohibits states from depriving any citizen of life, liberty, or property without due process of law. And the 14th establishes that every citizen in a state's jurisdiction shall have equal protection under the law.

The 15th Amendment removes all possible ambiguity from some of the provisions of the 14th. While the 14th Amendment enumerated penalties for prohibiting men over the age of 21 from voting, it didn't actually ban the practice. And there were plenty of abuses attempting to take advantage of that loophole, including poll taxes, literacy taxes and more.

One of the more straightforward amendments, it reads in its entirety as follows.

"The right of citizens of the United States to vote shall not be denied or abridged by the United States or any State on account of race, color, or previous condition of servitude."

Even under these new constitutional protections, abuses continued into the following century. We'll get into that later.

Some things just take time. The last state to finish ratifying the 13th Amendment was Mississippi. They completed the job on March 16, 1995. Yes, you read that correctly as 1995, not 1895.

Freedmen's Bureau: The First Safety Net

If the Civil War destroyed the direct practice of slavery through force, you might think of the Freedmen's Bureau as the cleanup crew for the aftermath.

Officially called the Bureau of Refugees, Freedmen, and Abandoned Lands, it was created in 1865 to help transition four million former slaves into free life. It maintained a secondary mission of assisting poor whites devastated by the war.

The Bureau was a federal agency under the War Department, which tells you something about how temporary its mission was supposed to be. Congress designed it as a one-year emergency program. Its head was General Oliver O. Howard, a man with both a reputation for piety and the nickname "the Christian General." His challenge? Distribute food and clothing, provide medical care, help negotiate labor contracts, establish schools, and generally make freedom something more than just a word. Piece of cake, right?

For a while, the Freedmen's Bureau made a significant dent in the problems, especially considering its limited resources. It fed millions during the chaotic aftermath of the Civil War. It set up hospitals and provided medical care. It invested in education infrastructure. With help from northern missionaries and black community leaders, the Bureau built thousands of schools, laying the foundation for the first real system of public education in much of the South. By 1870, an estimated 250,000 freedmen were learning to read and write. Remember, it was illegal to teach enslaved people to read and write just a few years prior.

Like many of the people and policies airlifted from the North, it was also somewhat of a lightning rod. Many white Southerners viewed the program as outside interference and Bureau officials were targeted by militant groups like the KKK and others. Even President

Andrew Johnson vetoed efforts to expand the Bureau's powers, though Congress overrode him.

Still, the Bureau never had enough money, manpower, or political backing to complete its grand mission. As Northern commitment to full Reconstruction waned, so did support for the Bureau. By the early 1870s, its schools and aid programs were handed off to state governments or private organizations, many of which lacked resources or commitment. By 1872, the Freedmen's Bureau was effectively shut down, leaving freed people to figure out the future on their own.

One of the Bureau's most transformative efforts was the push for education. In some Southern towns, freed slaves themselves built makeshift schools out of brush arbors (a temporary shelter made with poles and a brush or hay roof) or abandoned cabins, hiring teachers with whatever wages they could scrape together. In Richmond, Virginia, classes were held in the former Confederate Capitol building. Bureau agents and northern missionary groups helped scale this grassroots movement, and by 1870, the Bureau had established over 4,000 schools. Formerly enslaved parents were so determined to educate their children that they sometimes walked miles at night to attend classes themselves, sitting beside their kids on rough wooden benches.

Part Four

Industrializing and Immigrating

Chapter 14

Steam, Steel & Strikes

The Gilded Age brought together the unusual bedfellows of unfathomable power and wealth and abject poverty. Of course, there was a fair amount of representation between the two extremes.

The age of steel established a nationwide railroad network, which transformed the country's ability to do business, thereby launching its economic power into orbit.

But the journey wasn't easy. Much of the success was built on the backs of immigrant labor and, in many people's view, tough labor management practices. It was certainly a different time.

But with this incredible growth came growing pains: child labor, labor strikes, and frequent clashes between workers and industry titans like Carnegie and Rockefeller.

Captains or Robber Barons?

Coined by Mark Twain and Charles Dudley Warner in the satirical novel, "The Gilded Age: A Tale of Today," this era spanned the late 19th and early 20th centuries.

As the name implies, it was a period of prosperity on the surface while the underlying layers were far less glamorous. In other words, some incredible prosperity painted over the particle board of industrialization.

At the center of this transformation stood three men whose names became synonymous with both progress, success and controversy: Andrew Carnegie, John D. Rockefeller, and J.P. Morgan.

Carnegie, a poor Scottish immigrant, became one of the wealthiest men in America. As the country industrialized, his steel supplied the infrastructure. Think railroads, bridges, and skyscrapers.

Behind his incredible success was the business strategy of vertical integration. His companies controlled every step of production from raw materials to finished goods, allowing him to reduce overall costs and gain a big competitive advantage over rival companies.

He was Mr. Efficiency, and that's not necessarily a compliment, as he demanded it from his workforce, who didn't always agree with the idea of a "work more" mentality. Strikes at Carnegie Steel, most notably the Homestead Strike of 1892, highlighted the human side of the equation.

However, Carnegie also became one of history's greatest philanthropists. Believing in the "Gospel of Wealth," he argued that the rich had a duty to use their fortunes for the public good. And he did, eventually giving away 90% of his vast fortune. By the time of his death, he had funded over 2,500 libraries, as well as universities, cultural institutions, and foundations.

Starting his business career as a bookkeeper, Rockefeller showed a keen propensity for aggressive and often controversial business tactics. The combination paid off well for him, to say the least.

Starting in 1870, Rockefeller built Standard Oil into one of the most powerful corporations the world had ever seen. His business tactics, like secret railroad rebates, price wars, and the buyout of rivals, helped him achieve a functional monopoly on the oil business at a time when oil was the driver of the American economy. At its peak, Standard Oil controlled more than 90 percent of U.S. refining.

Critics saw Rockefeller as the ultimate "robber baron," using his money and power to crush competition. His monopoly power eventually provoked government action. In 1911, the Supreme Court ordered Standard Oil broken up into 38 different companies under the Sherman Antitrust Act.

Like Carnegie, Rockefeller turned to philanthropy later in life. His charitable contributions exceeded $500 million and funded medical research, universities, and global public health initiatives.

Carnegie and Rockefeller made their fortunes producing stuff. Morgan was a behind-the-scenes figure, with expertise in finance that was vital to business expansion. Unlike Carnegie and Rockefeller, Morgan was born into wealth, but I doubt anyone will argue that he didn't make the most of his situation.

A banker who founded J.P. Morgan and Company (Now J.P. Morgan Chase), he created the lasting templates of aggressive investment banking, instigating the consolidation of mega companies in railroads, steel, and more. His wealth and influence made him a driving force in stabilizing markets and even influencing the credit-worthiness of the United States as a country at times.

He was also the driver behind the first "billion-dollar" company, purchasing Carnegie's steel company for an estimated $500 million and merging it with other companies to create U.S. Steel.

Morgan's power was so great that in the Panic of 1907, he personally coordinated a rescue of the U.S. financial system by rallying banks and using his own resources to calm the markets. While the end result was favorable, this type of thing raised concerns about so much power in the hands of a small number of individuals.

Public opinion over men like these was mixed. Admirers praised them as "captains of industry" who fueled America's rise as an economic superpower. Critics condemned them as "robber barons" who exploited workers, corrupted politics, and concentrated wealth on an unprecedented scale.

Their legacies remain mixed. Carnegie's libraries, Rockefeller's foundations, and Morgan's art collections arguably benefitted public life. On the other hand, accusations of monopolistic practices and labor battles instigated the first real efforts to regulate big business, laying the groundwork for antitrust laws and governmental oversight.

Although none of the "big three" discussed here died on the Titanic, a number of other ultra-rich "billionaire types" (when you account for today's dollars) did. John Jacob Astor IV, with $2.7 billion in today's money, went down with the ship, as did Benjamin Guggenheim. He was the one with the famous line, "We've dressed up in our best and are prepared to go down like gentlemen."

J.P. Morgan was almost lost to the iceberg. He had a ticket for the transit, but canceled at the last minute. He died the following year, in 1913.

All Aboard the American Dream

Imagine trying to get from New York to San Francisco in 1860. You had three options, and, quite frankly, they all stunk.

Option one: a grueling wagon trek across plains, deserts, and mountains, complete with a forecast of disease, dysentery and arrows flying your way.

Option two: a months-long sailing trip all the way around South

America's southern tip, a route so dangerous sailors called it "the graveyard of ships."

Option three: a shortcut by boat to Panama, then a steamy jungle crossing before catching another ship north.

None of these options facilitated a family dinner table discussion of, "Let's move out west, I hear there's lots of opportunity. The kids will love it."

That's where the Transcontinental Railroad came in. It was a (relatively) efficient and massively time-saving connection between the coasts. Just the new Omaha to West Coast portion of the overall network represented about 1,900 miles of track. That's an incredible feat of engineering during a time before the widespread use of mechanized equipment.

And when the Union Pacific and Central Pacific railroads met at Promontory Summit, Utah, in 1869, the ceremonial golden spike wasn't just a piece of hardware. It was the beginning of a whole new means of expansion and economic growth. For the first time, people and goods could cross the entire country in about a week. A trip that once was a literal expedition became routine. Well, not as routine as today's air travel, but compared to what 19th-century travelers were used to...

Let's step away from the change in personal travel opportunities and think about the bigger commerce picture. The growing national railroad network rewired the nation's ability to do business. Farmers in Nebraska could ship wheat to New York. Miners in Nevada could send silver east. Chicago became a meat-packing empire largely because cattle could now be loaded onto trains in Texas and shipped north in train cars. And in these and many other cases, the risk of loss through theft or spoilage was dramatically reduced. While some never-do-wells still robbed the occasional train, the risk was far less than when traveling backwoods trails by wagon. Like waterfront port cities of old, towns along the rail routes turned into thriving cities.

And let's not forget the people factor. The railroad flung the doors wide open for westward migration. Immigrants from Europe and Asia found new opportunities in building out the infrastructure. The work was often brutal, but they got it done.

The Transcontinental Railroad jump-started the Industrial Revolution. Steel mills cranked out rails, building materials and raw stock for machinery manufacturing. Coal mines fed the locomotives. Inventors created better engines, brakes, and telegraph systems to keep trains safe and on schedule. The sheer scale of the railroad network turned the U.S. into an industrial powerhouse, making it easier to move not just goods but also ideas, labor, and capital across the country.

Of course, the expansion of the rail transportation network had a dark side, too. Native American lands were carved up, and buffalo herds nearly vanished under the relentless growth of rail travel.

Here's a fun fact that's not necessarily an obvious outcome of rail expansion. The railroads created something Americans hadn't really needed before: time zones. Before long-distance train travel, each town set its clock based on the sun. Noon in one town could be 12:15 in the next. With (relatively speaking) high-speed rail, that wasn't conducive to predictable schedules. In 1883, the railroads themselves established four standardized time zones. About five years later, the federal government adopted the system.

Strikes! When Workers Took on Titans

By the late 19th century, industrial capitalism was exploding across America. Steel mills, railroads, and factories powered economic growth but were also breeding grounds for tough labor policies that wore out workers through long hours, dangerous environments and low pay. Labor disputes were inevitable, and when they did boil over, things got ugly.

The Homestead Strike of 1892 unfolded at one of Andrew Carnegie's steel plants in Homestead, Pennsylvania. Carnegie had built his empire on efficiency and control, and his plant manager, Henry Clay Frick, shared his zeal for breaking unions. When the steelworkers' union contract expired, Frick announced pay cuts and fortified the plant with fences and armed guards. In other words, he made it clear he was here to play serious hardball.

Guess what happened? No surprise. The workers walked out. Frick responded by hiring armed Pinkerton agents to escort and protect strikebreakers entering the mill to continue the work. On July 6, 1892, the Pinkertons, landing in the area by barge, were met by striking workers and townspeople and lots of gunfire. The resulting battle left at least ten people dead and many more injured. Eventually, the state militia arrived to restore order, and the strike collapsed.

While it's hard to imagine in today's economy, the idea of company-sponsored private armies showed just how powerful the mega companies of the era were. Can you even imagine Mattress Firm or Burger King having and using a private army to keep employees in line?

Two years later, another strike erupted, but this time on the railroads. The Pullman Company, based near Chicago, manufactured luxury railcars. They also operated the stereotypical "company" store, in this case, more like a company town. You can probably guess the town name. Pullman! Workers and their families lived there for a price. And the price was set by George Pullman, of course.

It's 1893, and there is a nationwide depression. The Pullman company lowers wages in response. But somehow, they forgot to lower the rents for company housing and staple prices in the company store. Less money coming in and the same going out led to a shrinking of take-home pay for Pullman employees, and they were not at all happy. Employees tried to negotiate with Pullman management, but were ignored. On May 11, 1894, workers went on strike.

The American Railway Union (ARU), led by Eugene V. Debs, quickly joined the fight, calling for national boycotts of railroads using Pullman cars. Within days, some 125,000 railroad employees across the country, but mainly in the West, joined the strike in solidarity.

Here's where things get even more interesting. The ARU was very progressive for unions of the time because rather than segregate by skill or trade, it accepted all skilled and unskilled workers in the railroad business. Well, progressive to a point, and that's where they dropped the ball. The ARU and many other unions would not accept African American workers. And guess who the Pullman Company (and others) called to be replacement strikebreaker employees? That's right. African Americans. The replacements weren't all that sympathetic to the striking (and fired) union workers, as they'd never been welcomed into union ranks.

Things got ugly and violent until finally the courts and federal government stepped in with federal troops. By July 1894, the strike was squashed, and in the process, a new precedent for federal involvement was in place.

In both cases, the strikes technically failed, as most employees lost their jobs, the leaders were jailed or otherwise punished, and the federal government made it clear there would be little tolerance for such things.

However, both the Homestead and Pullman strikes underscored the fierce conflict between capital and labor in this Gilded Age. The power of organized labor was demonstrated for all to see, and there was renewed focus on the rights of workers. In fact, Congress established Labor Day later that year. Obviously, that wasn't of much value to workers who had fought and lost, but it did show the problems were starting to be recognized.

Eugene V. Debs entered the Pullman Strike as a respected labor organizer but came out a national figure and a convicted criminal. When the strike spread nationwide, federal courts issued an injunction ordering the ARU to call it off. Debs refused, arguing that the courts were siding with corporate power. For that defiance, he was jailed for contempt. While serving six months in prison, Debs read socialist works by Karl Marx and others, later saying it was the turning point of his life. He emerged as a committed socialist and ran for president five times, once in 1920 while still in prison, winning nearly a million votes.

Eight Hours, Fair Pay, and Fewer Kids in Coal Mines

The late 19th century was a tough time to be a blue-collar employee in the United States. Industrialization brought jobs, but they were often dangerous and carried long and exhausting hours. At least the pay was generally lousy. It was common for workers to put in ten to twelve-hour days, six days a week, with little protection against layoffs, injuries, or sometimes, death. Such were the conditions that led to the rise of labor unions.

The Knights of Labor started early, back in 1869, as a secret society to protect workers from employer retaliation and general bad behavior. Founded by Uriah Stephens, a Philadelphia garment cutter, the organization intended to represent nearly everyone: skilled and unskilled labor, men and women, and workers of different races. They did have standards, however, as they excluded gamblers and saloon keepers, along with a few other professions!

Their agenda was radical for the time, but table stakes in today's work environment. For example, the group hoped to implement eight-hour workdays, equal pay for women, the end of child labor, and broader social reforms that would level the playing field between workers and industrialists.

By the early 1880s, the secret part of the charter was over, and the Knights grew rapidly under the leadership of Terence V.

Powderly. Membership reached nearly a million workers, organized by offices in thousands of cities across the country.

But the momentum was short-lived. In May 1886, a labor rally in Chicago's Haymarket Square ended in tragedy when a bomb exploded, killing police officers and civilians. The Knights were not responsible, at least not directly, but the public wasn't having it and now viewed the group as violent and radical. Membership plummeted, and the Knights were no longer a force in the labor movement.

While the Knights were fizzling out, a new federated model burst on the scene. The American Federation of Labor (AFL) was founded in 1886 and led by Samuel Gompers for four decades. The AFL took a different approach from the Knights. Instead of aiming broadly to transform society, it focused more narrowly on direct worker benefits like improved wages, hours, and working conditions. The early strategy of the AFL was to focus on direct collective bargaining with corporations. Think of the original AFL as a federation of skilled craft unions representing workers like carpenters, machinists, and printers.

Gompers steered toward "pure and simple unionism." He argued that workers' immediate needs, like better paychecks and shorter hours, were more important than broader societal reforms. This more practical strategy focused on achievable goals, and as a result, it gained legitimacy and staying power. Today, it lives on as the AFL-CIO after its 1955 merger with the Congress of Industrial Organizations.

The rise of unions was not an easy hill to climb. Big, big money was at stake, and employers resisted fiercely. Many walkouts and strikes ended in violence. And, as we've seen with some of the more notable strikes, even corporate "armies" came into play.

By the turn of the century, organized labor had secured a foothold in American life. The Knights of Labor had shown the power of broad solidarity, even if their moment was brief. The AFL demonstrated the effectiveness of pursuing practical and tangible objectives. This progression set the stage for the modern labor movement.

The Haymarket affair of 1886 didn't just tarnish the Knights of Labor; it left a sour taste worldwide. After the bomb exploded in Chicago, police opened fire into the crowd, and 11 people ended up dead. Eight anarchists were arrested, but there was little evidence linking them to the bomb attack. Four were executed, and the trials were controversial, becoming symbols of injustice internationally.

The Muckrakers Stir the Pot

Just like the book, *Uncle Tom's Cabin* set fire to the slavery debate; another novel created quite the stir in the labor discussion. Although this one did have some interesting consequences, unintended by the author.

In 1906, an avowed socialist, Upton Sinclair, set out to change America. As a 27-year-old investigative journalist, Sinclair went undercover in Chicago's stockyards to expose the harsh realities of immigrant labor. The result was *The Jungle*, a novel that described the grueling, unsafe, and degrading conditions faced by workers in the meatpacking industry. Sinclair wanted readers to rally behind socialism.

However, in Sinclair's own words, "I aimed at the public's heart, and by accident I hit it in the stomach."

As the book's popularity spread, people focused more on the exposé of the gross realities of the meat-packing industry at the time. Readers learned about rotten meat ground into sausage, rats falling into processing vats, and filth being shoveled onto conveyor belts. President Theodore Roosevelt, never one to be squeamish, reportedly lost his appetite after reading the book.

The outrage was significant, and in 1906, Congress passed two new laws addressing the public's desire for clean and safe food: the Meat Inspection Act and the Pure Food and Drug Act.

Sinclair wasn't alone in this new muckraker journalism movement. Progressive writers explored and exposed corruption, abuse of power and various other injustices. Their mission was to illustrate the human cost of the industrialization movement and establish a higher degree of collaboration, voluntary or involuntary, between industry and government.

President Theodore Roosevelt privately dismissed Upton Sinclair as a "crackpot" and suspected his socialist agenda. But Roosevelt couldn't ignore the public uproar after The Jungle hit shelves. To test whether the shocking claims were true, he dispatched investigators to Chicago's stockyards. Their secret reports confirmed conditions even worse than Sinclair had described: meat stored in rooms reeking of urine, chemicals used to mask the smell of rot, and workers spitting tuberculosis germs onto carcasses. Roosevelt pushed Congress hard, and by summer 1906, the Meat Inspection Act and Pure Food and Drug Act were law. Sinclair's campaign for socialism had launched the modern era of consumer protection instead.

Chapter 15

Liberty... Imported!

If you're reading this book while sitting in the United States of America, there's a great chance that some members of your family immigrated here.

The U.S. has always had the reputation of being a melting pot of sorts, but the process of arriving at that final result wasn't always easy. Over centuries, waves of immigrants arrived on these shores, bringing different customs and languages, and were often unable to speak English. They came seeking opportunity, and many found it, but many also experienced resistance at various times throughout our history.

Let's explore how newcomers helped build the nation even as some were told they didn't belong.

Two Gates, Two Stories: Ellis vs. Angel

Between the late 19th and mid-20th centuries, millions of immigrants chasing the American dream arrived through two notable gateways: one in the East and the other in the West. In New York Harbor, Ellis Island was the arrival and processing facility, while in San Francisco Bay, it was Angel Island.

Ellis Island handled the heavy lifting for reasons we'll explore in just a bit. It processed an estimated 12 million immigrants from 1892 to 1954, while Angel Island processed about a million from 1910 to 1940.

After opening, Ellis Island quickly became the busiest immigration center in the United States, with the majority of people passing through arriving from Europe. The predominant nationalities included Italians, Poles, Germans, Jews, and many others. In many cases, they were fleeing poverty, political unrest, or persecution. And, of course, simply seeking better opportunities in this rapidly growing country.

Consistent with the high volume of individuals passing through, the process was relatively short and efficient. Inspectors checked for contagious diseases, asked questions about work plans and money, and, if nothing alarming came up, stamped them through. Most people cleared Ellis Island in hours or in some cases, days.

While quick, the process could be harsh. If a family member showed signs of some contagious sickness, separation was the next step. If inspectors became convinced one couldn't support themselves here and might become a burden on society, they were turned away and deported. Sometimes, standards of "moral fitness" would be applied. That immigration standard was likely as vaguely applied as it sounds.

On the West Coast, Angel Island operated somewhat differently. Opened in 1910, it processed mostly immigrants from Asia, including China, Japan, and the Philippines. The process coming through Angel Island was far stricter, and Angel Island became infamous for its interrogations and lengthy detentions. This was not a result of arbitrary behavior by inspectors or management. By the time Angel Island opened, the Chinese Exclusion Act of 1882 had taken effect, and most Chinese immigration had been halted as a result. We'll get more into that in just a bit.

Pending immigrants at Angel Island often spent weeks or even months waiting while inspectors evaluated and researched their paperwork and histories. The interrogations could be grueling: dozens of detailed questions about their home villages, family trees, and even the number of windows in their houses back in China. Any inconsistency could be grounds for rejection of their immigration application. While waiting at the facility, detainees often carved poetry into the wooden walls, voicing their fears and frustrations.

The stark differences between the Ellis and Angel experiences reflect some of the prejudices of the times. Ellis leaned towards representing hope, while Angel was arguably more about exclusion, as there seemed to be much stronger popular support, or at least tolerance, of Western European migration to the country.

By the mid-20th century, both faculties faded into oblivion as the less restrictive policies gave way to immigration quotas by country of origin. Now, Ellis Island is a museum celebrating immigrant heritage.

For many immigrants, Ellis Island's inspection line was their first real encounter with America and sometimes, the deciding moment of their future. About 2% of arrivals were denied entry, but that small percentage meant heartbreak for thousands. If one family member was sick or failed inspection, the entire family often faced a painful choice: return together or separate forever.

At Angel Island, the experience could be even harsher. One carved line in the wooden walls there read: "Imprisoned in the wooden building day after day, my freedom withheld; how can I bear to talk about it?" Those carvings, rediscovered decades later, survive as haunting reminders of both hope and despair at America's "gates."

Lady Liberty: Some Assembly Required

Apparently, the French didn't always hold nothing but scorn for Americans...

OK, I'm kidding. You have to admit, the whole Statue of Liberty gift was quite a meaningful gesture of national friendship. Is there anything more iconic to represent the melting pot heritage and foundations of freedom of the United States?

The idea for the Statue of Liberty was born in France. In 1865, French historian Édouard de Laboulaye suggested a monument be built as a gift to the United States to celebrate American independence and the enduring friendship between the two nations. It was to be both a tribute to American freedoms and a symbol of suppressed democratic values in France under Napoleon III. Sculptor Frédéric Auguste Bartholdi took the idea and ran with it, designing the massive neoclassical statue. Gustave Eiffel, later famous for his Paris tower, engineered the iron framework to support the copper skin.

The copper statue was shipped to New York in 350 pieces and reassembled on Bedloe's Island, now called Liberty Island. But there was a problem: while France paid for the statue as it was a gift, the Americans had to find a way to pay for the pedestal. Surprisingly, fundraising lagged until publisher Joseph Pulitzer launched a public campaign through his newspaper, *The World*. Readers sent in nickels and dimes, raising over $100,000 for the project. It was during this effort that poet Emma Lazarus was asked to contribute to the cause.

In 1883, she wrote "The New Colossus," a sonnet meant to inspire donors to support the building process. Her poem contrasted the Statue of Liberty with the ancient Colossus of Rhodes. Instead of a towering warrior looking intimidating and guarding a harbor, Lazarus envisioned Lady Liberty as a compassionate figure, sending a welcome message to those entering the country's primary immigration harbor. The message was iconic. "Give me your tired, your poor, your huddled masses yearning to breathe free."

Like many composers and painters, at the time, the poem didn't make a huge splash. It was only later, when a plaque bearing its words was installed on the pedestal in 1903, that Lazarus's vision became the inspirational message of the statue. For the millions arriving in the United States through Ellis Island, the towering figure was the first sign of America.

The Statue of Liberty, arm raised with a torch, and a tablet marked with July 4, 1776, spoke of independence and democracy. Lazarus's poem overlaid a second meaning: America as a refuge, an opportunity for those with nowhere else to go.

As we'll see, the sentiment of the country did not always reflect what the statue commemorated.

And one more thing. The original name of the statue was "Liberty Enlightening the World." That doesn't exactly roll off the tongue, so it's a good thing we ended up with the simpler descriptive name we use today.

The Statue of Liberty sure looks solid and eternal. While the meaning may be exactly that, the underlying construction is surprisingly lightweight. The exterior copper surface is just about 3/32 of an inch thick. For you metric types, that's about 2.4mm. To put this in perspective, this is roughly the same as three credit cards, 20 sheets of printer paper, or a little less than two dimes. Of course, that thin outer surface is supported by Eiffel's internal iron structure.

The Great American Potluck

Thirteen million people flocked to America from the mid-19th century into the early 20th. Considering the official population of the country according to the 1850 census was just 23,191,876, that's a massive influx of new residents.

America was flooded with newcomers chasing opportunity and, in many cases, simple survival. Among others, the Irish, Italians, Chinese, and Jewish immigrants pushed the country forward, reshaping the United States with each passing decade.

The Irish, including my great-grandfather (a bit later in the process), were among the first big waves. Between the 1840s and 1850s, over a million people fled possible starvation during the Great Famine (also known as the Great Hunger). This driving cause of emigration from Ireland was no trivial economic recession or depression. Potato disease destroyed crops in successive years from 1845 to 1849, leading to the starvation deaths of about 1 million Irish. That, in turn, led to the emigration of another one to two million, many of whom headed towards the United States.

They arrived poor, desperate, and overwhelmingly Catholic in a Protestant-dominated nation. The welcome wagon was not necessarily stocked and decorated for the new arrivals. Newspapers smeared them as lazy, drunk, and unfit for democracy. Job postings often carried the infamous tag: "No Irish Need Apply." While there's controversy about this being an urban legend, historians have found numerous examples in newspapers of the time to support the claim.

Despite that, Irish immigrants persevered, gained employment, and helped build this country. Out of the prejudice and poverty, the Irish carved out a path to acceptance, ultimately climbing from despised outsiders to mainstream middle-class Americans.

Italians arrived in heavy numbers later, from the 1880s through the 1920s. Most came from southern Italy, where poverty and limited farmland pushed people overseas in search of better opportunities.

The Italians also faced harsh stereotypes as criminals, anarchists, or untrustworthy foreigners. Lynchings of Italians were not uncommon in the South. On March 14, 1891, a mob lynched 11 Italian immigrants who had either been acquitted or not yet tried for the murder of Police Chief David Hennessy. This was the largest mass lynching in American history.

Like the Irish, the Italian immigrants persevered against the "Mafia" and other stereotypes and made their way, eventually becoming mainstream Americans.

On the opposite coast, the Chinese immigrants arrived initially chasing the California Gold Rush in the 1850s and, later, railroad jobs. Remember, the Transcontinental Railroad construction started from both sides, so Chinese immigrant workers started in California and steadily moved East. However, their success began to stir resentment. When economic cycles turned downward, politicians blamed Chinese workers for stealing jobs, fueling violent attacks and the 1882 Chinese Exclusion Act.

Even so, Chinatowns grew across the West, preserving their culture and identity while providing services, goods, and cuisine that would eventually influence all of America.

Jewish immigrants arrived mostly from Eastern Europe and Russia starting in the 1880s. They were escaping pogroms, persecution, and laws that made daily life in their homelands nearly impossible. Yet, after arriving in America, they still faced anti-Semitism and suspicion about their national loyalty. Like the other national and ethnic groups, they established thriving communities, as in New York, where they populated and built neighborhoods, started businesses, and played central roles in labor organizing. The garment industry, newspapers, and eventually entertainment were shaped heavily by Jewish workers and entrepreneurs. Despite social barriers at universities, clubs, and neighborhoods, they persisted, producing generations of leaders in culture, science, and politics.

Each of these groups hoped for opportunity while facing some of the ugly sides of the welcome mat. Yet they also integrated, contributed and stocked the melting pot called America with music, food, traditions, and political activism.

When Irish immigrants first arrived in big cities like New York and Boston, the hostility they faced was so fierce that they leaned into the one job no one else wanted: dangerous public service. Irish men flocked to police and fire departments, where long hours and high risks made the jobs unattractive to others. Over time, these positions became pipelines for stability and community respect. That's why, even today, the Irish identity is deeply tied to firefighting and policing in American cities, complete with St. Patrick's Day parades led by pipes and drums corps in full dress uniform.

The Door Slams Shut

Attitudes became law in 1882 with the passage of the Chinese Exclusion Act. For the first time, a federal law singled out one ethnic group for exclusion from the country.

Chinese laborers, who had arrived in large numbers during the Gold Rush and later to build the transcontinental railroad, were accused of taking jobs and driving down wages. In a timeless strategy of shifting blame, politicians capitalized on these fears, passing legislation that banned most Chinese immigration.

This was no short-term, knee-jerk strategy. The Act was renewed and expanded for decades, effectively halting Chinese integration in place. Family members were no longer able to immigrate to the U.S.

to join others who had already made the journey. Residents already here were stigmatized and viewed as outsiders.

It wasn't until World War II that the Act was finally repealed. Even then, it wasn't necessarily due to a fresh injection of conscience. The Americans needed increased Chinese support in the war against Japan.

The Immigration Act of 1924 widened the scope of exclusion. It imposed national origin quotas that heavily favored immigrants from Northern and Western Europe, while sharply limiting those from Southern and Eastern Europe. Lots of tricky math made things appear slightly less onerous, but the bottom line was that immigration was capped at 165,000 from countries outside the Western Hemisphere, which represents about an 80% reduction.

The act also banned nearly all immigration from Asia, targeting Japanese immigrants in particular. And the Immigration Act was one of the steps that reinforced and extended the Chinese Exclusion Act and its ban on Chinese immigrants. Africans were also largely excluded.

The law reflected racial and ethnic hierarchies of the era. Policymakers openly argued that America's character and future depended on maintaining a white, Anglo-Saxon majority. The 1924 quotas remained in place for four decades, shaping the nation's demographic makeup well into the mid-20th century.

After the Chinese Exclusion Act went into effect, many Chinese immigrants still tried to find ways into the United States, often through what became known as the "paper sons" system. Because the 1906 San Francisco earthquake and fire destroyed thousands of immigration and citizenship records, Chinese immigrants could claim (sometimes truthfully, sometimes not) that they were the children of U.S. citizens. Paper records became the golden ticket. When questioned by immigration officials, "paper sons" had to memorize elaborate family trees, floor plans of "their" supposed homes, and dozens of minute details in case they were grilled on arrival.

Assimilation Anxiety

All of this immigration caused contrarian reactions among established American citizens. As with nearly any political issue, some were ready to roll out the welcome mat, celebrating growth and offering a slice of the opportunity pie. Others, not so much, fearing flooding of the labor market and dilution of American culture.

For example, Nativist groups like the Know-Nothing Party of the 1850s railed against Irish Catholic immigration, fearing an undermining of Protestant values and cheap labor taking jobs. Later, the Immigration Restriction League, founded in 1894, promoted literacy tests and quota systems designed to discourage arrivals from Southern and Eastern Europe. The anxiety often boiled down to a fear that new immigrant groups would simply not assimilate into the American culture.

On the flip side was the "melting pot" crowd. The idea was that these diverse ethnic backgrounds could blend into one colorful national identity. Public schools provided English-language instruction, civic education, and patriotic messaging.

You know the rest. Most immigrant groups from this era gradually became as American as the immigrants who had come before them. The era of large-scale immigration was somewhat of a paradox. The country that was often hostile to incoming residents soon became defined by them.

Who says building a country from scratch can't be a bit messy at times?

The Know-Nothing Party got its odd name because members were sworn to secrecy. If asked about the group's activities, they were supposed to reply, "I know nothing." That cryptic answer became such a running gag in the press that the label stuck, and before long, everyone from newspapers to politicians was calling them the "Know-Nothings." Despite the silly-sounding nickname, they briefly became a serious force in the 1850s, winning dozens of congressional seats and even carrying Massachusetts in state elections. Their platform was anything but comic, though. It pushed for longer naturalization periods, restrictions on Catholic immigrants, and strict nativist policies. Ironically, for a party obsessed with being "truly American," they fizzled out within a decade, proving that secrecy and scapegoating don't make for lasting politics.

Chapter 16

Cowboys, Indians, and Hollywood Myths

The Old West wasn't all shootouts and saloons. In fact, gunfights in the streets were a pretty rare event indeed. Bar brawls on the other hand...

Anyway, the Old West was more about survival in tough conditions, building from the land, Native American resistance, and some frontier justice here and there. Let's reveal some of the myths to uncover a more complex and often sobering portrait of expansion beyond the Mississippi.

"Free Dirt! Get Your Free Dirt!"

A lot of things happened right smack in the middle of the Civil War. The Emancipation Proclamation was issued before the war was settled, and in 1862, President Abraham Lincoln signed one of the most sweeping land giveaways in American history: the Homestead Act. This deal really was one that people couldn't refuse. It offered 160 acres of free public land for anyone willing to live on it, build a home, and farm it for five years. For struggling families, immigrants chasing opportunity, and Civil War veterans looking to start fresh, it sounded like the deal of a lifetime.

Not surprisingly, a lot of people accepted the federal government's offer, sparking an enormous migration westward. The new railroads made it (relatively) easy for settlers to move into the new territories. The rumor mill shifted into overdrive about lands of opportunity in Nebraska, Kansas, the Dakotas, and beyond. By the end of the program in the 20th century, about 270 million acres had been claimed under the Homestead Act. That was about 10% of government-owned land. Talk about jumpstarting new local economies; entire towns, states, and agricultural regions grew directly from loads of promises of those 160 acres.

There was one small catch. The land wasn't empty. Native American tribes had lived in these areas for centuries—or longer. The Homestead Act ignored their claims entirely, treating the land as if it were unused and up for grabs. As settlers moved in, Indian communities were pushed off their homelands and often forced onto reservations. So, on one hand, the act did populate the West (with settlers), but at the same time, it depopulated it under that Manifest Destiny flag we described earlier.

Like most marketing pitches, the reality was just a bit different than the commercials. Life in the West was far from the romantic vision painted in recruitment posters. Conditions on the plains were brutal. Little rain, frequent droughts, and even locust swarms were all regular threats to crops. Any one of these could destroy a hard-earned livelihood in a heartbeat. Homes were often built of sod, as lumber was scarce on the plains. Neighbors were few and far away. Assuming these 160-acre plots were square and adjacent to one another, the nearest neighbor would be a half mile away.

Not all homesteaders were rugged white farm families. Thousands of African Americans, known as Exodusters, took advantage of the Homestead Act after the Civil War. In the late 1870s, waves of freedmen left the South, fleeing Black Codes, racial violence, and sharecropping debt. They headed for Kansas in particular, inspired by the biblical idea of an "Exodus" to a promised land. Whole communities like Nicodemus, Kansas, were founded by black homesteaders. Life was brutally hard, but these settlers saw owning land as the ultimate proof of freedom and self-determination. While many struggled, the Exoduster migration carved out a powerful chapter in the story of westward expansion, one often left out of Hollywood's cowboy myth.

Little Bighorn, Big Trouble

It was the summer of 1876, and the U.S. government, eager to corral Native tribes onto reservations and claim the Black Hills after gold was discovered there, found itself facing fierce resistance from Lakota Sioux and Cheyenne warriors.

The Native American forces were led by two "forces" of spiritual and tactical nature: Sitting Bull and Crazy Horse.

On the opposing side was a leader famous for many of his actions in the Civil War but infamous for his treatment of his troops and, on occasion, reckless decision making and overconfidence, General George Armstrong Custer.

To make a long story short, Custer, believing his opposition was light in numbers, split his forces and led an attack against (what he thought was) a small Indian village. The intelligence behind that assumption was tragically flawed. In fact, there were thousands of Indian warriors waiting for a fight. Custer's 200 men didn't stand a chance and were annihilated in the Battle of Little Bighorn.

For the Indian forces, Little Bighorn was an enormous triumph where their unity and resolve overwhelmed U.S. military power. Sitting Bull's vision and Crazy Horse's leadership inspired hope that the tide could be turned. But their victory carried a longer-term cost. The magnitude of the Army's defeat outraged the public and government alike, adding fuel to the fire of subduing the plains tribes once and for all. Little Bighorn turned out to be the last major Native American victory before the end of the Indian Wars.

Sitting Bull's role in the battle made him a symbol of Native American resistance and sovereignty. His defiance made him a marked man in the eyes of U.S. authorities. Within a few years, the Sioux and Cheyenne would face overwhelming military pressure, loss of their lands and confinement to reservations.

Before the battle, Sitting Bull performed a Sun Dance ritual in which he reportedly slashed his arms over a hundred times as an offering to the Great Spirit. During the trance, he envisioned soldiers "falling into his camp like grasshoppers from the sky." Many Lakota and Cheyenne took this as a prophecy of victory, and it bolstered their resolve in the days before Custer's arrival. When the Seventh Cavalry was wiped out, Sitting Bull's vision became legend.

When the West Went on Tour

Maybe we can describe William "Buffalo Bill" Cody as a "Western Renaissance Man" if there can be such a thing.

What was on his resume? Pony Express rider? Check. Army scout? Sure. Buffalo hunter? Duh. That's how he got the name. But his greatest job achievement was...frontier showman. Starting in the 1880s, Cody packaged the Wild West, put it under a tent, and took it on the road.

Buffalo Bill's Wild West show was part circus, part history lesson, and part pure marketing genius. City slickers who'd never been west of the Mississippi could suddenly watch a stagecoach get "robbed" right in front of them. Cowboys galloped, pistols shot stuff, and rope tricks whirled. Feats of "frontier skill" included sharpshooters who could knock the ashes off a cigarette (don't try this at home) and trick riders who dazzled crowds with their well-trained steeds.

No Western show would be complete without Native Americans. For this part, Cody didn't import Hollywood method actors. He recruited actual Lakota, Cheyenne, and others to play themselves. Yes, the scripts were likely exaggerated if not completely unrealistic. The headliner was Sitting Bull, the Lakota Chief, recently returned from his last gig defeating the U.S. Army at Little Bighorn. That had to be quite the marketing coup as, for one season, he toured with Buffalo Bill, and audiences lined up to see the "real deal" warrior.

It sure sounds like a logistical nightmare, but Buffalo Bill somehow managed to take this show, or more like a menagerie, overseas to European audiences. What could be more popular in Europe than a Wild West extravaganza? Word is that even Queen Victoria applauded. Really.

Some things never change. "Reality shows" were about as realistic as "reality TV" today. The Cowboys were always the noble good guys. Indians were fierce enemies or relics of an older world. Western life was portrayed as a non-stop, action-packed adventure, complete with plenty of shootouts.

Enthusiasm of the Native American performers was likely mixed, with some bristling at reinforcing the stereotypes, while others said, "Why not? It's a steady paycheck..."

Buffalo Bill Cody died in 1917. By that time, the stereotypical frontier life was gone, but the romance of the Wild West was just getting warmed up. While he didn't plan it, his shows almost certainly opened the door for Hollywood Westerns, rodeos and pulp cowboy novels. The appetite for the romantic Western adventure seems insatiable.

When Buffalo Bill took his Wild West show to London in 1887, it coincided with Queen Victoria's Golden Jubilee, and the spectacle caused a sensation. British newspapers raved about the sharpshooting of Annie Oakley, who could split playing cards in midair, and the drama of staged battles with Lakota performers. Queen Victoria herself attended, reportedly clapping enthusiastically during Sitting Bull's appearances, though he often refused to follow Cody's script, instead giving impromptu speeches about Native sovereignty. European royalty lined up for backstage visits, and even future Kaiser Wilhelm II got a lesson in Wild West bravado when Annie Oakley allegedly shot the ashes off a cigarette he held in his mouth. Whether or not the story is embellished, it shows how Cody's show blurred the line between history and myth, exporting America's frontier legend to the world.

Wounded Knee: America's Tragic Full Stop

On December 29th, 1890, U.S. troops surrounded a Lakota Sioux camp near Wounded Knee Creek in South Dakota. The Army's mission seemed simple, at least on the surface: disarm the Lakota and bring them back under government control.

The Army unit surrounded the encampment and accentuated their firepower with four Hotchkiss guns aimed at the Indian camp. A Hotchkiss gun is kind of a cross between a small cannon and a rotating-barrel Gatling gun, so it's quite intimidating when pointed at people.

As these events tend to go, someone, somewhere, fired a shot. One theory suggests that it started with a deaf Lakota warrior named Black Coyote. As the story goes, he was ordered to surrender his rifle and apparently refused, possibly because he couldn't hear it. No one knows for sure what started it, but once the shooting started, that was it.

Soldiers opened fire with rifles and the Hotchkiss guns at close range, and in short order, about 300 Lakota men, women and children were killed, with another 50 wounded. Some 25 U.S. soldiers died in the shooting, at least some as a result of friendly fire. The dead Lakota were buried in a mass grave.

The government initially heralded this a a great victory in battle. The Native Americans viewed it as nothing more than a massacre of defenseless people. Compounding the optics problems, the Army awarded some 20 Medals of Honor to U.S. Soldiers, thereby adding insult to injury.

Wounded Knee became a rallying cry referencing decades of broken treaties, forced removals, and relentless cultural destruction. As late as the 1970s, Native activists occupied the site to protest against ongoing injustices. For the U.S. government, it marked the end of organized Native resistance in the West.

The Wounded Knee tragedy was closely tied to the Ghost Dance movement, a spiritual revival that had spread among Plains tribes in the late 1880s. The Ghost Dance was a religious ritual promising that, if performed with enough devotion, Native peoples would see the return of the buffalo and the disappearance of white settlers. U.S. authorities saw the movement as a dangerous uprising, though it was largely nonviolent. The Army's decision to disarm the Lakota at Wounded Knee was partly fueled by fear of this ritual, which they didn't understand. Tragically, what was meant as a spiritual act of hope and renewal was treated as rebellion and met with devastating violence.

Cowboys, Camera, Action!

Is there anything more "Western" than a cowboy movie? The tumbleweed rolls across the screen, a rugged hero squints into the sun while scratching his six-day beard, and someone's about to learn the hard way that it's high noon. Even the ones made in Italy, yes, spaghetti with a side of six-shooters, carry the same dust-and-gunpowder romance.

As the real conquest of the West tapered off in the early 20th century, Hollywood discovered the West was the perfect soundstage. It had action, drama, and lots of cool hats. Silent pictures like *The Great Train Robbery* (1903) gave audiences their first cinematic taste of frontier lawlessness. By the time Surround Sound, Technicolor, and John Wayne came along, the cowboy had gone from a guy who happened to work on a ranch to America's ultimate hero, always saving the town, the girl, and occasionally the dog. Clint Eastwood later gave us the darker, squintier character, but the noble guy myth persisted.

No one has ever accused Hollywood of recognizing reality. In real life, the Western lifestyle was a tad different. For starters, real cowboys weren't all chiseled-jaw white men with an infinite pool of honorable intentions and perfect aim. Many were Mexican vaqueros, African American freedmen, Native guides, or just poor immigrants who figured herding cattle beat starving.

The "savage enemy" was usually an Indigenous nation defending land that had been theirs for centuries. The law-and-order sheriffs? Sometimes noble, sometimes just another flavor of outlaw with a badge. You know, real people. Good ones and bad ones. And vigilante justice, which Hollywood portrayed as frontier democracy, often looked more like mob violence.

The movies have always had a way of "softening" the truth. Conquest? Nah, it's entertainment. Raids on small towns? How about a shootout? Brave pioneer settlers? Brave, yes, but the previous residents might not agree with the "settler" labels.

To this day, if you ask someone to describe the West, they're more likely to mention Clint Eastwood's cigarette or John Wayne's drawl than the backbreaking grind of everyday survival on the frontier. The movies created an eternal cultural icon: the cowboy as America's knight, roaming the open plains with a six-shooter instead of a sword.

The Western has become much more than a film genre. It's really America's origin story on celluloid. The fact it's a bit embellished here and there? Well...

One of Hollywood's first true cowboy stars, Tom Mix, wasn't just acting, he'd actually worked as a ranch hand, rodeo performer, and even a marshal before hitting the screen in the 1910s. Mix made over 300 silent Westerns, performing many of his own stunts, from bronco riding to hanging off galloping horses. His fame was so great that his horse, Tony, got second billing on movie posters. Mix's blend of real cowboy grit and Hollywood showmanship helped cement the cowboy-as-hero myth, even though, in reality, cowboys earned about a dollar a day, ate beans for every meal, and spent more time fixing fences than chasing outlaws. The West may have been rough, but Hollywood knew how to make it glamorous.

Part Five

World Power and Progress

Chapter 17

Teddy Time: Roosevelt Rewires the Presidency

With a big stick and even bigger personality, Theodore Roosevelt redefined what it meant to be president. He busted trusts, built canals, saved forests, and scared off foreign powers, sometimes in the same week. This chapter covers how one energetic reformer changed the role of the presidency forever.

The Rough-Riding Spanish American War

The Spanish-American War was relatively minor in the scope of wars, if you can ever use the word "minor" and "war" in the same sentence. But it sure left a lasting impact. Who hasn't heard of the tale of the Rough Riders charging up that hill? Perhaps slightly lesser known is how this shifted one Theodore "Teddy" Roosevelt into political high gear.

Interestingly, for a guy with a lifelong reputation for being exceedingly energetic, he was born sickly, suffering from severe asthma. He decided to power his way through with a consistent regimen of tough physical workouts and clearly overcame his trouble. I'm not sure this is a doctor-recommended strategy, but somehow it seemed to work for him.

Shortly after graduating from Harvard, T.R. moved into public life, gaining posts in the New York legislature, the New York City Police and even Assistant Secretary of the Navy.

It was in his last role that he launched his career into the stratosphere. He had been publicly spoiling for a fight with Spain as he was convinced their extended territory in this half of the world was ripe for the taking. When war did break out in 1898, in part due to an unexplained explosion on the Battleship USS Maine in Havana Harbor, Roosevelt resigned his desk job with the Navy and started recruiting for a volunteer force to go fight.

Thus was born the 1st United States Volunteer Cavalry. You might know that unit as the Rough Riders. Like the country at large, this group was a military melting pot, comprised of everyone from Ivy League polo players to Texas cowboys and Native scouts, and even a sprinkling of lawmen and desperados.

As for that famous hill thing, The Rough Riders' earned their reputation during the assault on San Juan Heights outside Santiago, Cuba. You know, the charge up San Juan Hill.

Picture these rough and tumble guys charging up a hill on horseback, under withering fire. Then remove the horses because they actually did this on foot. As it turns out, the Army didn't plan for enough ships to bring all the horses along for the invasion. Oops.

Anyway, the photo op and resulting victory accomplished a few notable things. It helped put the "still relatively new" United States on the world map as a major power. The country had just taken on and defeated Spain, which had been a dominant force for centuries. As part of the spoils, the U.S. gained control of Puerto Rico, Guam and the Philippines. It also propelled Roosevelt into the White House, although a bit indirectly.

Soon after returning home, Teddy was elected governor of New York. Not too long after that, he became Vice President under William McKinley.

There's an interesting story there. As he was energetically progressive, the party bosses wanted to dampen his influence, so they pushed him into the normally "out of the picture" Vice President position. However, McKinley was assassinated in 1901, thereby launching Roosevelt into the big chair as President.

See what climbing a hill in Cuba can do? In his memoirs, he recalled the charge at San Juan as "the great day of my life." And perhaps it was. Without the spectacle of that hot July afternoon in Cuba, Roosevelt might never have gained the fame that propelled him to the presidency.

One of those lasting impacts left by Theodore Roosevelt was the most prevalent children's toy of all time, the teddy bear.

While on a hunt in Mississippi, the party's hunting guides thought it would be nifty to tie up a captured black bear, making it easy for the hunters to shoot and claim it. Roosevelt flat out refused, considering the act unsportsmanlike. The story spread, and before long, Washington Post cartoonist Clifford Berryman drew an image of Roosevelt sparing the bear. Brooklyn shop owners Rose and Morris Michtom created a stuffed bear and obtained Roosevelt's permission to call it

"Teddy's Bear." The toy and name caught on, and the couple soon founded the Ideal Toy Company to make and sell Teddy Bears, well, everywhere.

Trust-Busting and the Sherman Antitrust Act

Remember all those rich and powerful industrialists of the Gilded Age? Roosevelt wasn't too impressed with the imbalance of wealth, and in his view, the use and abuse of some of the rules of business. To be clear, he wasn't an anti-capitalist. He was more interested in establishing what he perceived as a level playing field, where government had more of a role as a referee to check some of the activities of big business, including anti-competitive practices, price fixing and use and abuse of the labor force and working class.

Passed before Roosevelt's presidency, back in 1880, the Sherman Antitrust Act wasn't in regular play. Roosevelt changed that.

For example, he took on J.P. Morgan's Northern Securities Company. This was a "trust" of other railroad companies, formed in 1901, that included the Northern Pacific, Great Northern, and Chicago, Burlington & Quincy railroads. In practical terms, this trust controlled virtually all railroad activity in the northern United States.

Roosevelt filed suit, using the Sherman Antitrust Act as his justification, and a Supreme Court 5-4 ruling agreed with him. Word has it that J.P. Morgan attempted to negotiate privately with Roosevelt, presumably to leverage the "good old boy" network, but Teddy refused, claiming the law applied equally, even to really rich and powerful guys, so the issue would be decided publicly in the courts.

And that's how Teddy Roosevelt picked up the "Trust Buster" nickname. He allegedly preferred the term "Trust Regulator." Again, being a capitalist himself, he agreed with good, aggressive business, but one that adhered to certain rules.

Consistent with his energetic persona, he was, at the time, a people's champion, demanding fairness, accountability, and markets available to all. Of course, many of his corporate targets didn't quite agree.

When J.P. Morgan learned Roosevelt's administration was about to sue Northern Securities, he reportedly requested a private meeting with the president. Morgan strolled into the White House and bluntly told him, "If we have done anything wrong, send your man to my man, and they can fix it up."

That kind of backroom deal had worked with presidents before, but Roosevelt wasn't having it. He shot back that the matter would be handled "by the government of the United States," not by "my man" and "your man." It was a moment that captured the shift of the era: the Gilded Age titans were no longer calling the shots unchallenged.

From Rough Rider to Park Ranger-in-Chief

Theodore Roosevelt was an avid outdoorsman. Perhaps an outcome of these intentional efforts to power through his childhood frailties, he was a guy who could take off into the woods on horseback and be right at home, for days, weeks or months.

It was this passion that he brought to the office of the President. Believing that the nation's land was a treasure worth preserving and protecting for future generations, he went to great lengths to carve out national forests and declare them off limits to use and abuse.

During his time in office, he created five national parks, 18 national monuments, and more than 150 national forests. Add all this up, and it came to somewhere over 230 million acres of land. To put that in perspective, it's not too much less than Texas and California combined.

You might recognize some of the areas he helped set aside: large parts of the Grand Canyon, Devil's Tower and the Petrified Forest, to name a few.

The real impact was a change in priorities for the powers in Washington. While large areas had been set aside before his time, like Yellowstone and Yosemite, he did change the dialogue and sense of priority, setting the stage for future conservation efforts.

In 1903, President Roosevelt ditched the White House for a three-day camping trip in Yosemite with famed naturalist John Muir. No Secret Service entourage, just two guys, bedrolls, and the Sierra Nevada wilderness. Roosevelt wanted to see the land firsthand, and Muir wanted to persuade him to protect it. They hiked through giant sequoias, camped under the stars, and talked late into the night about the importance of preserving America's natural wonders. By the time Roosevelt left Yosemite, he was even more convinced that conservation had to be a national mission. Out of that trip came policies that permanently protected huge swaths of wilderness, including the expansion of Yosemite itself into a full national park.

Panama or Bust: Slicing the Americas in Two

The idea of cutting a canal through that thin part of land between North and South America wasn't at all new. Here's why. Going by ship from New York to San Francisco is about a 13,000-mile trip if you have to travel around South America and through the nasty seas off Cape Horn. If you can cut through that bit of land in Panama by digging a ditch big enough for ships, the journey shortens by about 8,000 miles to, say, 5,200, give or take. That provides a lot of incentive to figure out a way to cut through the mountains and jungles where the oceans are only 40 or 50 miles apart.

It doesn't sound too hard, considering the French had cut the

Suez Canal starting in 1859, and it was just over 100 miles long at the time. The difference was the jungle environment. Oh, and a bunch of mountains. All that rain caused catastrophes like mudslides and gazillions of mosquitoes. And at the time, mosquitoes weren't just an annoyance; they were a death sentence. When the French attempted to create a "Panama Canal" starting in 1881, the environment alone killed some 20,000 workers. The guy who had built the Suez Canal, Ferdinand de Lesseps, was in charge and apparently was unable to internalize the dramatic geography and climate differences and how to overcome them. The effort failed by the late 1890s.

Enter the Americans.

In 1902, Congress passed the Spooner Act, which basically said, "Hey, let's build that canal, provided we can get suitable permission from Colombia, which controlled Panama at the time. Talks didn't go well, so Teddy Roosevelt resorted to his "carry a big stick" plan and backed Panama as they declared independence from Colombia. Conveniently, U.S. warships did some "exercises and training" in the area around that time, so Columbia wasn't really motivated to interfere. Of course, the newly minted Panamanians were happy to negotiate a deal for canal-building rights.

Learning from the poor experience of the French, a more open-minded team was assembled to design and build a more efficient lock-based system, leveraging lakes and rivers. And a Dr. William Gorgas joined the effort, spearheading work to drain swamps, add screen windows and fumigate buildings to kill off those dangerous mosquitoes.

Make no mistake, the work was still plenty hazardous, but rather than claiming 20,000 lives, the American construction effort resulted in about 5,600 fatalities over the ten-year job.

The result was nothing short of a modern wonder: a fifty-mile canal linking two oceans.

When the first ship, the SS Ancon, passed through in 1914, Roosevelt was no longer president, but his fingerprints were all over the project. The canal reshaped global trade and supercharged America's reach.

Technically, a French crane boat, the Alexandre La Valley, was the first to "pass through" the canal, but that was during construction. The SS Ancon was the first to go through the completed canal in an ocean-to-ocean crossing.

Today's canal is about 50 miles long and takes just under 10 hours to transit. About 52 million gallons of water are moved around for each ship to make it through the lock system, which moves ships up and down 85 feet in some places.

Roosevelt's Playbook: Talk Nice, Carry Muscle

An American highlight worth mentioning is the origin of some of those buzzwords we still hear today about this era, like "Speak softly and carry a big stick" and a "square deal." Let's explore.

When Theodore Roosevelt said, "Speak softly and carry a big stick—you will go far," he wasn't just tossing off a catchy phrase. It was basically his foreign policy blueprint, succinctly communicated in just 11 words. It's pretty much what it sounds like: negotiating is great, and do it when you can, but make sure the big, scary guy is standing behind you when you do.

It seems to me a bit similar to the Manifest Destiny concept, so when Roosevelt declared that the United States had the obligation to step in when nations in the Western Hemisphere couldn't get their act together, the position was likely not foreign to the American public.

Roosevelt's "big stick" also had a peaceful side. In 1905, he brokered an end to the Russo-Japanese War, hosting negotiations in Portsmouth, New Hampshire. The talks weren't easy, but Roosevelt managed to assist the two sides in hammering out an agreement. For his efforts, he won the Nobel Peace Prize, the first ever awarded to an American president.

At home, he applied a similar principle through his "Square Deal." The Square Deal wasn't exactly a law, but more of a guiding principle that claimed every American deserved a degree of fairness. That was to include all: workers, business owners, and consumers. Much like his diplomacy, the Square Deal balanced persuasion with action. Roosevelt believed in talking things out, as demonstrated through his help in arbitrations between miners and mine owners, but he rarely, if ever, shied away from using federal power to accomplish his goals. Right, wrong or indifferent, his message was clear: play fair, or the government will make sure you do.

Subtle? Not so much. Roosevelt wasn't kidding about the "carry a big stick" part. In 1907, he sent the Great White Fleet, consisting of 16 gleaming, white-painted battleships, on a world tour. Officially, it was about goodwill visits and showing the flag. Unofficially? It was pure muscle-flexing, a floating billboard of American naval power steaming past the coasts of Europe, Africa, Asia, and Latin America.

Chapter 18

World War I

As this is a practical guide to America, we're not going to dive into a comprehensive history of World War I. Instead, we're going to look at the people and events that reflect the United States' role in the global conflict.

At first, the U.S. sat out the Great War, watching Europe tear itself apart. But German U-boats and secret telegrams changed that. America entered late, but its arrival helped end the war and laid the groundwork for yet another World War in the not-too-distant future.

The Lusitania: A Warning Shot Across the Atlantic

One "side effect" of being an ocean away from the relative chaos of Europe and so many countries existing in close, and not always friendly, proximity is the isolation effect. Problems could be more easily viewed from a distance, as in, "It doesn't impact us; it's a European issue." The sentiment in the U.S. at the time was one of isolationism, and quite frankly, there were some benefits to that positioning.

The U.S. was an active trade partner of most of Europe at the time, so by remaining rabidly neutral in the conflict, it could continue trading with both sides. And then there was the immigration situation. America was freshly populated with (relatively) new arrivals from countries on both sides of World War I. The U.S. government wasn't keen on fanning the flames of conflict right here at home by taking sides with any geographic or ethnic group. So, the prevailing desire to stay out of it was a winning strategy, and why Woodrow Wilson won re-election in 1916, in part thanks to the "He kept us out of war" campaign slogan. By that time, however, he was talking to a population with a growing percentage of people fed up with Germany's behavior.

The year before, more gas had been added to the fires of war. On May 7, 1915, the British ocean liner RMS Lusitania set off on what was supposed to be a routine voyage across the Atlantic. Instead, the luxury ocean crossing ended in one of the most shocking maritime disasters of the 20th century. A single torpedo from a German U-boat slammed into the ship off the coast of Ireland, sending her to the bottom in just 18 minutes. Nearly 1,200 passengers and crew died, including 128 Americans.

That didn't sit well, anywhere, especially in the United States. People were shocked and horrified that Germany targeted a civilian passenger ship filled with women and children. Add the significant numbers of American citizens, and it was assumed Germany had raised the ante to unrestricted warfare, on, well, everyone.

On the flip side, Germany had publicly warned Americans not to sail on British ships, going so far as to take out advertisements in American newspapers to communicate the warnings. England and Germany were at war, after all. These things are rarely so cut and dried. Later, it was revealed that the Lusitania was carrying military supplies bound for Great Britain. Nonetheless, the American public only saw the victims. Wilson demanded an end to Germany's policy of unrestricted submarine warfare, and for a while, Germany backed off.

The Lusitania tragedy wasn't the sole reason the U.S. eventually entered World War I in April 1917. It did, however, change the conversation in the U.S. and greased the skids for Congress approving a declaration of war two years later. Europe's problem? Nope. The realities of a world now connected by sea and rail travel and near-instantaneous telegraph communication were apparent.

The resulting propaganda was powerful. The British used the disaster to help paint the Germans as ruthless villains. Photographs of drowned children drove men to enlist and fight with signs reminding people on both sides of the pond to "Remember the Lusitania!"

Among those who narrowly missed the Lusitania disaster was a young Winston Churchill. At the time, he was First Lord of the Admiralty, and although he toyed with traveling on the ship, he changed his plans. Later, critics accused him of deliberately avoiding the crossing because he knew the risks. Historians generally say it was a coincidence, not a conspiracy. Still, the rumor stuck and added another layer of intrigue to the already explosive tragedy. And speaking of brushes with fate, Alfred Vanderbilt, one of the richest men in America, did sail. Though he didn't survive, witnesses later recalled him giving his lifejacket to a woman holding a baby and calmly helping others into lifeboats until the final moments. His death turned him into a symbol of selfless courage in the press.

The Telegram Heard 'Round the World

One really should always think twice before sending a nuclear email. It hardly ever ends well.

While the Zimmerman telegram wasn't technically an email, it was a direct telegram from German Foreign Minister Arthur Zimmermann to Mexico. And, guess what? The British intercepted and decoded it. Those Bletchley Park chaps have always been really, really good at puzzles. OK, so some of you history nerds might have busted me here. Bletchley Park was a group of code breakers who worked in World War II, but the name is just so darned British, I had to say it here. Remind me when we get to the next war, and we'll talk about some of their exploits along with those of their American counterparts in Hawaii.

Anyway, Zimmermann was communicating a deal to Mexico. Ally with us in this war, and we'll help you get back all the territory you lost in the Mexican-American War. You know, Texas, Arizona, New Mexico...half your country and all that.

It wasn't as if Mexico had a lot to offer to the European war effort at the time, and they certainly weren't in any position to invade the United States, even if Germany did win World War I.

But, even if just a desperate move by Germany, the plan did have some remotely possible potential. If they could stir up trouble, or at least worry of trouble, between Mexico and the U.S., then maybe the United States would be too distracted to enter the war in Europe.

But, as you know, the Brits intercepted the secret offer and then promptly shared it with the Americans. Here's the best part. In war, there's plenty of deception and sneaky maneuvering to go around, and the British have always been absolute masters at that game. So, many on this side of the pond weren't sure if the message was real.

Enter pride.

Zimmermann himself publicly admitted the telegram was real, and let's just say that began the downfall of Germany in World War I. The American populace was royally ticked as suddenly, the "war over there" was right on our doorstep, as the U.S. shared plenty of border mileage with Mexico.

Remember in the last section where we discussed the growing sentiment against Germany's unrestricted warfare and the whole Lusitania thing? Even if it was carrying military supplies, people were still angry about the sinking.

America lost that isolationist feeling, and in April 1917, Woodrow Wilson went to Congress to ask for passage of a formal declaration of war. It was quickly granted.

America had just entered its first World War.

When Germany dangled the offer of Texas, New Mexico, and Arizona, you might think Mexico would at least consider it. In reality, Mexican officials knew it was a ridiculous proposal. Mexico had just come through years of revolution, its military was in tatters, and the U.S. Army was far stronger. Even if Germany could somehow defeat the U.S. Navy and supply Mexico with weapons (a huge "if"), Mexico would then have to govern millions of hostile English-speaking Americans in those "reclaimed" states. The Mexican president at the time, Venustiano Carranza, had his advisors study the offer, and their conclusion was blunt: not feasible.

10,000 Troops a Day Keeps the Kaiser Away

Is anyone, or any country, ever really ready for a world war? I suppose Germany's semi-secret buildup was one example of preparing in advance, but more often than not, it seems like nations are caught off guard and have to mobilize post haste.

Such was the case with the United States in World War I.

When the United States declared war on Germany in April of 1917, the U.S. Army was only the 17th largest in the world; for those counting, that's smaller than Portugal's. And at the time, most Americans had never actually seen a battlefield. Perhaps some of those clueless spectators who brought picnic lunches to the first major battle of the Civil War were still alive, but other than that...

However, as had been the pattern with the American military, the country was able to scale up fast. Within just one year, the United States had mobilized millions of soldiers. They had built ships to transport them and their equipment across the Atlantic Ocean. And the country was chock-full of training camps preparing young soldiers for war.

One figure stood tall amongst the mobilization chaos—General John J. Pershing. Nicknamed "Black Jack" from his earlier cavalry days, he was the stereotypical military "drill sergeant" type leader: stern, disciplined and prepared to take no guff from European military leadership.

Apparently, Britain and France had this idea that fresh U.S. troops would simply go straight into their divisions to replenish the millions they'd lost in the meat grinder called trench warfare. Black Jack's response was classic Pershing. In polite terms, his answer was something like "No, thanks," but probably with more four-letter-word equivalents of the times. Not willing to be a junior partner or assistant reserve force, Pershing insisted the U.S. Army would fight on its own terms and absolutely under its own command.

No one was really in a position to argue. Within months, by early 1918, American Doughboys were flooding into France at the rate of 10,000 troops per day.

Good thing. The German army, now getting desperate, had launched a last-ditch offensive and was getting dangerously close to Paris.

The American Army was green, no doubt, but it began to have success, initially by capturing a town at Cantigny, in its first offensive operation of the war.

Then came Belleau Wood.

U.S. Marines earned their fierce reputation by fighting so aggressively that the Germans nicknamed them "Teufel Hunden." That translates to something like "Devil Dogs," a name that proudly lives on to this day. Casualties were enormous, but there was no doubt the doughboys were here to fight and win. A few months later, the Meuse-Argonne Offensive became the largest battle in American history to that point. Approximately 1.2 million U.S. soldiers took part, slogging through forests, mud, and machine-gun fire. The fighting was brutal, but the Americans broke through German defenses and pushed the enemy back.

The cost was staggering, with over 26,000 Americans killed in that campaign alone, but the impact was clear. The infusion of American manpower, equipment and morale tipped the scales in favor of the Allies. By November, Germany was suing for peace. As the young American soldiers found themselves marching through French villages, they were cheered as liberators. They were, in Pershing's words, "an army unlike any the world had ever seen."

The Battle at Belleau Wood is Marine Corps lore. Facing an entrenched enemy, the Marines attacked six different times before finally dislodging the Germans. In the early days of the June 1–26, 1918, battle, Marines shocked the Germans with the effectiveness of their long-range, accurate rifle fire. Their marksmanship focus during training helped the Americans not only stun the attacking force into a halt, but also established the U.S. Marines as elite troops. Once stopped and forced to dig in, the Germans had to face the fighting Marines in vicious, often hand-to-hand combat.

A famous quote sums up the mentality that led to victory.

Marine First Sergeant Dan Daly reportedly rallied his men with the words, "Come on, you sons of bitches. Do you want to live forever?"

Woodrow Wilson: 14, World: Not So Much

As the war raged in Europe, Wilson delivered his aspirational speech to Congress on January 8, 1918 (the shooting didn't stop until November 11, 1918).

Embarking on a vision (some say a naive one) to prevent future "wars to end all wars," he offered up his world peace manifesto, hopeful that in the aftermath of this war, the world could figure out how to better behave.

Wilson's 14 Points were big ideas, including concepts like open diplomacy instead of secret treaties and agreements. And freedom of the seas and navigation to promote friction-free world trade. Add in the removal of trade barriers to provide an equal footing for all potential trading partners. Then there was the idea of arms reduction. The world had never seen carnage like that evidenced in World War I. The advance of military technology had enabled killing on a scale never imagined. And there were the ideas of re-evaluating and adjusting colonial claims to be more in line with the desires of the residents involved. The biggie was the creation of the League of Nations, which would establish an organized system of independence and territorial integrity for all nations. It would prevent future wars before they began through open communication and negotiation.

The short version of the reception to this message was that much of the populace loved it. Having lost sons, brothers, fathers, cousins and uncles to the Great War, people everywhere dreaded the prospect of another future World War. And that was just the soldiers. In Europe, civilians suffered too, and men, women and children were lost in stunning numbers. Who wouldn't support an end to wars?

On the other hand, more experienced political pundits saw it as naive and a pie-in-the-sky pipe dream, destined to fall under the weight of human nature, greed, and thirst for power.

While some of the ideas sounded nifty on paper, the reality was something different. European leaders wanted tangible guarantees, especially ones to clamp down on the possibility of future German aggression.

At home, Congress was reluctant to support anything that ran the risk of dragging the United States into foreign matters involuntarily. League of Nations? No thanks! The isolationist streak still ran deep.

In the end, the Fourteen Points were more influential as theoretical inspiration than as actual policy. The Treaty of Versailles incorporated few elements, as we'll see.

When Wilson unveiled his Fourteen Points in January 1918, the speech made such waves that German officials actually ordered it dropped over enemy lines in leaflet form. Thousands of copies fluttered down into the trenches, promising the outline of a just peace. Some German soldiers kept the pamphlets in their pockets, seeing them as a lifeline if they survived the war. Ironically, Wilson's ideas were more popular with enemy troops than with his own allies, many of whom thought the plan was far too lenient. For the men in the mud, though, "the American President's peace" sounded a whole lot better than another winter in the trenches.

Fourteen Points, Zero Wins

The official end of hostilities was at the 11th hour of the 11th day of the 11th month: 11 PM, November 11th, 1918.

The shooting may have stopped, but the battle over peace had just begun. It would take almost seven more months of fighting in conference rooms and representative chambers before the Treaty of Versailles was signed.

As the political reaction to Wilson's 14 Points foreshadowed, the prevailing sentiment was to punish Germany for the war in bold fashion. The treaty even included a "war guilt clause" that forced Germany to accept sole blame for the war and its consequences. Needless to say, that didn't sit well with the German populace.

Other provisions in the Treaty included massive reparations payments, territorial losses and strict limitations on future German military composition and buildup.

Wilson arrived in Paris with his 14 Points packed and ready to write into the Treaty, but it was not to be. European leaders like Georges Clemenceau of France had more tactical and immediate priorities. They wanted guarantees of security, punishment for Germany, and lots of reparations to rebuild from the war's destruction and economic damage. So, most of Wilson's 14 Points were ignored or rejected. He did manage to get the League of Nations bit in there, but in the end, not even the United States joined. That wasn't his doing. Official participation in such a treaty required ratification by Congress, and politics came into play. Some opponents were leery of becoming subject to foreign influence and even getting dragged into global conflicts without explicit congressional approval.

Wilson resorted to the Bully pulpit and hit the road, hoping to sell his vision to the public for the League of Nations. He traveled and spoke relentlessly until he literally collapsed from exhaustion and soon after suffered a stroke that left him partially paralyzed.

That was the end of the ratification battle, and the Senate rejected the treaty not once, but twice. The United States never did join the League of Nations.

When Woodrow Wilson arrived in Paris with his Fourteen Points, French Prime Minister Georges Clemenceau, nicknamed "The Tiger," was unimpressed. With his country devastated by German invasion, Clemenceau famously scoffed: "Fourteen Points? The good Lord only had ten!" To Clemenceau and other Europeans, Wilson's ideas sounded lofty but naïve compared to the blood-and-mud realities they'd endured.

Chapter 19

The Roaring Twenties: Fast Cars, Fast Money, and a Crash

The 1920s. The ultimate bubble, at least until it popped. Flappers, speakeasies, jazz, and sky-high stock prices made the 1920s feel like a non-stop party, at least for those with money. But beneath the dance floor was a shaky economic foundation and deep cultural divides. Let's explore the extremes that defined this famous decade and how the economy suffered a major hangover when the music stopped.

Prohibition: When Beer Went Underground

"Lips that touch liquor shall not touch ours."

So said many women of the Women's Christian Temperance Union and the Anti-Saloon League, campaigning in favor of the prohibition of alcoholic beverages back in the early 20th century.

Let's jump to the exciting conclusion. Those ladies, and their allies, won. The 18th Amendment was passed by Congress in December 1917 and ratified by the states on January 16, 1919.

Talk about last call. Hold my non-alcoholic beer and listen to this one. While most establishments sound the "get ready to get out of here" alarm 30 minutes or so before closing time, this motion shouted out "Last call!" a year in advance. That's right, the prohibition didn't take effect for a full year to give people time to get it out of their system.

Just to be clear, Prohibition didn't ban the consumption of alcohol, just the manufacture, sale and importation of it through the Volstead Act, which was the enforcement mechanism. And there were lots of loopholes: medicinal use, booze cruises off the coast, and more.

Let's get back to the idea behind all this and how it backfired...

The thinking by supporters was that alcohol led to moral decay, which led to all manner of bad behavior. Obviously, drunkenness, but also things like violence, poverty, robbery, sex-related crimes—you name it.

So, lose the gin and all those other things simply go away. Why didn't anyone think of that before?

How did the plan work out? Great... if by 'great' you mean something like the Titanic's maiden voyage.

First and foremost, Americans tend to have the capitalist bug. Apparently, it flows through the Mississippi and spreads in both directions. So, in many people's eyes, the government had just created the best business opportunity ever.

Enter an underground economy driven by waterways filled with, well, beer, wine, whiskey, gin and all the rest. Speakeasies—secret bars tucked behind soda fountains, barber shops, or mysterious unmarked doors, popped up by the tens of thousands. Bootleggers ferried barrels of whiskey across borders, down back roads, and even in hollowed-out loaves of bread. Meanwhile, police forces and federal agents, understaffed and often underpaid, found themselves overwhelmed trying to enforce this law against a very large percentage of the population.

Enter Alphonse "Al" Capone, and plenty of others like him.

I guess you could think of Capone as the Robber Baron of Prohibition, a dominant "business" figure, kind of like the Carnegies and Rockefellers before. Although, to my knowledge, those ultra-rich titans of business weren't quite as violent, or at least they paid others to do their dirty work.

Operating out of Chicago, Al Capone ran a vast operation of breweries, distilleries, and supply lines protected by his army of enforcers. By the mid-1920s, Capone was raking in tens of millions of dollars a year. To put that in perspective, $10 million back in the 20s is worth somewhere way over $100 million in today's dollars. All this money (and his sheer ruthlessness) allowed him to control not just liquor but also gambling, prostitution, and politics. Bribed cops looked the other way, judges suddenly forgot how to read indictments, and Chicago should have saved a fortune on civil servant payroll, as Capone paid nearly everyone in office.

Strangely, he was somewhat admired. He cultivated his image of a working-class Robin Hood, donating to charities, sponsoring soup kitchens, and making sure that poor Chicagoans remembered who to thank for their free Thanksgiving turkeys. The press ate it up, and the public often cheered him on, as if he were a magnanimous celebrity rather than a ruthless mob boss.

But there was that issue of the violence. Gangland wars erupted as rival mobs fought for control of the liquor trade. The most infamous moment came in 1929 with the St. Valentine's Day Massacre, when Capone's men gunned down seven rivals in broad daylight.

While he was never directly tied to the murders, his fingerprints were all over the bloody turf war.

Here's a life lesson: never mess with an accountant. After dodging charges and arrests for every crime imaginable, it wasn't bullets or billy clubs that brought Capone down. It was tax evasion.

In 1931, federal prosecutors proved that the IRS was mightier than all those bribes. He was sentenced to 11 years in prison, ending his reign as America's most infamous gangster.

After his appeals failed, he was sent to a federal prison in Atlanta, but in 1934, he was transferred to the "new" federal prison just off San Francisco—Alcatraz. There, he was treated like any other prisoner and even played banjo in the prisoner band, the "Rock Islanders."

While at Alcatraz, his health and mind deteriorated rapidly from advanced syphilis. By the time he was released in 1939, he had to be moved to a care facility.

As for Prohibition, it went away just after Capone. In 1933, with crime rampant and public opinion sour, the 21st Amendment repealed the ban on alcohol. The "noble experiment" had failed, showing that legislating morality is one thing; enforcing it is another.

Here's a fun fact about Prohibition. You can make your own call as to whether it's a causation or correlation relationship, but birth rates dropped like the proverbial lead balloon when the alcohol stopped flowing. It didn't drop that much again until those mile-long gas lines of the 1970s. OK, so maybe the Great Depression had something to do with that. You decide.

Because this is just so darn interesting, we'll share one more. When the 18th Amendment went live, vineyard owners got... creative. Enter the "grape brick," a block of concentrated grape juice that came with a big warning label: "After dissolving the brick in a gallon of water, do not place the liquid in a jug in a cool cupboard for 20 days, because it would turn into wine." Naturally, that's exactly what people did. Millions of gallons of "oops" wine were made in American kitchens during Prohibition, thanks to these bricks.

When Harlem Sang, America Listened

During the 1920s, Harlem wasn't just a neighborhood in New York City; it was a cultural movement of earth-shaking proportions.

The Harlem Renaissance, including its surge of African American art, music, and literature, was so powerful that the whole country sat up to pay attention. Disguised as an artistic movement, one might describe it as a declaration of pride and a challenge against racism and exclusion.

Writers like Langston Hughes, a highly influential American poet, novelist, playwright, social activist, and columnist, not only shared the black experience proudly himself, but also encouraged other artists to do likewise. His words capture the sentiment best.

"We younger Negro artists who create now intend to express our individual dark-skinned selves without fear or shame. If white people are pleased, we are glad. If they are not, it doesn't matter. We know we are beautiful. And ugly too".

At the same time, musicians like Louis Armstrong were redefining what American music could be. With his trumpet blazing and his epic, gravelly voice, Armstrong didn't just play jazz; he embodied its improvisational spirit. Harlem's clubs, from the Cotton Club to the Savoy Ballroom, pulsed with energy as jazz and blues reshaped American musical culture.

The Harlem Renaissance wasn't confined to music and literature. Painters like Aaron Douglas created bold, modernist works infused with African heritage, while intellectuals such as W.E.B. Du Bois used the movement as a platform to promote racial pride and equality. Every medium carried the same message: African American culture was not marginal or secondary. Rather, it was part of the American story.

The Cotton Club was the place to be in Harlem during the 1920s. Duke Ellington, Cab Calloway, and Louis Armstrong all lit up its stage. But here's the kicker: while black musicians made the place legendary, the club itself had a strict whites-only audience policy. That contradiction, black performers fueling white-only entertainment, was a perfect snapshot of the era.

Who Forgot the Women?

While many refer to the 15th Amendment as one of the "Reconstruction Amendments," I call it the "Everyone votes, period!" amendment.

Well, almost. It came close, but forgot literally half of the country. That would be all the women.

That "oversight" was rectified with the passage of the 19th Amendment, which was ratified in 1920. It's pretty simple. Here's the entire text:

"The right of citizens of the United States to vote shall not be denied or abridged by the United States or by any State on account of sex.

Congress shall have power to enforce this article by appropriate legislation."

While some states, primarily the western ones, about 15 in all, recognized the right for women to vote, most did not. And it took a long time to change that situation nationally.

The struggle began back in 1848 at Seneca Falls, New York, where Elizabeth Cady Stanton and Susan B. Anthony helped spark the women's rights movement. For decades, suffragists marched, petitioned, organized conventions, and endured ridicule from those who thought politics was no place for women. Some went even further. Alice Paul and her National Woman's Party staged dramatic protests, picketing outside the White House and going to jail for civil disobedience. Others focused on state-by-state campaigns, slowly winning victories that built momentum for a federal amendment.

World War I actually helped the movement because women kept the country running by working in factories, offices, and farms while so many of the nation's working-age men were called to armed service. By the war's end, after it was clear that women could run things too, it was much harder to argue that women were unfit for voting and other civic responsibilities. President Woodrow Wilson himself shifted under the pressure, eventually supporting the amendment as a matter of justice.

When the 19th Amendment was finally ratified on August 18, 1920, celebrations erupted. For many women, it was both a vindication and a new beginning with their "official" participation in the democratic process.

It wasn't all smooth, however. Discriminatory laws and practices, especially in the South, continued to block black women and other minorities from exercising their new rights, so there was still a long way to go.

The 1920s also saw a cultural revolution that went hand in hand with political change. Enter the "flapper." They were the young women who bobbed their hair, shortened their skirts, smoked cigarettes, and danced the Charleston. While not every woman embraced the style and its underlying meaning of protest and boundary stretching, the flapper symbolized a generation rejecting the idea that women should remain silent, wear homely floor-length dresses, or be homebodies.

The 19th Amendment squeaked into law by one vote. In August 1920, Tennessee became the 36th state needed for ratification, but only after 24-year-old legislator Harry Burn shocked everyone by switching sides. Up to the vote, he wore a red rose in his lapel, a symbol of the anti-suffrage camp. But tucked in his pocket was a note from his mother: "Hurrah, and vote for suffrage!" He listened to his mom, changed his vote at the last minute, and women across America finally gained the right to vote.

Radios, Roadsters, and Roaring 20s Living

Well, if people of the 1920s didn't (officially) have beer, then at least many of them had sound. For the first time, Americans could sit in their living rooms and listen to live music, breaking news, dramatic productions and even presidential speeches. By the end of the decade, more than 12 million households owned a radio. By 1929, there were 29.9 million total households in the country, so if you didn't have a radio (yet) the odds were good one of the neighbors on either side did.

Bringing entertainment and breaking news into the home was revolutionary. Now, a farmer in Nebraska and a banker in New York could tune in to the same baseball game or jazz concert at the same time. Everyone knew what was going on in the world as it happened, not days later when stories made the papers. The country felt smaller and more connected, and it was clear that the trend would continue.

But the radio wasn't the only invention turning heads shrinking the country. Henry Ford's "Tin Lizzie," better known as the Model T, rolled off assembly lines in nearly unbelievable quantities. In 1920, Ford was cranking out 1,270 cars per day, or 463,451 per year. By 1925, production had skyrocketed to over two million per year.

It all hinged on the continuing perfection of the moving assembly line. Mass production was the name of the game, and it not only put cars on the roads across the country but it also made them affordable. In the first year of production, 1908, the cost of a Model T was about

$850. By the mid-1920s, at the peak of production, the cost had been driven down to just $300. That's the rough equivalent of about $5,300 today.

The availability and accessibility through the affordable price gave millions of Americans freedom and mobility. Commuting to work was now a possibility. Visit relatives? No problem. The practical radius of one's life immediately expanded from a few miles to hundreds. The result was that suburbs became a thing as the country continued to get smaller.

The relative affordability, even for big-ticket items like cars, led to other "new" industries: advertising and credit buying. While a $300 car was a big deal, most people didn't walk around with that much disposable cash in their pockets. Enter the era of installment plans for larger ticket items like refrigerators, washing machines, and, you guessed it, automobiles.

To make all this spending possible, credit buying took off like never before. Americans embraced the idea of getting modern conveniences now and worrying about how to pay for them later.

The result was a new culture of consumerism. Work was still important, but so was what you did with your paycheck. Modern production technology helped people get past the "earn just enough to buy food" barrier and start thinking about the novel concept of "disposable income." This was another outcome of the glittery roaring 20s: a redefinition of prosperity and what it meant to live the "good life."

Then, like now, the attitudes created a layer of fragility. As people spent more of the money they did (and didn't) have, the economic bubble grew. And grew. And grew.

And that leads us to October 1929.

When Henry Ford gave America its first truly affordable car, he probably didn't picture the creativity of the accessories market. By the 1920s, aftermarket companies were selling "snowmobile conversion kits" that turned the humble Tin Lizzie into something like a Depression-era snowcat. The kits swapped out the front wheels for skis and added a set of tracks in place of the back tires. Suddenly, rural mail carriers, doctors, and adventurous farm kids could plow through blizzards where horses once struggled. They weren't cheap and cost almost as much as the original car.

Black Tuesday: Millionaire at Breakfast, Broke by Lunch

Throughout the 1920s, the stock market became America's new national hobby. Investing wasn't just for the financial industry titans, the Rockefellers and Morgans, anymore. Commoditization of investment products like stocks and bonds demystified the instruments to a degree. Now, ordinary Americans could own a piece (through shares) of steel mills, car companies, and appliance manufacturers.

Unfortunately, the credit frenzy of the consumer products market made its way to the financial sector. Brokers even made "investing" somewhat "affordable" through the concept of margin. If you put down 10%, you could borrow the rest. Why not? Stock prices were always going up, so what's to lose? OK, that was a bit cynical, but you know how the game works. Everyone is happy with the "buy on margin" model until prices dip or fall. Then the bottom falls out of the paper skyscraper, and the margin calls land in your mailbox.

But bubbles, while pretty and mesmerizing, tend to pop because they're constructed of mostly air. Farmers were drowning in debt. Factories were producing more goods than people could actually buy. Wealth was unevenly distributed, with much of the prosperity concentrated in the hands of a few. The market wasn't reflecting a healthy and stable economy. It was surviving off of Ponzi-like speculation.

Then came October 1929. The warning signs had started earlier that month, but Black Tuesday on October 29 was the breaking point. The floor of the New York Stock Exchange turned into a madhouse of panic and desperation as millions of shares flooded the market. Investors rushed to sell, but there were no buyers left. Stock values plummeted, often to virtually nothing in just hours. For many who came to work that morning, a millionaire on paper, they were destitute by lunchtime.

Then the dominoes began to fall.

The thing about economies is that they are just so darn interconnected. The price of stocks wasn't an abstract concept limited just to investors. Many banks had either invested their deposits in the market or loaned out money to speculators who fancied themselves investors. In both cases, that money, which represented the real dollars deposited by their customers, simply evaporated.

That led to credit for businesses drying up practically overnight. No purchases of raw materials meant production lines slowed or stopped, which led to layoffs and plant closures. And that led to unemployment in unprecedented numbers. With no one able to spend "actual" money from wages, the downward cycle was incestuous, making things even worse.

Enter the Great Depression. While the stock market crash wasn't fully responsible for the depression, it sure was a giant match that lit the dynamite. Any thriving economy relies on consumer confidence to work, and the ripple effects of the market crash destroyed that completely, leading to a downward spiral.

It was the end of the era of parties, prosperity, modern conveniences and the apparent ability of the everyday American to participate directly in the seemingly thriving economy.

Next up: desperate people selling apples on the streets, breadlines, and years of hardship.

On October 29, 1929, so many sell orders poured in that the stock ticker machines literally couldn't keep up. Normally, quotes were printed within a minute or two of the actual trade. On Black Tuesday, the ticker ran hours behind. Investors would look up, see a stock listed at $50, and rush to sell, not realizing it had already collapsed to $20. By the time the paper tape caught up, fortunes had already vanished. Desperate brokers resorted to runners sprinting across the trading floor to shout prices, while some investors just stood frozen, staring at the mechanical ticker as if it might spit out a miracle.

Part Six

Hard Times and Big Government

Chapter 20

FDR and the Alphabet Soup of Salvation

When the Great Depression hit, Franklin D. Roosevelt unleashed a blizzard of federal programs, including the CCC, WPA, TVA, and more. In this section, we'll explore how the New Deal reshaped the government's role, built infrastructure, offered jobs, and stirred fierce debate about the power of the presidency.

Franklin D. Roosevelt's First 100 Days

By the time Franklin Delano Roosevelt was inaugurated on March 4, 1933, the country was a mess. It was the lowest point of the Great Depression with a 25% national unemployment rate. That's about 12 million workers out of jobs with no way to support themselves and their families. The banking system was in shambles. The stock market was floating around at about 25% of its pre-Black Tuesday value. Farm incomes were down by half.

For the previous couple of years, President Herbert Hoover had been (mostly) favoring a "rugged individualist" policy and trying to keep government intervention out of the picture. He leaned on industry to maintain wage levels and urged private charity relief efforts. As things got worse, Hoover did support some government programs to ease the pain. For example, public works projects hired people to build things like the Hoover Dam and the Reconstruction Finance Corporation was formed to offer loans to banks and businesses.

So, by 1933, the Great Depression had been dragging on for nearly four years.

FDR didn't take much time to ponder the situation once he got into office. In what became known as the "First 100 Days," he unleashed a legislative blitz unlike anything the nation had ever seen. In those three months, he pushed 15 major bills through Congress. Forget the debates over the contents of the legislation; the velocity of passing that much of anything was impressive considering it takes Congress six months to decide if the cafeteria should change its menu.

The focal point piece of legislation was the Emergency Banking Act. Its purpose, and it was a big one, was to restore confidence in the banking system. After years of bank runs and failures, Americans had lost faith in the entire financial system and resorted to stuffing what money they had in the proverbial mattress. This Act did several things to help restore order.

First, it established a four-day bank "holiday," closing all banks for long enough to figure things out, inspect the books, and only allow solvent banks to reopen. It also expanded government authority to inspect and oversee banking activities and granted additional emergency powers to the President during financial crises. The Federal Reserve was empowered to issue currency during emergencies, and the Federal Deposit Insurance Corporation was created to reassure the public that their money was safe in the system.

Launched with one of Roosevelt's "Fireside Chats," the measures seemed to restore confidence in the system. The short version? "Trust me, your money is safer in the bank than buried in the backyard!" People began to deposit money in the banks, and the system began to regain its footing.

Other measures were aimed at putting people back to work, and with 25% unemployment, there were plenty of able bodies ready to go. The Civilian Conservation Corps (CCC) put young men to work planting trees, building parks, and restoring landscapes. The Tennessee Valley Authority (TVA) brought electricity and infrastructure to a region that was sorely lacking.

The Agricultural Adjustment Act attempted to stabilize crop prices by paying farmers to cut production. Roosevelt also pushed for new regulations on Wall Street to prevent the kind of reckless speculation that had fueled the 1929 crash.

FDR's intent wasn't all about immediate relief. His vision was for a broader "New Deal" that redefined the role of government with respect to business and the economy. As it happened, the timing and desperation of the Great Depression allowed him to sway the political pendulum toward his viewpoint of an expanded role of government, actively managing the economy and providing a safety net of sorts.

One lesser-known aspect of FDR's legacy is the performance of a new president during their first months in office. Since 1933, all Presidents have been publicly judged by how much they can get done in their first 100 days.

When banks started collapsing in the early 1930s, Americans improvised. Instead of depositing money in shaky institutions, people stashed it anywhere they thought it might be safe. Mattresses were the cliché, and plenty of cash really did end up under bedsprings. But farm families buried jars of money in the garden, tucked it into barn rafters, and even sealed it in tin cans and hid it in fence posts. Hardware stores reported a run on Mason jars, not for pickling but for "savings accounts." It's hard to blame them. In 1933 alone, more than 4,000 banks failed. Stories circulated for years about cash caches being found decades later, sometimes discovered only when an old farmhouse was torn down, or when a storm uprooted a tree and popped loose an old Mason jar.

New Deal? The Birth of Social Security

Arguably, the centerpiece of FDR's New Deal reforms was the Social Security Act.

Prior to this time, there was no formal, national social insurance system for elderly, unemployed, or disabled citizens. Before the Great Depression, American families did what they'd always done: care for their own and figure out how to make things work. The Great Depression put some serious pressure on that model, with so many out of work and without income, so FDR created a committee headed by Labor Secretary Frances Perkins to explore the problem and investigate solutions.

The result? The Social Security System.

In short, Social Security established unemployment insurance, old-age pensions, and aid for the disabled and poor. In FDR's view, it was to serve as a safety net during hard economic times and provide support for retirement and old age.

Signed into law on August 14, 1935, the program worked as

follows. Employers and employees would pay into the system through payroll taxes to fund future retirement benefits. The states would administer unemployment insurance programs to help with a safety net for hard times like the current Great Depression. And there were a handful of insurance-based support programs like Aid to Dependent Children, Aid to the Blind, and programs aimed at mothers and children.

Once established, the program as a whole was here to stay and revised every couple of decades to account for changing times. Arguably, this centerpiece of FDR's New Deal programs was one of the most significant legislative changes this country has ever seen, given the vast scope of the related programs and the longevity of the big ones, active to this day.

The very first monthly Social Security check went out in January 1940 to a woman named Ida May Fuller of Ludlow, Vermont. Ida was a retired legal secretary who had paid exactly $24.75 into the system during her working years. Her first check was for $22.54, nearly all of what she'd contributed in one shot. Here's the kicker: Ida lived to be 100 years old. By the time she passed away in 1975, she'd collected a grand total of $22,888.92 in benefits. That's quite a return on investment. She later joked that she never expected to get her money back, much less "so much of it."

The Original Oval Office Livestream

The advent of radio and its availability in so many homes led not just to an entertainment and news revolution, but also to an opportunity for the people's representatives to communicate directly with their constituents. Since the beginning of time, leaders had to walk, grab a nearby horse, or hop a train to speak face-to-face to a limited number of voters. No more. Radio brought Presidents into the home, face-to-ears, so to speak.

Franklin D. Roosevelt was a skilled communicator with a knack for making big, complex problems sound like something you and your neighbor could talk over the fence about. His radio addresses, quickly dubbed "fireside chats," let him bypass Congress, reporters, and critics to speak directly to the American people. Since radios were still a household appliance and not a personal device, families would literally gather around their living room radios as if the president himself had pulled up a chair next to the fireplace.

Clearly, some modern Presidents learned a thing or two from FDR's tone and style for these "personal" chats. He avoided lofty speeches and Washington jargon, choosing instead plain, conversational language. He called people "my friends" and explained policies step by step, as if tutoring the nation in real time. This was no accident. Given the anxiety of the times (The Great Depression and World War II), it was a deliberate way to calm nerves and build trust.

Consider the very first one in March 1933 as an example. The banking system was collapsing, and panicked Americans were pulling out what little savings they had left and literally hiding their meager funds in coffee cans or under their mattresses. Roosevelt calmly explained why he had declared a nationwide "bank holiday" to stop the bleeding and why people should trust that their money would be safe once banks reopened. The result? Within days, deposits flowed back in, and public confidence started to rebound.

Another memorable chat came in December 1940, as war raged in Europe. America wasn't yet committed to the war, but Roosevelt introduced the idea of the "arsenal of democracy." He explained why supplying Britain with weapons was vital to America's own security, even though the country was an ocean removed from the hostilities.

The fireside chats reshaped presidential communication. Today, when something happens that rocks the country, we expect to see the President delivering an update from the calm backdrop of the Oval Office.

The very first fireside chat on March 12, 1933, drew an audience of more than 60 million Americans. That was about half the population at the time. To put that in perspective, the modern Super Bowl draws 120 million Americans, which is far less than half the country. The impact was immediate: banks reported that deposits the next morning were higher than withdrawals for the first time in weeks. Some local bankers even sent thank-you notes to the White House. Roosevelt's voice alone had reversed a panic that no policy paper or press conference had been able to stop.

FDR's Supreme Scheme

By the mid-1930s, FDR was on a New Deal roll. He'd taken big steps to redefine the role of the federal government, not just during emergencies like the current depression, but for normal times in the future. New agencies with new missions were being formed at a record rate.

But not everyone saw this as a great idea, and many worried about the scales tipping too far towards the "too much government in your face" side. Representing part of that pushback on his policies, the Supreme Court was not keen on all of FDR's moves.

At the time, the Court had a conservative majority, and those justices took a dim view of FDR's experiments. In case after case, they struck down New Deal laws. The National Industrial Recovery Act? Unconstitutional. The Agricultural Adjustment Act? Nope. Roosevelt was all about the speed of action for his ideas and saw the Supreme Court as nothing more than a roadblock.

So in 1937, he unveiled a surprise plan, demonstrating once again, there is "nothing new under the Sun," according to the wise words of King Solomon.

Pack the Court.

In plain English, the idea was to add more Supreme Court justices. Not coincidentally, the new ones would be more amenable to Roosevelt's ideas. Of course, FDR couldn't exactly come out and admit that was the plan, so he worked up a "not very believable" cover story.

He claimed the Supreme Court was overworked and the poor, tired justices needed help. So, why not appoint a new justice for each one who is 70 or more years old and has thus far refused to retire? Who wouldn't want a little help?

Plausible deniability, right? There just happened to be six on the bench that met these criteria, so we were looking at six new justices under his plan.

Of course, critics called it for what it was: court packing. And they were fierce with charges of FDR trying to turn a coequal branch of government into his rubber stamp. Some in Roosevelt's own party were concerned the move would establish a dangerous precedent over the long term.

The end result was more of a fizzle than a bang as Congress didn't go along with the plan. But, for whatever reason, things did end up tilting in FDR's favor as the Court lowered its opposition bar and upheld other New Deal programs like Social Security. Some historians refer to this as the "switch in time that saved nine." That was a reference to Justice Owen Roberts's votes that preserved the Court's nine-member makeup.

The episode highlighted the "by design" fundamental tension in American government. Three branches of government are designed as checks and balances on each other. While Roosevelt tested the limits of Presidential Power, the other two branches acted as designed and established some guardrails over any single branch claiming a disproportionate amount of power.

The "switch in time that saved nine" wasn't just a clever rhyme. It may have literally saved the size of the Supreme

Court. Justice Owen Roberts, who had previously sided with conservatives striking down New Deal programs, suddenly voted in 1937 to uphold a Washington state minimum wage law. The timing was so uncanny that many believed Roberts flipped his vote to defuse Roosevelt's court-packing threat. Historians still debate whether his change of heart was a political calculation or genuine legal reasoning, but the effect was clear: the Court's legitimacy and its nine-member tradition remained intact.

Eleanor: First Lady of Activism

Since the inaugural First Lady, Martha Washington, set the precedent of active participation in White House activities, the role has expanded and now most First Ladies (so far, no men have had the honor of First Gentleman) have staked a claim on causes near and dear to their hearts.

Prior to Eleanor Roosevelt's move into the White House, most First Ladies had limited their "politics" to directing and hosting formal functions, welcoming foreign dignitaries, and such.

Eleanor rose above the mostly ceremonial role. While Martha Washington only delivered one significant public speech during her tenure, Eleanor held regular press conferences and, on occasion, only allowed female reporters. This was a 3-D chess move as it forced some news publications to hire women reporters for the first time. She also wrote a widely read syndicated newspaper column called "My Day," and logged thousands of miles traveling the country to visit ordinary Americans during the Depression and later, World War II.

Her travels served a dual purpose. In addition to getting out into the communities, she was FDR's "feet on the street" as he was mobility-limited by polio. Eleanor became his eyes and ears, relaying back to the White House conditions throughout the country.

Unlike many of her First Lady predecessors, she didn't shy away from taking public political positions. When the Daughters of the American Revolution barred black singer Marian Anderson from performing in Constitution Hall, Eleanor resigned her membership and helped arrange for Anderson's iconic 1939 concert at the Lincoln Memorial.

Her work reshaped expectations of the First Lady forever. After Eleanor, the president's spouse was almost expected to become involved in some way.

Eleanor Roosevelt held 348 press conferences during her time as First Lady, far more than most presidents! To encourage gender equality in journalism, she famously invited only women reporters at first, forcing newspapers to hire female staff if they wanted White House access. She also became the first First Lady to speak at a national political convention (1940), and her newspaper column "My Day" ran six days a week for 26 years, totaling more than 8,000 columns. By sheer output and reach, she was one of the most widely read political voices in the country.

Chapter 21

World War II: When America Went All-In

Pearl Harbor changed everything. Prior to the attack, America was a spectator to the growing tensions and later direct conflicts in Europe and Asia. The war was someone else's problem. The U.S. mobilized at warp speed, turning factories into war machines and citizens into soldiers. This chapter tells how America helped defeat fascism abroad while grappling with internal struggles related to the multi-national makeup of the country.

Isolation With a Side of Lend-Lease

If you ever look at social media, you might have seen one of those passenger brawls on one of the budget airlines. Or perhaps a fight over the last big screen TV at the local Walmart. In both cases, you're watching the altercation from a safe distance, wondering what on earth all those people are throwing punches over.

The late 1930s in the United States were vaguely similar.

Since this book is about the United States of America, we'll have to gloss over the world situation, but the highlights are important background for America's entry into World War II. Here's the short version...

The world, not just Europe, but Asia as well, was on fire. Hitler's Germany was steadily pushing against the boundaries established by the Versailles Treaty. Re-militarization kicked into high gear in 1936. Germany annexed Austria in 1938 and was trying to reclaim the Sudetenland in Czechoslovakia. Europe was tired of big wars and pursued an appeasement strategy, giving Germany the Sudetenland. That didn't go well. In 1939, Germany took the rest of Czecho-slovakia by force and then Poland. This was a bridge too far, and England and France declared war on the Germans.

Meanwhile, on the other side of the world, Japan, with its limited natural resources, was on an outward expansion binge, invading Manchuria in 1931 and China at large in 1937.

Here at home, the United States was doing the "watch the brawls on video" thing and not at all interested in getting involved in another bloody and costly war.

The overwhelming mood was: "Not our problem." Congress even passed a series of Neutrality Acts in the 1930s that prevented sales of arms and financial backing to countries at war.

But by the late 30s, in 1937 and again in 1939, the Neutrality Acts began to recognize the potential consequences of allowing Europe to fall to Nazi Germany. The trick was helping them survive without actually declaring war. That's where Franklin Roosevelt came in. He was a master at reading the national mood and nudging it forward. First came "Cash and Carry," which let Allies buy U.S. war goods if they picked them up and took them home themselves. A military gear drive through, so to speak. The next step closer to active involvement was the Lend-Lease program. That ratcheted up the process to direct support by the U.S., supplying military gear assistance.

In a rewind/replay scenario, in 1939, the U.S. military was no global threat, being ranked 19th or so in the world in size. Americans still relied on the vast oceans and isolationist predispositions for their defensive posture.

During all this time, Japan was still on the move in Asia, occupying China, and heading who-knows-where next. The U.S. tried tough economic sanctions by cutting off oil and metal, but that strategy increased the desperation of the Japanese.

So, before Pearl Harbor, America was clearly supporting defense against Germany and Japan, but was still trying hard not to cross the line into direct combat. Then, on December 7, 1941, the attack on Pearl Harbor struck the nation like a lightning bolt. Overnight, the debate ended, and the United States was at war.

One of the weirdest Lend-Lease deliveries was a flock of pigeons. Yes, birds. Alongside tanks, planes, and food, the U.S. sent 3,000 carrier pigeons to Britain. Radio equipment was still bulky and unreliable in battlefield conditions, but pigeons had a 95% success rate at delivering messages through smoke, gunfire, and blackout zones. They were used on D-Day and in countless covert operations. Some even became decorated "war heroes," like G.I. Joe, a pigeon who saved over 1,000 British troops in Italy by carrying a last-minute message that stopped an accidental Allied bombing run.

Pearl Harbor: America at War. Again.

At 7:55 a.m. on a quiet Sunday morning, the sky over Pearl Harbor filled with the roar of 353 Japanese warplanes, organized into two attack waves. The American Navy base, the focal point of all naval activity in the Pacific, was caught completely by surprise.

Within minutes, bombs and torpedoes rained down on the fleet anchored in the Hawaii harbor. Battleships, cruisers, and destroyers erupted in fire and smoke. Planes, which had been lined up together on airfields to protect against sabotage, were destroyed. The USS Arizona took a direct hit that detonated her forward magazine, splitting the ship apart and entombing more than a thousand sailors inside.

In less than two hours, more than 2,400 Americans were killed, another 1,000 wounded, and much of the fleet lay in ruins. As for the Japanese force, only 29 planes, five midget submarines and 100 personnel were lost. It was a rout.

The only "good" news was that America's aircraft carriers were at sea. As the predominant tool to project force over the seas, they were vital to any hope the United States had to stand up to the powerful Japanese navy.

This one twist turned out to be a really big deal.

Japan knew it couldn't take on the United States in a traditional, full-blown war. The natural resources of materials and people, combined with infinite production capacity, would make a long-term struggle hopeless. The hope, and basis of the Pearl Harbor surprise attack plan, was to stun the United States, destroy the majority of its Pacific naval infrastructure (ships and support facilities) in one move, and sue for a favorable negotiated settlement.

With the American aircraft carriers still in play, that was not gonna happen. In fact, the Japanese attack force was considering a follow-up strike to destroy repair facilities, submarines and the oil reserves, based on the overwhelming success of the initial attack. Instead, they elected to follow the path of caution and withdraw their forces. It probably wouldn't have mattered anyway, as the carriers would still not have been destroyed. But the still intact repair facilities would now be used to rebuild the American Pacific Fleet.

Imagine the reports of this surprise attack and the devastating toll on equipment and service members spreading across the country like wildfire. The sentiment of "this isn't our war" changed in an instant. Like it or not, the country was now part of a new world war.

President Roosevelt wasted no time. On December 8, he appeared before a joint session of Congress to deliver what became one of the most famous speeches in American history. You've likely heard some of his words, including his declaration that December 7 was "a date which will live in infamy." The speech was just a few minutes long but direct. He shared the facts of the attack and declared that the country was at war.

Congress agreed. The vote supporting the declaration of war in the House of Representatives was 388 to 1; the Senate vote was unanimous. The lone opposition vote in the House was from pacifist Congresswoman Jeannette Rankin of Montana, who had also voted against entering World War I.

It was no surprise that Germany and Italy, who were allied with Japan, returned the favor and declared war on the United States. So now, the country was officially involved in the European conflict, too.

Pearl Harbor unified the country and lit a fire under the wartime economy. It didn't take long for factories to shift into high gear, producing planes, tanks and ships. And the affront of the Pearl Harbor surprise attack inspired hundreds of thousands of young men to flood recruiting stations, seeking to enlist. This led to women entering the workforce in unprecedented numbers.

The American carriers were at sea, but eight battleships were in port during the attack on Pearl Harbor. Six were repaired and returned to fight in the war. Only two were completely destroyed. In total, 15 damaged ships were repaired and returned to service, so in the longer term, the Japanese attack turned out to be a temporary setback. A significant one, but its long-term impact on the war was limited.

American Citizens or the Enemy Within?

Not long after Pearl Harbor, fear and suspicion swept across the United States. Suddenly, anyone of Japanese ancestry, even those born and raised in America, was branded as a potential threat. Even in a country made of immigrants, the hard-earned label of "American" for those who had come to this country to become citizens was lost to panic, fear and emotion.

In February 1942, President Franklin Roosevelt signed Executive Order 9066, authorizing the forced relocation of over 120,000 Japanese Americans from the West Coast. Two-thirds of them were already established U.S. citizens. Their "crime" was simply looking like the Japanese enemy.

Families were given short windows of days or even just hours to pack what they could carry. Homes, farms, and businesses had to be sold off for pennies on the dollar or simply abandoned altogether. Armed guards escorted them to remote camps surrounded by barbed wire and watchtowers.

In an effort to sugarcoat the truth of what was happening, the government called them "relocation centers," but it was clear to all that they were really just prison camps. Life inside meant cramped barracks, communal bathrooms, and harsh conditions that stripped away dignity as much as freedom.

Even in the face of this treatment, many young Americans of Japanese descent volunteered for the U.S. military. Generally speaking, they were assigned to the European theater, far from the battlefields of Japan. And while they fought and died, their families remained in the camps.

Credible evidence of potential danger from these American "spies" was rare, if even present. The internment program was fueled by wartime hysteria, racial prejudice, and political pressure. It wasn't until decades later that the nation began to reckon with this injustice. In 1988, President Ronald Reagan signed the Civil Liberties Act, issuing a formal apology and $20,000 in reparations to each surviving internee.

It was a hard-earned lesson learned at great cost to these Japanese Americans about the importance of recognizing and protecting rights.

The 442nd Regimental Combat Team was a segregated U.S. Army unit composed almost entirely of second-generation Japanese Americans. Drawn from Hawaii and internees of west coast camps, the 442nd earned the distinction of being one of the most decorated units ever, considering its duration. Fighting in Italy and participating in the invasion of southern France, the unit was awarded 21 Medals of Honor, over 9,486 Purple Hearts, seven (or maybe eight) Presidential Unit Citations and over 18,000 total awards for valor.

Omaha, Ardennes, and the Road to Victory

Some participants described the English Channel crossing for the D-Day landings as "being able to walk across the English Channel, hopping from ship to ship." That's not much of an exaggeration, as over 5,000 ships and other vessels from Allied forces brought the soldiers and equipment to Normandy. It was the largest amphibious invasion the world had ever seen. Operation Overlord, the landings on mainland Europe, were underway.

D-Day certainly wasn't the beginning, but it was the beginning of the end. From the American perspective, participation in the European theater up til this point had been primarily in the Mediterranean with Operation Torch landings in Morocco and Algeria. Joining with British forces there in North Africa, the Allies, while having a rough go at the beginning, began to gain their footing as a fighting force and ultimately defeated Rommel, causing a surrender of German and Italian forces in Tunisia.

Next up were the landings in 1943 and 1944 in Sicily and Italy. After capturing Sicily in '43, the Allies landed in Italy and headed for Rome and parts north. It was a brutal campaign against determined Axis defenses through the Italian countryside and mountains. While the Allies captured the first Axis capital, Rome, on June 5, 1944, and the Italians surrendered, the Germans fought on. The campaign in northern Italy continued right into 1945 as the invasion landings and march through France took place.

Now back to D-Day.

Starting in 1942, Americans had started the buildup in the UK, preparing to launch the offensive into Europe and support the air war (more on that shortly). By mid-1944, there were about 1.6 million American servicemen and women stationed there in 1,200 different camps and 133 airfields. The country was somewhat overrun, and British soldiers, who were paid somewhat less than their American counterparts, commented on the yanks' presence as, "Overpaid, over-sexed and over here."

On June 6th, 1944, Allied Supreme Commander Dwight D. Eisenhower pulled the trigger and ordered the landing of 59,000 assault troops for the first day. About 15,000 elite paratroopers dropped into the French countryside the night before to prepare the way and disrupt German defensive efforts. By the end of the first week, some 326,000 Allied troops had landed.

Five beaches were chosen as landing sites for British, Canadian and American troops, with Omaha and Utah being assigned to the US forces. The landings at Omaha and Utah were horrific beyond belief, with complete failure hanging in the balance for much of the morning of that first day. Persistence and acts of bravery finally tipped the scales, and a beachhead was secured.

Total Allied casualties on D-Day numbered about 10,000 killed, wounded, and missing across all of the Allied forces. Of that number, 4,414 were killed outright. Of those, almost 2,500 were killed on Omaha Beach alone.

But as the Allies established a foothold and landing site for reinforcements, the door to Europe was now cracked open.

From that beachhead in France, the U.S. military machine rolled forward. To be clear, it came at great cost as the Germans mounted a strong defense and the Allies struggled to fight through the difficult French hedgerow country, encountering major obstacles every few hundred yards.

American forces, backed by overwhelming logistical support, plowed onward towards Berlin, freeing towns across France. By late summer, Paris was liberated, and the next stops were Belgium and Germany.

But Hitler wasn't keen on admitting defeat. In a last-ditch effort to split the Allied forces, he ordered a massive offensive through the Ardennes forest in December 1944, busting through Allied lines and forming a "bulge" in the battle line.

The Battle of the Bulge was some of the coldest, most miserable, and brutal fighting of the war. American troops, many of them young and barely out of training, bore the brunt of the assault. In places like Bastogne, surrounded and outnumbered, elite U.S. Airborne and other forces held on with staggering courage until reinforcements arrived. While there was plenty of dangerous work yet to do, the German offensive was the last gasp of major resistance.

By spring 1945, American troops were streaming into Germany itself. They liberated concentration camps, confronted the full horror of Nazi atrocities, and helped capture cities that had once seemed untouchable. Alongside their British, Canadian, and other Allied counterparts, U.S. forces drove the war in Europe to its conclusion. Hitler was finished.

The European Theater represented the best of America at its most determined and resourceful. From the chaos of Omaha Beach to the frozen forests of the Ardennes, U.S. soldiers, commanders, and industry played indispensable roles. Without American leadership, manpower, and supplies, the liberation of Europe would have been far slower, if even possible at all. That famous American industry we've talked about leading up to this point answered the call when it mattered and produced the supplies of military might the world had never seen.

In May 1945, Adolf Hitler unknowingly hosted quite a party, complete with take-home party favors for troops of the 101st Airborne Division. Tucked high in the Bavarian Alps near the little town of Berchtesgaden was the Eagle's Nest, a mountaintop retreat built as a 50th birthday gift for Hitler. When the U.S. 101st Airborne Division "Screaming Eagles" rolled into the place, they discovered a retreat stuffed with German high command luxury: wine cellars, silverware, marble decor and the like. And lots of it. The party started, with the war-weary soldiers drinking wines, champagnes and liquor older than the United States itself and eating with Swastika-stamped silver. Plenty of souvenirs and lots of silver place settings made it back home, stuffed into duffel bags. So, yes, there are families in the United States eating Thanksgiving dinners with Hitler's silver, brought home by a Screaming Eagle grandfather or great uncle.

Brains, Bombes, and Broken Codes

The outcomes of wars, even really big ones, can turn on secrecy and deception.

All sides rely on radio and landline communications for the distribution of orders, reports, and intelligence. Since most anything can be intercepted with enough effort and ingenuity, the players have to resort to sophisticated code scenarios to protect their secrets. Knowing the enemy's plans in advance is perhaps the biggest possible advantage in wartime.

In a scenario straight out of a James Bond movie, British intelligence service MI6 bought the massive Bletchley Park estate, isolated on its sizable and private grounds, in 1938 to serve as a center for intelligence gathering and codebreaking work. Staffed by math geniuses like Alan Turing, the team of Brits was joined by a growing number of Americans starting in 1941.

The mission was simple in description, but near impossible to complete. Crack the Enigma and Lorenz ciphers. Oh, and do that so the Nazis didn't know, so they would continue to use the code systems for transmission of their deepest secrets.

Their primary tools were brains, both organic and mechanical. The world's first programmable digital computer, Colossus, was put to work alongside the hundreds of Bombe machines, which were electromechanical workhorses designed specially to figure out the days settings of the Enigma machines used by the Germans. With billions of possible setting combinations, this was a crucial step in breaking the codes.

The intelligence output of this operation, code-named Ultra, made all the difference. Knowing invasion plans in advance, and the locations of German navy assets like the feared U-Boat packs, and troop movements, arguably shortened the war by years.

A similar effort took place in Honolulu at Station HYPO. The roles were simply reversed. Run by the U.S. Navy, the resident team was led by Commander Joseph Rochefort. He was a less-than-traditional Navy officer with a special talent for puzzles and led a slightly eccentric team tasked with breaking Japanese Naval codes. Located in a chilly basement in Pearl Harbor, he often worked while wearing a smoking jacket.

Like Bletchley Park, this team shared and cooperated with British counterparts, located both at Bletchley and other stations in the far east. By 1944, the group was intercepting tens of thousands of

Japanese communications per month.

So while Bletchley Park was the intelligence brain of Allied strategy in Europe, the code-girls and code-boys in Hawaii were the team secretly listening in to activities in the Pacific theater.

Arguably, the turning point of the Pacific War was the Battle of Midway, where the US Navy landed a crippling blow on Japan's fleet, sinking four of Japan's carriers. How that successful ambush by the smaller US Navy force happened is an amazing story. The Station HYPO codebreakers were seeing repeated references in Japanese message traffic referencing something called "AF." Rochefort and team believed that AF referred to Midway Island, then held by the Americans. Needing to prove this theory, they devised a plan and instructed the Midway garrison to transmit a message in the clear (no code) that their water distillation plant was broken. It wasn't, of course, so the command on Midway was mighty confused by this order. Soon after, HYPO decoded a Japanese message instructing the Japanese attacking force to bring extra water to "AF." The code was confirmed, and the Americans even deciphered the attack date. That allowed US Navy carriers to set up an ambush and later destroy the Japanese carrier fleet.

The Skies of Fire: America's Air War in Europe

The background war, possibly even worse than the ground and island-hopping campaigns in Europe and the Pacific, was the air war in Europe.

All of southern England during World War II heard the daily sound of droning aircraft engines. That was the 8th Air Force, America's long-range bombing group.

The "Mighty Eighth" grew into one of the largest air fleets ever assembled, with over 200,000 personnel and thousands of aircraft. Its mission was simple but costly. Take off from England, fly to the European continent and bomb the German war-fighting machine into submission.

Consisting primarily of B-17 Flying Fortress and B-24 Liberator four-engine bombers, these planes flew in tight formations into enemy territory, sticking together to provide some protection against German fighter planes. But that wasn't the only danger. Thousands and thousands of anti-aircraft guns on the ground sent millions of rounds of explosive flak projectiles into the formations, causing horrific losses.

In fact, the British stopped flying in daylight hours because the losses were too great to bear. Both fighters and flak took too much of a toll. On the other hand, the Americans believed night bombing to be too inaccurate and accepted the astronomical daylight loss ratios in return for precision bombing capability.

The cost was staggering by any measure. Early missions in 1943, like the infamous raids on Schweinfurt, saw entire bomber groups shot from the sky. Loss rates of 20 percent in a single mission weren't uncommon. Crews had a saying: "You only have to make 25 missions" because the policy was that you got to go home if you survived that many. But few believed they'd actually live long enough to finish those 25 runs.

As the war progressed. Things got a little better. New aircraft developments, such as the P-51 Mustang fighter, enabled American fighter planes to escort bombers deep into Germany, providing at least some protection against enemy fighters. However, nothing could be done about the flak.

By 1944, the Mighty Eighth was flying thousands of sorties a day, softening up German defenses ahead of D-Day and crippling the Luftwaffe before it could ever contest Allied landings in Normandy.

By the war's end, the 8th Air Force had dropped over 600,000 tons of bombs on Europe. The cost was beyond belief, with more than 26,000 airmen killed. That's more than the U.S. Marine Corps lost in the entire war. Every time a plane was shot down, 10 men were either captured, injured or killed.

The 8th Air Force suffered the losses of 5,100 bombers over Europe between 1942 and 1945. Consider that each plane carried an average of 10 crewmen, and the impact becomes stunning. In just one day's raid, "Black Thursday" at Schweinfurt, 60 bombers were shot down and lost.

From Midway to Iwo: The Long Road to Japan

The war in the Pacific was a different kind of battle, horrific in its own way. Given the geography, the "ground war" against the Japanese Army really meant planning and executing successful amphibious assault landings against entrenched Japanese forces. Over, and over, and over again. Each island between Hawaii and the mainland of Japan represented a potential strong point for Japanese forces that had to be conquered. Oh, and these island fortresses were spread across thousands of miles of ocean.

The "island hopping" strategy involved skipping heavily defended islands and instead seizing those with airfields or harbors that could support the next leap forward. If the "hopped" island had no air or sea power threat, enemy forces could be left alone and bypassed.

The island campaigns were brutal. At Guadalcanal in 1942, Marines endured months of savage fighting in mosquito-infested jungles. As with the Panama Canal construction, the bugs weren't just irritating; they spread debilitating tropical diseases like wildfire, taking thousands of troops out of the fight.

At Tarawa in 1943, Marines waded ashore in chest-deep water for hundreds of yards while under withering machine-gun fire, suffering massive casualties that shocked the people back at home. And on all these islands, the Japanese defenders had spent months digging impenetrable tunnel and fortification systems that were all but resistant to pre-invasion shelling and bombing. Each and every emplacement had to be rooted out by soldiers on the ground, and the network allowed the enemy to pop up and attack from in front, behind, or beside the Marines. Threats came from all directions, day and night.

Saipan, Iwo Jima, and Okinawa became infamous names, each representing horrific close-quarters combat. On Iwo Jima, nearly 7,000 Americans were killed and 20,000 wounded to capture a tiny volcanic island. Allied command felt the cost necessary as its airfields provided a crucial base for bombing runs over Japan. Okinawa, the last great battle of the Pacific, claimed more than 12,000 American lives and hinted at how costly a full-scale invasion of Japan might be.

Each victory brought the Allies closer, and each battle taught hard lessons about amphibious landings, logistics, and the sheer determination of Japanese defenders.

By the summer of 1945, American bombers could strike Japan directly from captured islands, and the bloody experiences of the campaign heavily influenced the decision to use atomic bombs instead of invading the mainland. Based on the island campaigns thus far, the Allied command estimated that over a million Allied casualties and tens of millions of Japanese casualties would have resulted if a land invasion had been required to end the war.

The iconic photo of the flag raising on Iwo Jima—taken by Associated Press photographer Joe Rosenthal on February 23, 1945—was so powerful that it won the Pulitzer Prize within the same year. But here's the twist: it wasn't the first flag raised on Mount Suribachi. Marines had already planted a smaller flag earlier that morning, but commanders decided it was too small to be seen across the island. So a second, larger flag went up—and that's the moment Rosenthal captured. The image became one of the most reproduced photographs in history and inspired the Marine Corps War Memorial in Arlington, Virginia.

The Bomb That Ended (and Began) an Era

Talk about secret projects...

The Manhattan Project took secrecy to a whole new level. With, at its peak, 130,000 people in on at least some of the details, it was perhaps World War II's greatest secret operation. In fairness, the whole operation was extraordinarily compartmentalized, so many involved in the day-to-day operations didn't exactly know what they were doing. Like the public, they only learned the full scope of the project with the public news of the Hiroshima bombing.

Started all the way back in 1942, not long after America entered the war, the project brought together the best scientific minds of the day, including future Nobel Prize winners and European émigrés fleeing Nazi persecution. At hidden sites in Los Alamos, Oak Ridge, and Hanford, they worked to harness the theoretical power of the atom by figuring out how to split them and unleash unimaginable energy in the process.

The physicists did, in fact, figure it out. On July 16, 1945, in the New Mexico desert, a test bomb explosion codenamed "Trinity" exploded with the power of 20,000 tons of TNT. J. Robert Oppenheimer, the project's scientific leader, recalled a line from Hindu scripture: "Now I am become Death, the destroyer of worlds."

The team had built two different types of nuclear bombs, one based on a uranium reaction and the other based on plutonium.

Just weeks later, President Harry Truman made the decision to use the new weapon to force Japan's surrender. Facing an imminent invasion of the main islands of Japan, he'd heard the casualty estimates of 220,000 to 500,000 Allied deaths, with total casualties (killed, wounded, missing) potentially between 1.7 and 4 million. On the Japanese side, estimates ranged from 5 to 10 million for total casualties. Japanese military leaders had previously estimated 20 million. His logic considered the unforgiving math of the human cost. Perhaps the war could be ended with less overall destruction and death by using the new weapons.

On August 6, 1945, the B-29 bomber *Enola Gay* dropped the first atomic bomb on Hiroshima. The blast leveled the city, killing tens of thousands instantly, with many more succumbing to burns and radiation as the days and weeks progressed. Three days later, a second bomb destroyed Nagasaki. Faced with such devastation and the threat of more, Japan announced its surrender on August 15, ending World War II.

At its peak, the Manhattan Project employed about 130,000 people. Over its duration, it cost about $2 billion in 1940s dollars, which is somewhere in the $35 billion vicinity in today's money. It represented about 1% of the overall cost of World War II for the United States, and surprisingly, it's not even the largest single-item expense. That plaque goes to the B-29 bomber program. America built just under 4,000 of those during the war.

Rosie the Riveter: From Aprons to Assembly Lines

At the peak of World War II, over 16 million Americans, mostly men, were serving in uniform overseas. Considering the population of adults in the U.S. at the time was about 75 million, that's an enormous percentage of the workforce.

Enter Rosie the Riveter.

No, she wasn't real, but she represented the millions of women who flooded the factories and offices of America, picking up the slack created by the departure of all those men.

Women traded aprons for overalls, taking on jobs that had long been considered "men's work." You know, like building tanks, bombs and airplanes. Oh, and doing stuff like driving and flying them to ports of embarkation so they could be delivered to military units in the field. These women became the cultural icon of Rosie the Riveter.

Rosie appeared in posters with her red bandana and rolled-up sleeves, flexing her muscles under the slogan "We Can Do It!" She became the face of the women who flooded into factories, shipyards, and munitions plants. Suddenly, women were welding, riveting, and operating heavy machinery. They built B-24 bombers in Michigan, Liberty ships in California, and tens of thousands of tanks, trucks, and rifles across the country.

The scale of production was staggering. American factories turned out planes faster than the enemy could shoot them down. Detroit earned the nickname "Arsenal of Democracy" as auto plants shifted from making cars to building war machines. By the war's end, the U.S. had produced nearly 300,000 aircraft, 88,000 tanks, and millions of tons of munitions. This industrial miracle not only helped defeat the Axis but also finally pulled the United States out of the Great Depression. Jobs were plentiful, paychecks steady, and the economy was on a roll.

Many women's lives changed. They learned new workplace skills, enjoyed new independence, and made money. Simply put, they proved beyond doubt that they could run a factory just as well as the men.

Yet when the war ended in 1945 and the soldiers returned home, most women were pushed back into traditional domestic roles. Factories cut jobs when the war contracts dried up, and even the proud Rosie ad campaigns gradually shifted to more domestic themes.

Even still, Rosie the Riveter became a symbol of female strength and possibility, a reminder that women could, and did, step up when the country needed them most.

The most famous "Rosie" wasn't the original one. The first Rosie appeared in a Norman Rockwell painting on the cover of the Saturday Evening Post in 1943, depicting a muscular woman in overalls with a lunchbox labeled "Rosie." But the image most people know today, the "We Can Do It!" poster, wasn't widely seen during the war at all. It was created by J. Howard Miller for Westinghouse Electric, intended only to boost morale inside their factories. The poster resurfaced decades later during the women's rights movement of the 1980s and became the enduring feminist icon we know today.

Soldiers, Students, and Suburbs

When those 16 million Americans were finished fighting World War II, they came back home to a country that had figured out how to keep running without them.

The country learned something after World War I, when a similar challenge arose: how to "re-integrate" all those people back into the economy.

To smooth this transition, Congress passed the Servicemen's Readjustment Act of 1944. You know it as the GI Bill. It was one of the most ambitious pieces of social legislation in American history, designed not just to reward veterans but to reshape society.

Before they left for the war, those service members lived in a country where only about 15% of young Americans went to college. The GI bill changed that, offering tuition assistance and living stipends for veterans interested in college, vocational schools and graduate programs.

Not surprisingly, with the offer of going to college via government assistance, the percentage of college graduates skyrocketed. By 1956, nearly eight million veterans had taken advantage of the GI Bill, building a more educated future workforce in the process.

The GI Bill didn't just address higher education. It also provided for low-interest home loans, making it possible for millions of veterans to buy houses with little or no down payment. This drove the postwar suburban construction and relocation boom. All the new homes drove the construction industry and helped move people out of the cities.

And there was more. The GI Bill also provided unemployment insurance and business loans, helping veterans stabilize financially as they transitioned back to civilian life.

The results of the programs, taken together, represented a massive upward mobility movement. Soldiers coming back who would have competed for limited jobs instead became doctors, engineers, teachers, lawyers and homeowners.

It wasn't all perfect. Discrimination still existed, and black veterans faced challenges accessing the many benefits of the GI Bill due to barriers in the education system and home ownership.

Military commercials still tout the services as a life training ground, enabling personal growth, and in this case, the promise came true, at least for many. The GI Bill not only prevented an economic crash but also built the modern middle class.

The very first recipient of the GI Bill was Sergeant Dominic Bartolini, a World War II veteran who enrolled at the University of Illinois in fall 1944. His tuition and fees were paid in full, and he received $50 a month for living expenses (worth about $900 today). Within months, campuses across the country were flooded with veterans, many still in uniform, carrying books instead of rifles. College presidents scrambled to find housing, sometimes turning barracks, trailers, and even chicken coops into dorms to meet the demand.

Part Seven

The Cold War Era

Chapter 22

Reds, Rockets, and Refrigerator Spies

The Cold War brought space races, proxy wars, and duck-and-cover drills. Paranoia ran hot, spies ran rampant, and schoolkids practiced hiding under desks. Let's explore McCarthyism, nuclear standoffs, and the global chess game that dominated half a century.

The Great Communist Witch Hunt

If you were alive in the 1950s, the chances are that you were a communist.

No, let's revise that. The chances are that pretty much everyone was accusing pretty much everyone else of being a communist. There, that's better; we're all about being factually accurate here.

OK, I'm exaggerating a touch, but the idea was deeply ingrained in American society thanks to the Red Scare. From the tail end of World War II onwards, the nation was afraid of the Soviet influence and threat.

At the center of the circular firing squad of paranoia and accusations was one Senator Joseph McCarthy of Wisconsin. In 1950, he claimed he had a list of communists working inside the U.S. government, secretly toiling away to end the Great American Experiment. He never actually produced that list or cited any real sources, but that explosive claim launched years of televised hearings, accusations, and political theater. You know, like politics has always been, but for different reasons.

Government officials, military officers, professors, and Hollywood writers found themselves hauled before committees to answer one "shake-in-your-boots" question: "Are you now or have you ever been a member of the Communist Party?"

Your answer didn't much matter because with a question like that, an accusation was a pronouncement of guilt, whether or not it was justified. It's kind of like, "When did you stop shoplifting?"

McCarthy's aggressive and usually baseless tactics ruined careers and reputations. People lost jobs, were blacklisted, or lived in fear of being labeled "un-American." It didn't help that this was all happening during the early Cold War, when tensions with the Soviet Union were sky-high and nuclear war paranoia was in full swing.

The witch hunt movement came to a head in 1954, during the Army-McCarthy hearings. Televised to the nation, these hearings brought the source material for the stories straight to the American people. McCarthy's bullying and wild, often baseless accusations revealed the flimsy underpinnings and lack of real evidence behind all the questioning. In a now-famous exchange, Army attorney Joseph Welch asked McCarthy, "Have you no sense of decency, sir?" That moment helped turn public opinion. McCarthy's credibility crumbled, and the Senate formally censured him later that year.

But some of the ripples continued to spread through society. Teachers and government workers often had to take loyalty oaths. The entertainment industry blacklisted suspected communists from work. And far too many citizens had one eye on their neighbor and the other watching their own back.

The Red Scare, like the Japanese American Internment program before, was a stark reminder of how people can, well, lose their minds when they're afraid.

Even America's favorite redhead, Lucille Ball, got tangled in the Red Scare. In 1936, years before I Love Lucy, she registered to vote as a Communist, though she later explained she only did it to please her grandfather, who admired the party during the Depression. When investigators came calling in the 1950s, Ball insisted she had never attended meetings or believed in communist ideology. The public sided with her, and Desi Arnaz even joked at a press conference, "The only thing red about Lucy is her hair, and even that's not real!"

Atomic Spies: The Rosenbergs

Sometimes the Red Scare fears were at least partially justified.

David Greenglass worked as a machinist on the Manhattan Project. He was the brother of one Ethel Rosenberg, married to Julius Rosenberg.

So far, so good. At least until Julius and Ethel were arrested and tried for selling nuclear secrets to the Soviet Union, partly based on the testimony of David Greenglass.

At the time, secrecy of how to make "the bomb" was paramount. At the end of World War II, the United States was the only country with nuclear capability, and everyone was keen to keep it that way for as long as possible. But in 1949, the Soviets tested their first bomb. It was way ahead of schedule according to the Americans. They believed stolen secrets allowed the Soviets to accelerate their program.

In 1951, both Rosenbergs were convicted of espionage and sentenced to death. It seemed pretty clear that Julius was guilty, as he had connections to a Soviet spy ring, but the evidence against Ethel was far less direct. To this day, controversy remains over whether she was as guilty as the trial indicated. Some believe the evidence against her was amplified to put more pressure on Julius. The conviction happened based on the Espionage Act of 1917 back in 1951.

Even at the time, there was a global movement to commute the couple's sentences, but President Eisenhower refused. Whatever the truth, the couple was, in fact, executed by electric chair at Sing Sing Prison on June 19, 1953.

Justice, Cold War paranoia or both?

The Rosenbergs' execution in 1953 was the first time civilians in the United States had ever been executed for espionage during peacetime. Their case was so controversial that even Pope Pius XII and Albert Einstein appealed for clemency. On the night of their execution, thousands gathered in Paris, London, and New York to protest the decision. At Sing Sing Prison, hundreds of demonstrators held vigil outside the walls as the couple went to the electric chair.

Beep, Beep! Sputnik!

In an era of mass paranoia, there's nothing like an overhead threat you can't see but you know is there.

On October 4, 1957, Americans looked up and collectively

gasped, not because of what they saw, but because of what they could hear.

Somewhere above in the heavens, circling the Earth every 98 minutes, was a metal beach ball called Sputnik. Launched by America's arch-enemy, the Soviet Union, it was the world's first artificial satellite, and it scared the heck out of everyone below.

Sputnik itself wasn't a threat. It was just a 24-inch diameter, 184-pound ball with a battery-powered radio inside. It's not like it was bristling with missiles and space lasers or anything. But the "Sputnik Shock" was very real because of what this Red Menace achievement meant. The Soviets could launch things into space, at will, and control them. Who knows what would be next? Perhaps orbital threats bristling with missiles and space lasers. Or worse.

The fear was compounded because here at home, we didn't have the capability to launch anything into space.

Theoretically, the U.S. had a rocket that could drop something into space as early as 1956, the Juno I, but the program stalled. In December 1957, the Vanguard blew up on the pad, illustrating for all to see that the Soviets had taken the space race lead. It wasn't until the end of January 1958 that the Explorer satellite made it into space.

It's important to note that the fear of the Soviets controlling space was very real, but it was the practical meaning of their program that warranted the national freak-out in the United States. If the Soviets had the technology to launch rockets into space, then they certainly were capable of building missiles that could deliver atomic bombs to any target in the world.

Time to act. In 1958, Congress created the National Aeronautics and Space Administration (NASA) to head up America's space program. The charter was simple. Beat the Soviets. To meet the brainpower need, the country overhauled the education program to produce more rocket scientists. The focus on math, engineering, and general sciences was expanded.

Sputnik was the starter's gun of the Space Race. There was a long way to go before it tapered off, but we'll revisit those topics a bit later.

Sound? What sound? Sputnik was designed with that battery-powered radio to beep on two shortwave frequencies, 20.005 MHz and 40.002 MHz. The purpose was to monitor and track the satellite and study how radio waves behaved from space. That would be valuable knowledge for future space exploits. However, the beep had to have some planned propaganda value. Its little 1-watt radio was detectable by most any amateur radio operator, so the whole world was subjected to about 22 days of the Soviets broadcasting their space superiority. By about day 23, the batteries ran out and Sputnik spoke no more.

Kennedy, Khrushchev, and the Poker Game of the Century

Beaches, white sand, communism and...nuclear missiles?

In October 1962, the Cold War nearly turned really, really hot. American U-2 spy planes flying over Cuba captured photos that shocked government and military leadership to its core. Soviet nuclear missiles were being installed on the island of Cuba. That's just 90 short miles from Florida. The distance was less important than the time. From Cuba, nuclear missiles could reach most anywhere in the Eastern United States in just minutes. That allowed virtually no time to detect launches and respond. The Soviets would have an incredible advantage in a first-strike scenario.

It was immediately clear that President John F. Kennedy had to respond. But this was poker of the highest stakes. One false move and we're looking at the potential for nuclear war. Let it slide, and the nation lives under the threat of surprise annihilation forevermore.

Kennedy and team opted for what they called a "quarantine," which was basically a naval blockade to stop Soviet ships from delivering more missile components. He then demanded that the existing missiles be removed. Last and perhaps most important, he stated publicly that any attack from Cuba would be treated as an attack by the Soviet Union itself.

The standoff lasted for 13 days while the nation held its breath. The military was on high alert as fighting could easily break out at any moment.

We came really close.

The U.S. Navy was dropping signaling depth charges around one Soviet submarine nearing the blockade line. That sub, B-59, had been cut off from Soviet command, and they thought war had already started. The captain ordered the onboard nuclear torpedo to be armed. It carried about the same explosive power as the Hiroshima bomb, and at the time, the United States had no idea Soviet subs had nuclear capability. The Soviet plan was to launch the torpedo towards the U.S. Navy ships and destroy them en masse.

Fortunately, the launch protocol for a nuclear weapon called for the three senior officers to agree and sign off on the action. Captain Savitsky and Political Officer Maslennikov agreed, but the second-in-command and brigade chief of staff, Vasily Arkhipov, refused to cooperate, and there was no launch. Firing that torpedo would have almost certainly started a nuclear conflict.

Meanwhile, back on land, President Kennedy and Soviet Premier Nikita Khrushchev were engaged in some unofficial back-channel diplomacy and reached an agreement. The U.S. agreed to remove its missiles from Turkey and not invade Cuba. Khrushchev agreed to remove his missiles from Cuba. Interestingly, the U.S. agreement to remove its arms from Turkey was kept hush-hush at the time. That situation was somewhat the inverse of the Soviet missiles being set up in Cuba.

The Cuban Missile Crisis was the most dangerous confrontation of the Cold War, a moment when mutual destruction was literally one signature or errant move away. But some good came out of the event. The two superpowers established a new hotline between Washington and Moscow to help prevent any future misunderstandings that could lead to grave consequences.

The U-2, nicknamed the "Dragon Lady," was a spyplane specifically designed to fly so high it couldn't be caught or shot down by missiles or enemy fighter planes. With its glider-like extra-long wings, it could operate at 70,000 feet for very long flights. To put that in perspective, the Concord flew at 60,000 feet, and most modern airlines fly at 35,000 or so feet, although they can go as high as 44,000. For most of its operational life, it did, in fact, fly high enough to evade enemy defenses. Most of the time. Just ask Francis Gary Powers, who was shot down while flying one over the Soviet Union back in 1960.

Concrete Curtain: Berlin Divided

At the close of World War II, Berlin ended up in the Soviet-controlled part of Germany, but from a prior agreement among the Allies, Berlin was controlled by the Soviet Union, the United States, France, and Britain. By 1949, Berlin had settled into two areas of control, east and west. The Allies backed the Federal Republic of Germany (FRG), while the Soviet Union controlled the German Democratic Republic (GDR).

In August 1961, Berlin woke up to the noise of construction crews. East German authorities had quickly put up barbed wire and roadblocks during the night, separating the eastern and western zones. In short order, the temporary barricades were upgraded to walls, guard towers and minefields. The Berlin Wall was born, cutting the city in half.

The PR explanation was to protect the East from infiltrating fascists, but the truth was obvious. The move was really more about stopping East Germans from escaping to West Berlin and freedom. Thousands had been crossing to the west daily before the wall went up.

The wall didn't stop desperate people from trying to escape communist rule. Some tried tunneling under. Others tried flying over, literally with homemade hot air balloons. Others made daring dashes across the barriers, and many were killed in the process of trying to escape.

This concrete barrier remained a stark symbol of the Cold War for over two decades.

Throughout this time, the United States and the Soviet Union were engaged in a one-upmanship contest using nuclear weapons to keep score. Pride, ego, paranoia or perhaps all three increased the collective nuclear stockpiles to a quantity capable of destroying the planet many times over. By the mid-1960s, both had thousands of warheads.

The goal was bizarrely logical in hindsight. The threat of "mutually assured destruction" was supposed to keep both sides from doing something stupid, as each had the capability to inflict mortal damage on the other under any imaginable scenario. No one could strike first, even by surprise, without suffering complete and utter destruction in the retaliation strikes. So, simply put, peace depended on catastrophe.

The cultural impacts on both sides were equally bizarre. The Soviets feared music, Levi's jeans, stylish clothing and tennis shoes. Americans built bomb shelters in their backyards while their children practiced "duck and cover" drills in school so they could better "survive" a nuclear attack.

Unable to fight each other for fear of escalation to nuclear bombs, the two countries engaged in endless proxy warfare, supporting different sides of conflicts around the globe in the name of defeating or spreading communism.

One of the most dramatic escape attempts across the Berlin Wall came just two days after it was built. On August 15, 1961, 19-year-old East German border guard Conrad Schumann made a split-second decision that stunned the world. While patrolling a newly strung barbed wire fence, he dropped his weapon and leapt over the coils into West Berlin. A photographer snapped the exact moment he jumped—legs midair, cap flying back—which became an iconic Cold War image.

Chapter 23

Back to the Civil Rights Movement

While, in theory, the Civil War resolved the slavery issue and related civil rights disparities, in actuality, it... didn't. There was plenty of civil rights abuse and racial tension to go around. More work was in order, and the Civil Rights movement of the 50s and 60s brought the issue to the table once again.

The promises of equality finally faced a true test. With sit-ins, marches, court cases, and speeches that still echo today, Americans of all races fought to dismantle segregation and fulfill the Constitution's ideals. This chapter highlights the courage, backlash, and break-throughs of the Civil Rights Movement.

Classrooms of Change

Until the mid-1950s, much of the country had been operating under a "separate but equal" doctrine. The Reconstruction Amendments, primarily the 14th in this case, mandated equal protection under the law for all citizens.

However, some jurisdictions developed the concept that segregation was fine, provided all segregated groups had equal access, opportunity, etc, etc. This led to situations like segregated schools, segregated public transportation, and so on.

In 1896, Homer Plessy, who was 7/8 white and 1/8 black, chose to sit in a whites-only train car in Louisiana, willingly choosing to challenge the Separate Car Act of 1890. Plessy's logic was simple. This policy (and law in this case) violated the 13th and 14th Amendments.

The case made its way to the Supreme Court, and on May 18, 1896, the court ruled against Plessy in a 7-1 majority, basically stating that segregation was constitutional provided the facilities were equal and that segregation did not imply inferiority.

This set the stage for a consolidated case aimed at desegregating schools in the mid-1950s. Led by Oliver Brown in Topeka, Kansas, a group of black families challenged the existing policy calling for black students to be sent to distant, segregated schools while white students attended nearby schools. Backed by the NAACP and Thurgood Marshall, its Chief Counsel, the case made its way to the Supreme Court.

On May 17, 1954, a landmark ruling was issued by the Supreme Court. Chief Justice Earl Warren, speaking for a unanimous Court, wrote: "Separate educational facilities are inherently unequal." The Plessy precedent was destroyed in one fell swoop, and the entire legal framework upholding segregation policies was dismantled. The net-

net? This was an order from the highest court to desegregate, well, everything.

The problem was that the Court didn't specify how that was to be done. A ruling was one thing, but implementation on the ground was another. Some districts slow-walked the policy change for years, while others simply closed down schools to avoid integration.

A follow-up case in 1955, Brown II, increased the pressure on desegregation with an order instructing schools to desegregate "with a deliberate speed." Even that phrasing left segregationists too much wiggle room, but the tides had shifted. Now, the growing Civil Rights movement had solid backing. The African American community had a legal backstop for their claims that equality delayed was equality denied.

There was still plenty of work to do ending Jim Crow, but the war against inequality was in full swing.

When the Supreme Court handed down Brown v. Board of Education in 1954, it wasn't one case; it was actually a bundle of five lawsuits from Kansas, Delaware, South Carolina, Virginia, and Washington, D.C. One of the most striking came from South Carolina, where parents in Briggs v. Elliott initially only asked for a school bus. Black children had to walk up to nine miles each day to class, while white students rode buses. The case expanded into a challenge to segregation itself, and though those families faced threats, firings, and even violence, their push became part of the ruling that ended Plessy v. Ferguson.

Rosa's Ride to Revolution

Here's a life lesson. Don't mess with a quiet seamstress. They just might surprise you with their inner fighting spirit.

Like Linda Brown, her father and their neighbors, Rosa Parks wasn't taking segregation sitting down. Well, on second thought, she kind of did. By sitting and staying put, she brought the issue of segregation on city buses into the open. For her and the black community in Montgomery, Alabama, enough was enough.

Rosa Parks was an activist and secretary for the NAACP when she was sitting in the "colored" section of a bus. A white man asked for her seat, and she politely refused. She was tired, and along with thousands of other black residents, tired of putting up with the pervasive injustice.

The result? She was arrested for violating the city's segregation laws.

Rosa Parks drove her stake into the bus seat on December 1, 1955. By December 5th, the black community had organized a widespread boycott of buses in Montgomery. For over a year, 381 long days, black residents developed other ways to get to and from work and their daily business. They established carpool systems, used black-owned taxi cabs, and many simply walked, often for miles. They'd had enough, so this was no flash-in-the-pan protest, fizzling out when things got difficult.

The effect on the bus company was crippling. The publicity was nationwide.

The city tried to outlast the protest, but the economic pressure was crushing. Black bus riders represented a majority of overall customers, and the business was simply not sustainable without them.

Shortly after the boycott started, four other women, who had also refused to give up seats to white passengers and been arrested, filed a lawsuit targeting the city ordinances regarding bus segregation. Aurelia Browder, Claudette Colvin, Susie McDonald, and Mary Louise Smith pursued the case, backed by the NAACP. Rosa Parks wasn't involved in this particular case due to a technicality.

After a long legal battle, the Supreme Court ruled in November

1956 that segregation on public buses was unconstitutional. In short order, the city of Montgomery was forced to integrate its buses.

The movement also introduced a new national leader of the Civil Rights movement: Martin Luther King, Jr. A 26-year-old Baptist Minister, King preached the philosophy of non-violent protest, keeping the community united and focused on the ultimate goal. It didn't take long for him to become the voice of the movement.

A single, quiet act of resistance had become the spark igniting a national protest. While others called Rosa Parks the "Mother of the Civil Rights Movement," she always insisted she was just tired of giving in.

Rosa Parks wasn't actually the first person arrested for refusing to give up her seat on a Montgomery bus. Nine months earlier, 15-year-old Claudette Colvin had done the very same thing. A high school student, Colvin refused to move when asked, declaring that it was her constitutional right to stay seated. She was arrested and briefly jailed. Civil rights leaders, however, worried that Colvin, who was young, unmarried, and pregnant, would not be the best test case to rally broad support. Parks, with her reputation as a quiet, respectable NAACP secretary, became the perfect figure to ignite the boycott.

I Have a Dream

For 13 years, Martin Luther King, Jr. was the face of the Civil Rights Movement.

After earning a Doctorate in Theology, King moved into a career pastoring the Dexter Avenue Baptist Church in Montgomery, Alabama. After joining the Rosa Parks Bus Boycott, he founded the Southern Christian Leadership Conference (SCLC) to help guide non-violent activism. From that point forward, his life mission was clear, and he never looked back from his new calling.

By 1963, the Civil Rights Movement was in full swing, having been active for the past eight years. Boycotts, sit-ins and civil protests by countless ordinary citizens were slowly but surely making a dent in the segregation culture.

King's defining moment came on August 28, 1963.

The March on Washington for Jobs and Freedom was the largest demonstration America had ever seen at the time. More than 250,000 people flooded the National Mall in Washington, D.C., having arrived from all across the country. They came under a banner of now being the time for the realization of true equality and freedom for all.

Speaking from the foot of the Lincoln Memorial, King delivered his most famous speech, talking of how the promises defined in the founding documents would be at long last realized.

As for the enduring and iconic "I have a dream" segments of King's speech, they were largely improvised. Gospel singer Mahalia Jackson, standing nearby, urged Martin Luther King, Jr. to "Tell 'em about the dream, Martin!"

King was in the moment and responded with these timeless lines:

"So even though we face the difficulties of today and tomorrow, I still have a dream. It is a dream deeply rooted in the American dream.

I have a dream that one day this nation will rise up and live out the true meaning of its creed: 'We hold these truths to be self-evident, that all men are created equal.'

I have a dream that one day on the red hills of Georgia, the sons of former slaves and the sons of former slave owners will be able to sit down together at the table of brotherhood.

I have a dream that one day even the state of Mississippi, a state sweltering with the heat of injustice, sweltering with the heat of oppression, will be transformed into an oasis of freedom and justice.

I have a dream that my four little children will one day live in a nation where they will not be judged by the color of their skin but by the content of their character. I have a dream today.

I have a dream that one day down in Alabama, with its vicious racists, with its governor having his lips dripping with the words of interposition and nullification; one day right down in Alabama little black boys and black girls will be able to join hands with little white boys and white girls as sisters and brothers. I have a dream today.

I have a dream that one day every valley shall be exalted, every hill and mountain shall be made low, the rough places will be made plain, and the crooked places will be made straight; 'and the glory of the Lord shall be revealed and all flesh shall see it together.'"

The speech did more than inspire the large crowd. It inspired action in Washington, too. Within a year, Congress passed the Civil Rights Act of 1964, outlawing segregation and discrimination.

When King shifted gears into the "I have a dream" refrain, the effect on the crowd was electric. Eyewitnesses described people breaking into cheers, waving their hats, and some openly weeping as his words blanketed the National Mall. Clarence Jones, one of King's advisers, later said, "I turned to the person standing next to me and said, 'These people out there don't know it yet, but they're about to go to church.'" It was no longer a policy speech; it had become a sermon to the nation. That unscripted pivot transformed the march from a protest rally into one of the most spiritually uplifting moments in American history.

From Jim Crow to Justice

Years of protests, marches, and speeches finally forced the government to take definitive action. Again.

The Civil Rights Act of 1964 was a broad piece of legislation addressing a host of discrimination-related topics.

It ended discrimination in hotels, restaurants, schools, theaters, and other public places.

It addressed employment-related discrimination and established the Equal Employment Opportunity Commission (EEOC).

It empowered the federal government (even more) to enforce discrimination in the education system.

It attempted to address discrimination in voting by outlawing unequal procedures in voter registration.

The effects were sweeping. It was the legal end of "whites only" signage and blatant employment discrimination practices. It took a prolonged fight in Congress, but President Lyndon Johnson finally signed it into law on July 2, 1964.

The following year, Congress addressed a host of voting-related issues. While the Reconstruction Amendments were intended to fix equality in voting rights once and for all, many jurisdictions created all sorts of obstacles and hurdles designed to prevent minorities from participating freely in the election process. Literacy tests, poll taxes, impossible penalties and "interest" on poll taxes and lost, delayed or even rejected paperwork all served to suppress the black vote.

The Voting Rights Act of 1965 looked to put an end, once and for all, to those tactics. It banned literacy tests, outlawed poll taxes in federal elections, and gave the federal government authority to oversee elections in places with a record of discrimination. In short, although it took a full century, it made the promise of the Fifteenth Amendment real with legislative teeth.

When President Lyndon B. Johnson signed the Voting Rights Act of 1965, the impact was immediate and dramatic. In Selma, Alabama, where peaceful marchers had been brutally attacked just months earlier on "Bloody Sunday," black voter registration jumped from less than 1% to nearly 60% within two years. Across the South, hundreds of thousands of African Americans who had been locked out of the democratic process for generations were finally able to cast ballots. Within a decade, the number of black elected officials in the U.S. rose from fewer than 500 to over 4,000.

Malcolm X and the Black Power Movement

The Civil Rights Movement wasn't all about peaceful protests. While Martin Luther King Jr. called for nonviolence, integration, and reconciliation, Malcolm X inspired followers with a different approach of active self-defense, pride, and empowerment. His speeches challenged America to confront not only the current segregation but also centuries of exploitation and humiliation.

Malcolm X's early rise came through the Nation of Islam, where he sharpened his fiery oratory and preached separation rather than integration. For many, his message of pride and resistance was a shock to the system, a counterbalance to King's appeals to America's conscience. He urged African Americans to reclaim their dignity through economic independence, self-discipline, and, if necessary, the willingness to defend themselves "by any means necessary."

In 1964, Malcolm broke with the Nation of Islam and broadened his vision. His call was not for hate, but for solidarity among oppressed peoples everywhere.

Malcolm X's mission was cut short by his assassination in 1965.

In the years that followed, his legacy fueled the rise of the Black Power movement. This new wave of activism, embodied by groups like the Black Panther Party, demanded not just access to lunch counters and ballots but community control, cultural pride, and an end to police brutality. Panthers in leather jackets and berets became symbols of resistance, even as their community outreach efforts, like free breakfasts, health clinics, and neighborhood patrols, quietly reshaped lives.

The movement certainly wasn't all roses, as internal organiza-
tional strife and apparent pro-violence stances discouraged more
mainstream acceptance and adoption. Some civil rights leaders
feared that the more aggressive and separatist stance was promoting a
form of "reverse racism."

The Black Panther Party's free breakfast program, launched in
Oakland in 1969, became one of its most influential legacies.
At its height, the program was serving over 20,000 meals a
week to children in cities across America. Local businesses,
churches, and even sympathetic grocery store owners donated
food. The effort was so effective that FBI Director J. Edgar
Hoover labeled the breakfast program as one of the "greatest
threats" to U.S. security. Why? Because it showed the
Panthers could provide what the government would not,
winning loyalty through community care as much as through
defiance.

Chapter 24

Vietnam and the Limits of Power

The U.S. entered Vietnam to stop the spread of communism. In a global chess match aimed at keeping as many of the countries on the world map anything but "red," it seemed the right thing to do under that strategy. However, the country learned a hard lesson with 58,000 dead, a divided home front, and a shattered illusion of invincibility. Let's examine how a jungle war challenged America's might and morale and changed the nation's view of itself.

When 'Just Helping' Became a War

The United States' involvement in Vietnam was a classic example of the dangers of a slippery slope.

American military aid began all the way back in 1950 with the Military Assistance Advisory Group, formed to help the French, who were at the time fighting the communist insurgents in the region. While the Americans didn't have strategy and leadership responsibility at the time, they ended up providing about one-third of the money and equipment for the campaign effort.

In 1955, the French were defeated and withdrew, leaving American aid and assistance to shoulder the burden of enabling South Vietnam's military. This took the form not only of money and equipment, but a growing number of military advisors there to train and direct South Vietnamese forces.

By 1961, the number of U.S. Military advisors had grown to thousands, and the United States began sending bigger and more sophisticated gear, like helicopters and other aircraft.

By the end of 1962, the American advisory force had grown to about 11,000, and these troops slipped into the role of joint participation with their South Vietnamese counterparts.

While unofficial, there were American "boots on the ground" engaged in active fighting against communist forces.

By the early 1960s, U.S. "advisors" weren't just giving lectures in classrooms; they were flying combat missions. A striking example is the Battle of Ap Bac in January 1963. About 350 Viet Cong fighters ambushed a much larger South Vietnamese force supported by American helicopters, armored vehicles, and U.S. advisors on the ground. Despite the overwhelming firepower, the Viet Cong held their ground and inflicted heavy losses, downing five helicopters and killing three American advisors. The battle stunned Washington and underscored a grim truth: U.S. involvement had already shifted from "helping" to fighting, even if no one officially admitted it yet.

Operation Blank Check: The Tonkin Resolution

In the summer of 1964, the subtle and plausibly deniable "war" blew up. On August 2, the USS Maddox reported being fired upon by North Vietnamese patrol boats. Two days later, another incident was reported, although there is controversy to this day over whether it actually happened. Whatever the details, American politicians saw this as acts of unprovoked aggression.

President Lyndon B. Johnson went before Congress asking for authority to respond militarily. The result was the Gulf of Tonkin Resolution, passed on August 7, 1964, with almost-unanimous support. Senators Ernest Gruening of Alaska and Wayne Morse of Oregon voted against the resolution, fearing that Congress was giving up its constitutional authority and responsibility to authorize and oversee matters of war.

The Gulf of Tonkin Resolution granted the president sweeping authority to handle the situation in Vietnam. He could take "all necessary measures" to repel attacks and prevent further aggression in Southeast Asia. Practically speaking, it was a bank check to do what he wanted.

It didn't take long for the situation on the ground to escalate— dramatically. In the first year, Johnson ordered the launch of Operation Rolling Thunder, a massive and sustained bombing campaign. Troops began to arrive in growing numbers. Every month, more and more were required. It was a game of "we just need a little more to get over the hump and end this conflict." By the late 1960s, hundreds of thousands of U.S. soldiers were in Vietnam, and the war continued to expand with no clear signs of victory in sight.

In hindsight, the Gulf of Tonkin Resolution was a classic

example of why the government was designed with so many offsetting checks and balances. Arguably, in this case, Congress gave in to fear and anxiety, and as a result, handed too much power to the executive branch. But it was too late. The nation was stuck in a seemingly endless war, taking a massive toll on the country in terms of resources and lives.

It wasn't until 1971 that Congress repealed the resolution, but by then it was too late.

When the Tonkin Gulf incidents first hit the news in 1964, Americans largely trusted the official story that U.S. ships were attacked without provocation. But years later, declassified documents and the Pentagon Papers revealed something different: the second reported attack on August 4th almost certainly never happened. Even Secretary of Defense Robert McNamara later admitted the evidence was shaky at best. Despite this, Johnson told Congress that America had been a victim of "open aggression," helping secure the sweeping resolution. Historians now often cite the Tonkin episode as a case study in how murky intelligence can snowball into major war-making authority.

Tet: When the Homefront Lost Faith

For years, military leaders had been telling the politicians and public back home that the situation in Vietnam was under control and a conclusive end was "right around the corner."

In 1968, Tet, the Vietnamese New Year, which started January 30, saw the launch of a massive offensive by the North Vietnamese Army and the Viet Cong. So much for the end of the war being close at hand.

More than 80,000 communist troops struck over 100 cities,

towns, and military bases across South Vietnam. The fighting was everywhere: from the ancient city of Hue to the U.S. Embassy compound in Saigon, where Viet Cong sappers stormed the gates and fought their way inside before being stopped.

After weeks of brutal fighting, the offensive was finally beaten back. The cost to the North Vietnamese was immense: tens of thousands of their soldiers were killed, and the Viet Cong's strength as a fighting force never fully recovered. By conventional measures, the United States and the South Vietnamese had won a military victory. But the Vietnam War was anything but conventional. The North Vietnamese were committed to fighting until the bitter end, no matter what the ultimate cost.

Back home in the U.S., Tet didn't look like much of a victory. Remember, the official reports constantly spoke of an enemy almost beaten. The simple fact that the North Vietnamese and Viet Cong were able to mount such a large-scale operation and do so much damage blew that narrative away. Fighting in Saigon? Oh, and literally everywhere else? That didn't look much like the situation being under control. Had the official reports simply been too optimistic? Or were the reports intentionally dishonest? The public began to wonder.

From the American soldier's perspective, the war was a grind of constant danger from any direction. In places like Hue, Marines and Army units encountered and fought through some of the most vicious urban combat since World War II. Every alley and building might hide snipers, booby traps, or worse. In the countryside, every patrol carried the possibility of a massive firefight. In both environments, after a vicious attack, enemy combatants literally dissolved back into the civilian population. It's impossible to fight when the enemy is unidentifiable. With few, if any, lines, fronts or meaningful long-term objectives, every day was a fight simply to survive for American troops.

At the height of America's involvement, over half a million U.S. troops were in Vietnam. For them, the war meant long stretches of monotony punctuated by bursts of chaos. Oppressive heat, endless patrols, the distant thump of artillery and surprise attacks were the norm. Nights could explode into terror with mortar attacks or ambushes at any moment. Soldiers spoke of fighting an enemy that was everywhere and nowhere. The Viet Cong, and to a degree, the North Vietnamese regulars, seemed able to vanish into the jungle at will.

Tet brought all these issues into the limelight back home. It became clear that millions of pounds of bombs, infinite bullets and artillery shells, and hundreds of thousands of troops might not be enough to break the will of the North. In addition to the physical costs, Tet represented a loss of confidence in the war and its leaders.

One of the most iconic images of the Tet Offensive came from Saigon itself. On February 1, 1968, Associated Press photographer Eddie Adams captured a South Vietnamese general executing a captured Viet Cong fighter in the street right in front of cameras. The photo won the Pulitzer Prize and became one of the most famous pictures of the war, instantly splashed across American newspapers. While the context was complex, as the prisoner had reportedly just murdered a South Vietnamese officer's family, the raw brutality of the image stunned Americans and further eroded support for the war. Adams later said the photo "killed the general" as surely as the bullet had killed the prisoner.

The My Lai Massacre: Stories That Broke the War

The Tet Offensive eroded confidence in the war, military leaders and Washington politicians. The hamlet of My Lai and the release of the Pentagon Papers were possibly the breaking point for the American public. In a public relations war fought on living room TVs and newspaper headlines back at home, knowledge of what was really going on was the ammunition.

In March 1968, U.S. soldiers entered the small Vietnamese hamlet of My Lai on a search-and-destroy mission like those happening all across the country on any given day. Go out into the jungle. Look for signs of the invisible enemy, destroy any evidence related to enemy activity, capture or kill the enemy, and hope you survive the day. But in this case, the fear, frustration and anger boiled over and led to the killing of hundreds of civilians, including men, women and children.

Initially reported as a great victory over Viet Cong forces with some 20 civilian casualties related to the battle, the Army claimed 128 Viet Cong fighters were also killed in the operation. As future investigations would show, the reality was far different. Over 300 civilians had been killed in the event, and it soon became clear that an organized cover-up, at all levels of the military, was underway.

Over a year after the event, in November of 1969, the American public learned of the massacre through investigative reporting by journalist Seymour Hersh, photographic evidence by Army photographer Ron Haeberle, along with eyewitness reports by American soldiers and helicopter pilot Hugh Thompson. The stories highlighted how the Army had suppressed evidence, applied pressure to whistleblowers and checked off half-hearted investigations in efforts to keep the scale of the killings out of the public eye.

The truth ultimately came out, and 26 Army soldiers were charged, but only one was convicted, serving four years under house arrest.

Two years later, in 1971, came another surprise to the public. The New York Times began publishing the Pentagon Papers, a top-secret Department of Defense study that traced years of U.S. involvement in Vietnam. The documents revealed that multiple presidential administrations, representing both political parties, had misled Congress and the public about the war's goals and prospects for success. The suspicions that had been growing about the misrepresentations were confirmed.

My Lai might never have come to light without helicopter pilot Hugh Thompson Jr. and his crew. Flying overhead during the massacre, Thompson reported seeing American soldiers gunning down unarmed villagers. He landed his helicopter between the soldiers and fleeing civilians, ordering his door gunner to open fire on fellow Americans if they kept shooting. Thompson then helped evacuate survivors, including a group of terrified children, airlifting them to safety. At the time, he was vilified by some in the military as a traitor. Decades later, however, he was recognized as a hero, awarded the Soldier's Medal in 1998 for his courage in stopping further bloodshed.

Hell No, We Won't Go!

The collection of events makes it clear what fueled the anti-war protests of the late 1960s and the first half of the 70s. The erosion of trust, combined with the seemingly endless delivery of body bags back to the United States from some distant and, in many people's view, incomprehensible war, set the stage for widespread protest.

By the late 1960s, Vietnam had become a daily part of American life. Unlike World War II and Korea, where more curated reports of the war made their way to the populace less directly, the Vietnam conflict was delivered, in living color, to their living room televisions. It was a constant presence on nightly news broadcasts, dinner table debates, and campus rallies.

America's youth, the generation most directly affected through the draft and subsequent shipment overseas, took to the streets in growing numbers. The anti-war movement wasn't confined to students either. Veterans returned home to speak out against the conflict, and they carried the voice of authority. They'd been there and seen the war's impact and prognosis first-hand.

In May 1970, then-President Richard Nixon had just announced the expansion of the war into Cambodia, sparking a fresh wave of protests. At Ohio's Kent State University, students gathered to voice their outrage. What began as demonstrations escalated into confrontations with local authorities, and the Ohio National Guard was called in. On May 4, guardsmen fired into a crowd of unarmed students. Within seconds, four young people lay dead, and nine others were wounded.

The shootings stunned the nation. For many Americans, seeing college students gunned down on their own campus was a bridge too far, regardless of the circumstances. Newspapers brought the tragedy to America's front doorstep. Photos like that of a young woman kneeling beside the body of a dead student were simply too much.

The Kent State incident became a defining moment for the anti-war protest movement. Demonstrations not only continued but intensified on campuses across the country.

The shock of Kent State spread so widely that nearly 4 million students at colleges and high schools across the country walked out in protest within days of the shootings. More than 450 campuses had to shut down, some for the rest of the semester. It was the largest student strike in American history. Even musicians joined in. Most famously, Crosby, Stills, Nash & Young released the song "Ohio" just weeks later, calling out the tragedy in raw, unfiltered terms.

The Last Flight from Saigon

We're seeing the writing on the wall, aren't we? A war with no end.

The loss of trust by the American public. Revolt in the streets at home opposing the war and its cost in young American lives.

The end had to be near. And it was.

By the early 1970s, the political will for the Vietnam War was fading fast. The Nixon administration began steadily withdrawing troops from the region. On the surface, it was simply a "Vietnamization" strategy. "We're still intent on winning, but we're going to do that by enabling the Vietnamese leadership and military to do that on their own."

But South Vietnam didn't have the will or means either, and everyone knew that. The Vietnamization strategy was simply a way to get out while maintaining a facade of the exodus being a planned and ultimately win-win scenario.

North Vietnam certainly wasn't fooled by this move, and by 1975, the endgame was underway. North Vietnamese troops continued to advance, capturing cities one after another. South Vietnamese resistance crumbled in the face of the North's determined onslaught, and confidence in the South Vietnamese government evaporated.

In April, the North closed in on Saigon. What followed was a scene unlike anything in American history. Helicopters shuttled frantically from the U.S. embassy roof and other key sites, ferrying out diplomats, soldiers, and desperate South Vietnamese allies to Navy ships offshore. Thousands of South Vietnamese, who had worked with Americans as translators, drivers, and clerks, crowded the embassy gates, hoping for a seat on the departing flights. Knowing they would face severe retribution for aiding the "enemy," they were desperate to escape, but many were left behind as the last helicopters pulled away.

On April 30, 1975, North Vietnamese tanks rolled into the capital. The South Vietnamese president surrendered unconditionally, and Saigon was quickly renamed Ho Chi Minh City. Just like that, America's longest war ended with images of helicopters lifting off embassy rooftops in chaos and retreat.

It was a hard lesson. By now familiar with conventional wars, the United States was accustomed to building lots of guns, tanks, ships and planes...and winning. But Vietnam was different. A war with no little definition and a determined, invisible enemy was not easily winnable by conventional means. It was a national moment of surprise. The world's largest military didn't necessarily give the United States the ability to bend foreign policy and events to its will in a complicated regional civil war.

The end result was tragic. Over 58,000 American service members died in Vietnam. Millions of Vietnamese civilians and soldiers were killed either directly or indirectly, even when they desperately tried to remain uninvolved.

The final evacuation of Saigon, codenamed Operation Frequent Wind, was the largest helicopter airlift in history. Over just two frantic days, American pilots flew more than 600 helicopter sorties, carrying out nearly 7,000 people. Things got so desperate on U.S. Navy ships offshore that crews began shoving helicopters into the sea to make room for more landings. Some South Vietnamese pilots even flew their own helicopters packed with family onto American carriers, then jumped out as their aircraft were pushed overboard.

Part Eight

Modern Times

Chapter 25

From Hippies to Yuppies

The Sixties were loud, colorful, and chaotic. They gave us Woodstock, another round of the military draft, the moon landing, assassinations, and social revolution. This chapter tracks how that rebellious energy shaped the decades that followed, from disco to Wall Street.

The First Campaign in Prime Time

Live television changed politics and elections forever. Until the 1960 presidential debates between John F. Kennedy and Richard Nixon, the only way American families heard these events was by sound only over the radio. Without a picture to accompany the experience, the words were all that mattered.

All that changed when these two debated on live television in front of a record audience. Nearly 70 million people tuned in. That was more than watched the Super Bowl and the moon landing later in 1969.

Kennedy, at a youthful 43 years old, looked great by comparison. He appeared tan, confident, and sharp. Nixon, recovering from illness and refusing makeup, appeared pale and visibly sweating under the studio lights.

Proving the power of the visual image, radio listeners thought Nixon performed better in the debates. Television viewers, however, preferred Kennedy. He looked better. He was relaxed and poised, exuding confidence. The visual contrast underscored a new reality in politics. Policy arguments matter, but the image in front of the camera was just as important.

It didn't take long for campaign strategists to bring media training, image consultants, and choreographed words and demeanor into the mix.

The old guard of more traditional politicians was uncomfortable in this new world of image. Lyndon Johnson avoided televised debates in 1964, fearing that the risks outweighed the rewards. On the flip side, Ronald Reagan, a former actor, later mastered the medium with easygoing humor and hard-hitting and often funny one-liners. By the 1980s, television ads, sound bites, and carefully staged events dominated campaigns.

The first Kennedy–Nixon debate in 1960 drew such a massive audience that studies later estimated it swung as many as 4 million votes. One fun fact: Nixon refused to wear stage makeup, insisting it wasn't "manly." Instead, he dabbed on a drugstore product called Lazy Shave to cover his beard stubble. Under the hot studio lights, it melted and streaked, making him look even worse on TV. Meanwhile, Kennedy's team had worked with a professional makeup artist.

JFK, RFK, and MLK: A Nation in Mourning

We've discussed the growing tensions from the Civil Rights Movement and the Vietnam War. It's time to put that under the lens of stark reality. The 1960s also brought a rash of high-profile assassinations, including that of a President, his brother, and the nation's preeminent civil rights leader.

World War II PT boat hero John F. Kennedy became President at the young age of just 43, making him the youngest to ever assume the duties of the Oval Office. Together with his elegant bride, he brought a picture of youthful enthusiasm to the traditionally stodgy role of Washington politics.

But on November 22, 1963, President John F. Kennedy's political career, and the nation's hopes, were cut short by a sniper's bullet while driving through Dallas, Texas. While people may never agree on whether Lee Harvey Oswald acted alone or was even the killer, one thing is clear. The assassination of a sitting President is something that rocks the nation to its core, especially in an era where the events unfold in real time on televisions across the country.

Robert F. Kennedy was appointed to the post of Attorney General at the beginning of the Kennedy administration and served until 1964 in that position. He then ran for the Senate, representing New York, until he entered the presidential race in 1968.

Many viewed RFK as the continuation of the JFK legacy and the path to complete his unfinished work. However, it was not to be.

Just hours after winning the California Democratic primary, Robert Kennedy was gunned down in a Los Angeles hotel kitchen. America was shocked yet again. A president and a presidential candidate, and brothers at that, both assassinated within five years of each other? Unthinkable. And it made many think no conspiracy theory was too far "out there."

But that wasn't all; there was more tragedy to come.

Dr. Martin Luther King, Jr. had been electrifying the nation for the past 13 years, ever since the Rosa Parks-inspired Montgomery bus boycott.

But on April 4, 1968, King was assassinated in Memphis, Tennessee. He had traveled there to support striking sanitation workers.

King's murder sent shockwaves far beyond the black community. Riots erupted in over 100 cities, from Washington, D.C., to Chicago and Kansas City. The national grief was not just for a great man, but for the dreams he had so eloquently shared with the nation: a world free from racism, hatred, and injustice. It was oddly and terribly ironic that the man who championed peaceful protest and demonstration was shot down.

The murders of Kennedy, King, and Kennedy again left America reeling. The sixties had begun with optimism and a sense that progress was in motion. However, by the end of the decade, these assassinations, the emergence of a war without foreseeable end and violence in the streets became the reality.

The office of the President of the United States is not one left unattended for very long in times of national emergency. Just hours after President Kennedy was killed, Lyndon B. Johnson took the oath of office on board an airplane at Dallas Love Field. The plane literally became "Air Force One" mid-sentence. President Kennedy's new widow, Jacqueline Kennedy, stood by Johnson's side, still wearing her bloody clothes from the shooting. This was also the first time the Presidential oath was administered by a woman, U.S. District Judge Sarah T. Hughes. Oh, and in the hurry, it turned out Johnson laid his hand on a Catholic missal inadvertently mistaken for a bible.

Uncle Sam Wants You

Like the Internal Revenue Service, the draft has always hovered in the background, not necessarily front and center during your daily life, but from time to time, it rears its head and turns your world upside down.

The Vietnam War was the last time America relied on a mandatory draft to build up its military forces. At first, U.S. involvement in Vietnam was limited. At the peak of the advisory stage, there were about 11,000 military members in the country. But as the conflict escalated in the mid-1960s, so did the need for more soldiers. Lots more.

The Selective Service System, the government authority in charge of conscription, was activated, and the country's most unpopular game of "Duck, Duck, Goose!" was on.

From 1964 to 1973, about 2.2 million American men were drafted into service. The official draft eligibility age range was 18 to 26. At the time, there were about 27 million men in the country within that bracket, so a cursory look might indicate that about one in twelve were actually drafted into active service. But that's a misleading picture. A host of often discretionary exemptions and deferments cut down the pool immensely, making the probability within some demographics quite high. College students? Usually exempt. Working-class men? Not so much. The distinction led to accusations of the "haves" avoiding the war while the "have-nots" were disproportionately impacted and more likely to be drafted.

The result of the perceived injustice, combined with the growing unpopularity of the war, led to draft protests. "Why should I go to the other side of the world to die for a cause that's not mine?" was a common sentiment. And the "Hell no, we won't go!" chants echoed across the nation.

Many young men fled to Canada. Others simply burned their draft cards, risking prison instead of the possibility of death overseas.

In 1969, the draft lottery was introduced in an attempt to make the system fairer; birthdays were drawn at random to determine the order of call-up. Still, controversy continued, and public pressure mounted.

Nixon eventually shifted the mechanisms back to a voluntary enlistment system. The last draft call was issued in December 1972. In January 1973, with U.S. combat operations winding down, the draft officially came to an end.

The draft has never been popular, but some went to extreme lengths during the Vietnam War to avoid the service. For example, at the time, homosexuality was a disqualifying attribute, so more than one man wore women's underwear to their exams, hoping that examiners would make an association between their undergarments and sexual orientation. Others took drugs, including amphetamines or endured extreme sleep deprivation to appear "unhealthy" or "unfit" for service. More than a few resorted to self-harm, like shooting off a finger.

America Sticks the (Moon) Landing

If you're old enough to have eaten Space Food Sticks as a kid, you know something about the national excitement, nervous tension and pride of the moon landings.

In a September 12, 1962, speech at Rice University, President John F. Kennedy made a promise, which the nation fulfilled, about five and a half years after his death.

"We choose to go to the Moon in this decade and do the other things, not because they are easy, but because they are hard, because that goal will serve to organize and measure the best of our energies and skills, because that challenge is one that we are willing to accept, one we are unwilling to postpone, and one which we intend to win."

On July 20, 1969, at 21:56 EST, the world collectively held its breath as grainy black-and-white images flickered across television screens. Millions tuned in to see astronaut Neil Armstrong climb down the ladder of the lunar module Eagle and place his boot on the dusty surface of the moon. His words, "That's one small step for man, one giant leap for mankind," were simple, but they captured the enormity of the moment most eloquently. For the first time in history, human beings had left their home planet and walked on another world. OK, it's not so much a planet, but a moon held captive by Earth, but still.

Apollo 11 was the dramatic climax of a decade-long effort that began with Kennedy's bold promise. This goal likely freaked out the folks at NASA because, at the time, the United States was reeling and trying to play catch-up to the Soviet Union's string of successes in space. They'd stunned the world with Sputnik in 1957 and Yuri Gagarin's first human orbit in 1961. The U.S. barely lobbed a man into suborbital space for just 15 minutes later that same year.

But the nation mobilized behind the effort, believing America had to win the space race. Thousands of scientists, engineers, and factory workers threw themselves into the effort, producing a program that consumed roughly 4% of the federal budget and employed over 400,000 people.

On July 16, 1969, three NASA astronauts, Armstrong, Buzz Aldrin, and Michael Collins, blasted off in the most powerful machine ever built, the Saturn V rocket, generating some seven million pounds of thrust. About three days later, the men reached lunar orbit and the landing was cleared to go.

The lander was built for two, and someone needed to remain in the Command Module in lunar orbit to keep the lights on and coordinate the return trip rendezvous. That was Collins. Aldrin and Armstrong hopped in the Lunar Lander and headed for the surface.

The landing had the world biting its nails as Armstrong had to manually steer the machine over unexpected craters and boulders and almost ran out of fuel in the process. Keep in mind, this was a one-try deal. Any miscalculation or problem would have left the two stranded on the moon until the end of time. Collins would have had to leave them and make the trip back to Earth alone.

When mission control confirmed "The Eagle has landed," cheers erupted not just in Houston, but around the world.

The pair were on the lunar surface for just over 21 hours, with only a few hours out hopping around the surface, running experiments and gathering 47 pounds of lunar rocks to bring home. They also left behind a plaque that read, "We came in peace for all mankind," reminding everyone that while the moon landing was an American achievement, it was a human endeavor.

Apollo 11 astronaut Neil Armstrong insisted his famous words were a bit different from what history recorded, and that a single letter was lost in transmission. It was a quarter-million-mile radio signal after all. Armstrong claims he actually said the following, which is grammatically correct: "That's one small step for **a** man, one giant leap for mankind." Most recordings don't capture the additional word, "a," but some analyses indicated it might have been there and lost or garbled, while making its way back to Earth.

Three Days of Peace, Mud, and Music

In August 1969, a dairy farm in upstate New York suddenly became the place to be seen.

Nearly half a million people made their way to Max Yasgur's fields for three days of music, mud, peace and protest. The Woodstock Music and Art Fair, as it was officially called, was billed as "three days of peace and music." What unfolded was far more than a concert. It was a far-out defining symbol of a generation that wanted to reimagine the world.

The lineup was epic: Jimi Hendrix shredding "The Star-Spangled Banner," Janis Joplin, the Who, Joe Cocker, Jefferson Airplane, Santana, The Grateful Dead, and more.

It was the counterculture of the '60s set to music, live and in person.

This counterculture questioned nearly everything mainstream America stood for. It was about civil rights, women's liberation, environmental awareness, and a deep suspicion of the government and corporate America. Young people experimented with alternative lifestyles, communal living, and psychedelic drugs. Tie-dye shirts, long hair, and protest songs weren't just fashion fads; they had meaning and were badges of identity.

Today, it's easy to "remember" Woodstock as some sort of proof that utopia is, in fact, possible. In reality, there were elements of that, but any massive event like this has its share of challenges. The crowd was far larger than anyone planned for, so food, medical supplies and capability were in short supply. Sanitation? Who needs it, really? Lots and lots of rain turned the place into mud. It was a dairy farm after all, not a parking lot. But, in fairness, there was a notable lack of violence. People shared, cooperated and made the best of the challenges, generally speaking.

The counterculture movement didn't really die off. Its fading was more like elements of it being absorbed into the mainstream. For example, social activism and environmentalism aren't considered countercultural anymore; they're just part of the American dialogue.

Woodstock organizers were struggling to find a place for the music festival. Expecting tens of thousands of attendees, many farms and towns had no interest in allowing "all those hippies" to overrun the place. A local realtor connected the organizers with Max Yasgur, a dairy farmer in Bethel, New York. He agreed to lease 600 acres of his land for the event, believing 20 or 30 thousand could show up. As we know, the attendance was more like half a million.

You might think Max was a farmer hippie himself, agreeing to such a thing over the strenuous objections of neighbors and the town. Nope. He was a conservative and a Vietnam War supporter. Yes, he was having a rough year and needed the money, but he also believed people of the counterculture ought to have an opportunity to gather and celebrate peace, share their views and enjoy some music. Even with all the controversy between him and other locals and the extensive property damage, he never expressed regret about hosting the event.

The Other Civil Rights Revolutions

The first wave of feminism was mostly about legal rights, including the right to vote. The second wave, active in the 1960s, was more about broadening the concept of equality in the workplace, home and the bedroom.

One spark behind this renewed movement was Betty Friedan's 1963 book, *The Feminine Mystique*. It called out the "problem that has no name." That was the boredom, lack of fulfillment and the general frustration felt by many women about being boxed into traditional roles in the workplace and at home. The book brought frustrations to light, especially in middle-class households and turned housewives into activists.

In the mid-60s, the National Organization for Women was formed to lead the charge for women's rights. The movement struggled, in part due to internal disagreements about which issues were the priorities. Some favored negotiation and the solidification of basic principles like equality in the workplace. Others took a more revolutionary stance. Initially supported by unions, NOW lost much of that support when it publicly supported the Equal Rights Amendment.

Amidst the strife of the movement, big gains were made in the 60s, while some efforts ended up falling flat. In 1963, the Equal Pay Act outlawed pay discrimination based on gender. In 1964, Title VII of the Civil Rights Act made workplace discrimination illegal. Court cases like Griswold v. Connecticut in 1965 addressed access to contraception. Congress passed Title IX of the Higher Education Act in 1972. That addressed educational programs, making discrimination based on sex illegal in any school that received federal funds. That also opened the door for increased equality in athletic programs.

First introduced way back in 1923, the Equal Rights Amendment aimed to establish broad legal equality between men and women. Resurrected in the 60s, the proposed constitutional amendment passed Congress in 1972. However, to take effect as a permanent adjustment to the United States Constitution, it required ratification in the states. Ultimately, that process fell three states short, and ratification never happened.

Meanwhile, another equal rights movement was taking shape.

As a sign of the times, the Stonewall Inn, a New York City gay bar, was raided by police. This was nothing unusual at the time, as homosexuality was illegal in much of the United States.

However, by now, the gay rights movement had gained some steam, drawing inspiration and tactics from the civil rights and women's rights movements. While the Stonewall Inn wasn't the first raid (there were plenty in cities across the U.S.), it did represent the first time the gay community fought back in force. For six nights, riots in the streets inspired nationwide activism and established the basis for pushback and the repeal of the sodomy laws, which had been used to enforce the de facto ban on homosexuality.

Together, feminism and gay rights expanded the nation's civil rights frontier, forcing citizens and government alike to step back and think more broadly about concepts of equality.

When Title IX became law in 1972, some colleges panicked about how it might affect sports. One unintended consequence? Women's rowing became a varsity powerhouse almost overnight. Why? Because football programs had (and still have) massive rosters, schools needed a women's sport with equally large numbers to balance scholarship opportunities under Title IX. Rowing, with its eight-person crews plus alternates, fit the bill. Within a decade, women's rowing exploded across American campuses, and today it's one of the NCAA's largest women's sports. Row, row, row your boat!

Watergate: When the Cover-Up Cracked

Political pundits always say the cover-up is worse than whatever caused the need for sweeping things under the rug in the first place.

As you might expect from a real-life Washington, D.C. conspiracy, this one is uber-complicated, but we'll try to boil it down to the basics here.

On June 17, 1972, police caught and captured five burglars at the Democratic National Committee offices located in the Watergate office and apartment complex. Some of the burglars were identified as previously having interaction with the Central Intelligence Agency, but the fifth was even more interesting. That was James W.

McCord, Jr. He was the security chief of the Committee to Re-elect the President. People would later refer to this committee as CREEP. Yes, really.

Anyway, a couple of junior reporters at the time, including Carl Bernstein and Bob Woodward, put the story in the Washington Post the next day. And they kept tugging on threads. A quick side note here. Both reporters really were very junior, covering back-page crime beats and such. What a way to launch a career...

It soon seemed there might be more going on here than the White House initially claimed, referring to the event as a "third-rate burglary attempt." The White House, through minions, began to muddy the story, create alibis, and pressure the FBI to cool it on the investigation. But Bernstein, Woodward and the FBI persevered. As the campaign season continued, it started to become clear that these shenanigans were not a singular event, but more of a regular pattern.

Things dragged on as government scandals tend to do. The reporters continued dropping a steady stream of stories, making bigger and bigger claims of White House involvement in this shady (and illegal) re-election strategy. On October 10th, the Post launched its front page story claiming White House aides were directly involved.

And things dragged on more. The five burglars went to trial, and Judge John J. Sirica kept the pressure on, arguably stepping far over the boundaries of a simple burglary case. His strategy was to "encourage" the defendants to speak more freely. In other words, spill the beans on who ordered them to do what.

The election came and went. Nixon won in a landslide, and the investigation continued. By mid-1973, Congress was holding the obligatory hearings and continuing to dig. Throughout the rest of that year, underlings in the administration were getting fired in hopes they could be blamed and shield the President.

Then there were the tapes. Nixon recorded all goings on in the Oval Office for posterity, but that came back to bite him. Resisting all attempts to provide the investigation with copies of the tapes related to these events, he finally delivered some of the subpoenaed tapes, but one had a mysterious and unexplainable 18.5-minute gap. Hmm. As we moved into 1974, the Supreme Court ordered the White House to release the tapes.

On August 8, 1974, it's finally over. Facing impeachment and certain eviction from office, Nixon resigned. He's the first and only President ever to do so.

The results were predictable. Growing distrust of the government. Recognition that maybe too much power does corrupt. Perhaps the founders were onto something with those ideas of balancing power to prevent just this sort of thing. Last but not least, Watergate proved, very publicly, that even the President is not above the law.

The identity of the famous Watergate whistleblower "Deep Throat" remained a mystery for over 30 years. The nickname wasn't some clever code name dreamed up in a smoke-filled newsroom. It really was a cheeky reference to the hit 1972 adult film *Deep Throat*. Washington Post editor Howard Simons coined it as a private newsroom joke, and it stuck. For decades, speculation ran wild about Deep Throat's identity, with guesses ranging from White House insiders to the CIA. It wasn't until 2005 that former FBI Associate Director Mark Felt revealed himself as the source.

Chapter 26

Reagan, Gorbachev, and the End of the Cold War

One was a cowboy, the other a reformer. Together, they helped thaw a 40-year freeze. This chapter explores Reagan's rhetoric, Gorbachev's glasnost, and how the Cold War collapsed with more speeches than shots.

Ronald Reagan's Evil Insults

Doesn't it seem like enduring quotes always seem to come from some peripheral conversation? For example, the phrase "separation of church and state" is nowhere to be found in the Constitution, but rather, it came from a personal letter written by Thomas Jefferson. And this one, the "Evil Empire," was taken from a March 1983 speech by President Ronald Reagan to the National Association of Evangelicals in Orlando, Florida.

When he branded the Soviet Union as an "Evil Empire," no one was particularly shocked, as they kind of had acted like weenies for quite some time. The phrase had a ring to it, both as a sound bite and a ring of truth, and so it stuck, becoming a newspaper headline phrase everywhere.

Whether or not President Reagan hoped for the widespread adoption of the phrase, it turned out to be quite an effective characterization. Instead of framing the Cold War as the United States and its allies against some other geopolitical foe, it turned the standoff into a moral issue. You know, good versus evil. Communism wasn't just another abstract government; it was a moral threat to everything clean and wholesome. Everyone could understand that at the time.

Supporters, tired of years of appeasement and, in their view, allowing the Soviet Union to grow unchecked, loved the clear rejection in simple moral terms. Critics feared the consequences of what they saw as reckless language, not appropriate for international diplomacy. Was this cowboy president trying to start a nuclear war or something?

Reagan's "Evil Empire" speech symbolized a sharp and deliberate pivot from timid coexistence to direct confrontation, even if it was just in words. At a time when Reagan's policy was a military buildup of peace through strength, it helped clarify his argument to the American people.

Reagan's "Evil Empire" speech got another round of headlines in 1987 thanks to Hollywood. George Lucas, already annoyed that his Star Wars films had been linked to the Strategic Defense Initiative, wasn't thrilled about journalists suddenly calling the Soviets the "Evil Empire" either. Lucasfilm even joked that both sides of the Cold War were hijacking his galaxy far, far away. The phrase, however, took on a life of its own, used by newspapers, commentators, and even comedians. By the end of the decade, it had become one of Reagan's most famous one-liners.

Star Wars, For Real?

Doesn't it always seem like things taken for granted today were mocked not so long ago?

One such example was the Strategic Defense Initiative, not-very-lovingly mocked and criticized as "Star Wars" back when it was in the idea stage.

When it became a public mission back in 1983, remember the global conditions. The Cold War was still going strong. Everyone and their brother were building enough nuclear weapons to vaporize the Sun, with a few bombs left over. The only "defense" against nuclear war was the concept of Mutually Assured Destruction (MAD). Which, while effective so far, sounds kind of silly. The other guy won't attack you because you'll blow him up too, then he'll blow you up some more, and so on. No one wins in the end, so it's not worth starting a fight in the first place.

Anyway, the idea behind SDI was to develop and construct an actual defense against a future rainstorm of incoming nuclear missiles. Simply put, the plan was to develop defensive satellites armed with lasers in space to shoot down or otherwise destroy incoming missiles before they reached the United States.

People laughed because the technology didn't exist at the time, and it was tough for the average person to comprehend how such a pervasive and futuristic system could be implemented. Remember, this was long before WiFi and the iPhone.

Others recognized how technology has this recurring habit of marching forward and shocking people with new capabilities. For example, when this program was announced, who wouldn't have laughed at the idea of someone having a televised conversation with a friend across the globe using a pocket-sized device with no wires? Yet billions of us do that every day. And, as we know, lots of militaries are in fact shooting screaming missiles out of the sky one way or another. It may not be with laser beams (yet), but few would argue that's not far off.

Among the "I'm worried about this" crowd were the Soviets. Any such system, even if only partially effective, would undermine their strategy of nuclear deterrence and, in their view, give the United States the possible advantage of preemptive strike capability.

At the time, SDI never became a reality in the way Reagan described. Lasers in space couldn't zap missiles from the sky, at least in that era. But the program did put serious pressure on the Soviet Union at a time when it simply couldn't afford to keep up. The result? In the not-too-distant future, that pressure helped bring them to the bargaining table and into arms control agreements.

When President Reagan announced the Strategic Defense Initiative in 1983, the nickname "Star Wars" wasn't just a political jab—it became a pop-culture phenomenon. Star Wars creator George Lucas wasn't thrilled about his blockbuster title being hijacked for missile defense, and Lucasfilm even filed a lawsuit to stop its use in connection with SDI. The suit failed when judges ruled that "Star Wars" had already become part of the public vocabulary.

Glasnost & Perestroika: The Soviet Makeover

By the mid-1980s, the folks in the Communist Soviet Union were getting a bit out of control. Economic decline, unrest at home, and a populace seeing freedom around the rest of the world put pressure on the Kremlin to make some adjustments.

Mikhail Gorbachev became the General Secretary of the Soviet Union in 1985, and in short order, he launched two areas of reform.

Glasnost was, with only a slight risk of oversimplification, kind of like deciding to quell some of the festering unrest by treating the Soviet population like adults. For decades, censorship had been the norm. Criticize the government? Not allowed. Speak freely about social issues? No. That was discouraged as well. One couldn't even speak ill of previous government foibles, like Stalin's behavior decades earlier. Think "Big Brother" everywhere.

Glasnost eased the pressure on such things. While it would be a stretch to describe the new environment as "free speech" friendly, the new rules were far less restrictive than anything in the recent past. Pre-publication censorship of the media, while not eliminated, was greatly reduced. Public debate was even encouraged, and at least moderate criticism of the government was tolerated.

A parallel effort, perestroika, started the long, slow process of opening up the markets. For decades, production and industry had been centrally planned. If the Kremlin said to produce 100 pierogis, you produced 100 pierogis, whether or not there was a market for them. Oh, and they set the prices, costs and wages.

It didn't work. Products were junk. Either over- or under-produced. Bread lines were a real thing. The concept of a Western grocery store, chock full of, well, everything, was a foreign concept, unimaginable to most Soviet citizens.

Under perestroika, local facilities could make more of the market and production decisions based on need and availability. That included negotiating contracts and setting prices. The program even allowed for private ownership of some types of businesses.

All of this radical reform was accompanied by increased dialogue with the West and reluctance to use the Soviet military to quash unrest, especially in the satellite states of the time, including Poland and East Germany. This set the stage for some of them to break free of the Soviet system later.

Glasnost didn't just open up politics; it opened up culture. For the first time, Soviet citizens got official access to Western pop music, films, and books that had long been banned or hidden away. Lines formed outside Moscow theaters showing "forbidden" movies, and albums by artists like Bruce Springsteen and the Beatles, which had previously been black-market-only items, started selling openly. One Soviet journalist even joked that Gorbachev's reforms would be remembered less for politics and more as "the time we finally got to watch Rambo without fear of arrest."

Mr. Gorbachev, About That Wall...

Remember that part of perestroika where Gorbachev was reluctant to continue using force to quell unrest in the satellite regions of the Soviet Union? One of those was East Germany.

The Berlin Wall, erected in 1961, had stood for over 28 years, but unrest was growing on the Eastern side of the wall. In 1987, President Reagan, in a speech delivered at a wall border crossing, even demanded, "Mr. Gorbachev, tear down this wall!"

Glasnost and reform demands spread across Eastern Europe, including East Germany. Protests demanding democracy were spreading in Hungary, Estonia, Latvia and Lithuania. Now it was Easy Germany's turn.

On November 4, half a million people gathered at the Alexanderplatz in the heart of East Berlin. Just days later, a hasty response of loosening travel restrictions for East Germans inadvertently knocked down the wall.

The announcement was intended to communicate that there would be minor changes coming to the travel system on November 10. But the simple message delivered to the East German spokesperson Günter Schabowski didn't have all the requisite details. He read it to the press, clearly unprepared with the full story and the underlying logistical details.

"Private travel outside the country can now be applied for without prerequisites."

When asked by reporters when that was to take effect, he replied that, as far as he knew, it was effective immediately.

The dam burst, and thousands of East Berliners rushed to the border crossings, overwhelming the guards, who had received premature and incomplete news. Without orders, the border guards had no real choice other than to open the gates and allow passage.

That was it.

The botched communication of minor loosening of the crossing regulations had become a stampede, and the crowds turned it into a wall-destruction party. Out came the hammers and pickaxes, followed by heavy equipment and bulldozers. There was no containing the exodus and destruction of the wall.

The greatest symbol of the Iron Curtain was no more, and President Reagan's demand from two and a half years earlier was fulfilled.

After the Berlin Wall came down, Berliners discovered a new cottage industry: selling chunks of the Wall itself. Street vendors chipped off colorful fragments covered in graffiti and offered them as souvenirs to tourists who wanted to take home a piece of history. The demand was so high that some vendors ran out of "authentic" wall rubble and started selling ordinary bits of concrete painted to look like Wall pieces.

Cold War? What Cold War?

Cracks had been appearing in the Soviet empire far beyond those created in the Berlin Wall in 1989. Years of systemic failure, shortages, hard living, and oppressive government had taken a toll.

Now that the government was less prone to harsh retribution and violence under the Glasnost policy, republics under the Soviet umbrella began to fall like dominoes in favor of independence and rejection of Kremlin control.

One by one, Soviet republics declared sovereignty. In August 1991, hardline communists attempted a coup to stop and reverse the new reforms, but the effort failed and only served to accelerate the process.

Once feared, the Soviet Union was now a lame duck.

On December 25, 1991, Gorbachev resigned as president of the USSR, and the iconic hammer and sickle flag was lowered from the Kremlin for the last time. In its place rose the Russian tricolor.

The United States and its allies had seemingly won the Cold War without a battle or a shot fired. Simply put, the Soviet Union ceased to exist. Like those old buildings set for demolition, it just quietly imploded.

Fifteen new nations emerged from the chaos, including Russia, Ukraine, and the Baltic states of Estonia, Latvia, and Lithuania.

Now, the United States was the last superpower standing. For a time. A new world order was on the horizon, but what would that look like, and what would be America's role in it?

When the Soviet Union collapsed in December 1991, it left behind the world's largest nuclear arsenal of over 27,000 nuclear weapons scattered across four newly independent countries: Russia, Ukraine, Belarus, and Kazakhstan. Suddenly, the U.S. faced a terrifying question: who controlled all those bombs? To prevent loose nukes from ending up on the black market, Washington rushed to act. The result was the Nunn–Lugar Cooperative Threat Reduction Program, which provided U.S. funding and expertise to dismantle thousands of warheads and secure materials.

Chapter 27

21st Century War

From terrorists to bio-threats, modern wars re-shaped the country's understanding of conflicts. The new "traditional" wars were anything but, with a lack of battle lines and clear objectives. Invisible enemies who were often indistinguishable from the population increased the challenges and dangers to U.S. warfighters.

Get ready to explore America's modern wars, including the one against invisible germs, and how those impacted life here at home forever.

Desert Shield, Desert Storm, Desert Done

As the Soviet Union was steadily fading, things got a little heated in the Middle East, and the United States was faced with a dilemma.

In August 1990, Iraqi dictator Saddam Hussein ordered his army to invade and occupy neighboring Kuwait, a small but very oil-rich nation. The attack not only surprised the world, but it also rocked the global oil markets. The United States, under President George H. W. Bush, quickly condemned the aggression and began assembling a broad international coalition to push Iraq back behind its own borders.

At first, the efforts to thwart Iraq were limited to the conference table. U.S. diplomats worked with counterparts at the United Nations to pass resolutions demanding Iraq's withdrawal. Iraq, led by Saddam Hussein, flat-out refused. Whether Hussein didn't believe the U.S. and the remainder of the coalition would actually resort to force or had an inflated view of his own military capability, he continued to play hardball and seemed unconcerned about the growing pressure.

Cue up Operation Desert Shield. Step one was a massive military buildup in Saudi Arabia, ostensibly to protect it from invasion, too. It was no big secret that this buildup of forces also provided a great launching pad for a future attack to liberate Kuwait.

In January 1991, the operation shifted to Desert Storm, a relentless air campaign to be followed by a powerful ground assault. The bombing continued for weeks while the world watched video clips of precision smart weapons methodically destroying Iraqi infrastructure. With no real opposition in the air, the coalition took its time dismantling Iraqi defensive capability.

By the time the ground campaign started, Iraqi forces had had enough, and the invasion forces liberated Kuwait in just 100 hours.

Consistent with the public mission to liberate Kuwait, President Bush elected to hold back and not march on Baghdad, ousting Saddam Hussein in the process. It's unlikely the Iraqi army could have mounted any serious defense. It's more likely that coalition leaders and Bush feared the uncertainty of a power vacuum and had little desire to take on an extended presence in what was certain to become an even more chaotic Iraq.

If the Vietnam War was brought into Americans' living rooms every evening via the nightly news, the Gulf War was delivered in real time, 7x24. With smart bombs equipped with cameras and pilot views of air strike runs, viewers literally saw the bombs hit. Modern war had become a video game.

The Gulf War introduced Americans to something new: "the video game war." CNN, still a relatively young cable network, broadcast live from Baghdad as U.S. cruise missiles lit up the night sky. Millions of viewers tuned in around the clock, making the Gulf War the first real 24-hour televised war. One of the most striking visuals was footage from smart bombs equipped with cameras that showed the weapon guiding itself straight into a target. For many Americans, the war felt both distant and strangely close. They were safe on the couch, but with a front-row seat to precision warfare.

9/11: The Day the Sky Fell

Everything changed on a September morning in 2001.

The world had grown accustomed to occasional airline hijacking attempts. Enough were successful that the normal response was to do what the hijackers wanted until, if and when the situation allowed a peaceful resolution or a rescue operation could be mounted.

But this event ended that traditional "hijacking agreement." Nineteen al-Qaeda terrorists, who'd infiltrated the United States, boarded four commercial flights, prepared to do something the world had never seen.

Years in the planning, these terrorists went deep undercover, entering he country on student and other visas and going to great lengths to distance themselves from extremist communities and did their best to blend in, or at least not draw attention.

As their plot was a new one, no one sounded alarms when these young men took flight training at various centers, some of them going so far as to learn via simulators how to fly commercial airlines of the types they intended to attack.

The planning was meticulous, up to the point of carefully vetted and developed IDs and even dry runs to practice navigating the U.S. air travel system.

On the morning of September 11, 2001, they boarded those four flights and commenced their attack. Seizing control of the planes shortly after takeoff with nothing more than box cutters, the team encountered relatively little resistance at first. Passengers and crew were operating under the old paradigm of thinking that the events were hijacking initiatives by a group with political or other demands.

Sadly, the plan was far more lethal. Two of the four planes struck the World Trade Center towers in New York City. Within hours, both had collapsed, killing nearly 3,000 office workers and emergency responders.

The third plane struck the U.S. Pentagon, the nerve center of the entire military complex.

The fourth flight, United 93, never reached its target, likely the United States Capitol. It's probable the White House was an alternate target for that attack. By then, passengers had gotten word through cell phone calls about the other three planes and knew they had to fight back. A group stormed the cockpit, and in the ensuing struggle, the plane crashed into a Pennsylvania field.

Who was responsible? The credit went to Osama bin Laden, leader of al-Qaeda. From his base in Afghanistan, bin Laden had declared a new kind of war on the United States, blaming the country for propping up regimes in the Middle East and for stationing troops near Islam's holy sites. His goal was more than one-time destruction. He desired a long and costly war.

He got it.

The response was near immediate as the U.S. launched Operation Enduring Freedom. The goal was simple, but the execution complex: topple the Taliban regime that had sheltered and enabled al-Qaeda while they planned the 9/11 attacks.

At home, air travel was forever changed. A new federal department under Homeland Security, the Transportation Security Administration, was created and staffed at record speed. While metal detectors were nothing new, the federal machine took over at airports across the country, establishing new procedures, hiring tens of thousands of agents, and buying loads of new equipment. In addition to striking the heart of America's economic center, the attacks had cost the country untold billions related to new security procedures and delays.

While it's difficult to compare to other shockwave events in American history, the 9/11 attacks and resulting actions became a before-and-after dividing line. The attacks and the government response raised questions we're still grappling with today over the balance between civil liberties and national security.

On the morning of September 11, 2001, every civilian aircraft flying in U.S. airspace, about 4,500 planes, was ordered to land immediately. It was the first time in history that the Federal Aviation Administration grounded the entire national airspace. Pilots diverted to the nearest airports, sometimes landing massive jets at small regional fields never designed for jumbo jets. In Canada, the sudden arrival of 38 flights carrying nearly 7,000 passengers in the tiny town of Gander, Newfoundland, inspired a days-long act of hospitality that later became the Broadway musical *Come From Away*.

The War on Terror, Times Two

It didn't take long after the attacks on 9/11 for things to go kinetic on the other side of the world.

In a move aimed at attacking the people and places that had enabled terrorist safe harbors for planning and training, the United States launched Operation Enduring Freedom on October 7, 2001. The initial plan was, along with British forces, to execute a massive air campaign combined with advisory and support functions, helping the Northern Alliance in Afghanistan to reclaim the country from the Taliban.

It didn't take long for the al-Qaeda camps to scatter and to remove the Taliban from power. But scattering the enemy is not historically the same as defeat in Afghanistan. The operation turned into a long-term conflict of insurgency and terror within the rugged country. Al-Qaeda and Taliban forces continued a campaign of resistance from within the population, and the initial lightning strike campaign became one of winning the peace, with building a new nation becoming a requirement.

Over the 20-year campaign, the American troops on the ground levels changed dramatically, reflecting the current strategy. For example, in 2001, there were fewer than 1,300 Americans in the country, consistent with the goal of helping the Northern Alliance achieve mutually beneficial objectives. U.S. presence grew over the next ten years, reflecting a growing need to crush the insurgency. By 2010, the "surge" strategy had about 100,000 troops in country. From that point, until the end in 2021, troop levels were gradually reduced until they reached just 2,500.

As the objectives expanded in Afghanistan, so did the War on Terror.

On March 20, 2003, U.S., British and other Allied forces invaded Iraq in a campaign to oust Iraqi Dictator Saddam Hussein and seize suspected weapons of mass destruction.

Over 100,000 troops were in Iraq during the early years of the conflict. Considering rotations in and out, over a million American soldiers served in the country at some point. During the peak "surge" campaigns in 2007, the U.S. had some 170,000 troops present.

As in Afghanistan, initial objectives were achieved quickly, although weapons of mass destruction were never found. Baghdad fell in just three weeks, with other major cities taken in short order. By May 1, 2003, President Bush announced the end of major combat operations. But, as in Afghanistan, the insurgency continued, and it became clear the Iraqi people weren't ready to self-govern under a democratic structure. By December 2011, U.S. combat operations ended, and most troops were returned home, leaving a small training and counterterrorism force of about 2,500.

The two wars left plenty of scars at home. The financial costs were astronomical, with some studies placing the price tag in the four to six trillion dollar range, counting direct military operations, infrastructure and nation building, veterans' medical and long-term support programs and homeland security costs.

But the real costs were to the American soldiers who fought in both countries. Military deaths numbered over 7,000 in the two wars. Direct physical injuries numbered over 53,000, while those with long-term health issues, including PTSD and traumatic brain injuries, could be as high as hundreds of thousands.

In modern history, no country has ever achieved a sustained victory against Afghanistan. In the 19th and 20th centuries, Britain fought three wars there, achieving tactical successes, but nothing that lasted. Forces eventually withdrew in all three conflicts. The Soviets fought in Afghanistan for a decade, from 1979 to 1989, but never achieved a lasting victory. The United States and allies fought in the country for 20 years and ended up leaving in 2021.

The combination of brutal terrain and decentralized tribal

society has kept the country a seemingly impossible target of conquest.

Osama bin Laden: America's Most Wanted Man

What about the ultimate bad guy? What happened to him after 9/11?

If there was ever a guy more wanted dead or alive than Osama bin Laden, I can't remember who it was. OK, maybe Hitler, but bin Laden instantly became America's most despised villain after the 9/11 attacks.

From day one, the United States intelligence and military machines were on a full-time hunt for the guy who had masterminded the deadliest attacks on American soil, ever.

As U.S. forces moved into Afghanistan to dismantle the terrorist-supporting regime there, it was believed he was hiding out in the rugged Tora Bora mountain complex. U.S. forces bombed and, in conjunction with Afghan units, attacked the cave complexes for weeks in an effort to kill or dislodge him and his followers. At some point during the chaos, bin Laden managed to escape the tightening noose and slip into Pakistan. His escape from the world's most powerful military shows how difficult it is to find and capture one man in such an unfriendly environment.

Then he became a virtual ghost. While he continued to smuggle out video messages and inspiration to his followers, no one could find him for almost a decade. Bin Laden's refusal to use forms of communication like cell phones thwarted modern surveillance efforts.

But in 2010, the Central Intelligence Agency caught a break through good old detective work. They identified a courier known to be associated with the movement and tracked him to a compound in Abbottabad, Pakistan. It was an unusual complex with no phones, big walls and hermit-like residents who never left the place. That raised suspicions.

On May 1, 2011, almost ten years after the 9/11 attacks, then-President Barack Obama authorized a strike mission. U.S. Navy SEALs executed a daring raid on the target. Flying into the compound on stealth-modified Blackhawk helicopters, with the Pakistani government having no knowledge of the raid, they quickly seized the complex from within. In less than 40 minutes, bin Laden was finally dead, and the SEALs retrieved his body for proof.

In a world of satellite surveillance and smart bombs and missiles, it was old-fashioned detective work and brave troops with rifles who finally ended the manhunt.

The raid on bin Laden's compound, named Operation Neptune Spear, was very nearly a disaster. One of the two helicopters crash landed inside the compound. There were no serious injuries, but the aircraft was unflyable and had to be destroyed with explosives as the assault teams left. There is some controversy about what happened. Official accounts say the helicopter experienced what's known as a vortex ring state on the way in and became unstable when just off the ground. The pilot forced it down to prevent it from flipping over, and it ended up leaning against the compound wall. A conflicting account claims that the helicopter had already dropped an assault team on a roof and was repositioning when it crashed.

Freedom vs. Fear: The Patriot Act Debate

Earlier, we discussed how fear caused the nation to turn against its own Japanese American citizens after the attack on Pearl Harbor. When the war on Terror began in New York City on September 11, 2001, a similar scenario replayed.

While there was certainly backlash against Muslim citizens and visitors after 9/11, other lasting effects were the result of legislative changes that changed the balance of freedom and security.

Passed almost immediately after 9/11 in October 2001, the PATRIOT Act dramatically expanded the government's ability and authority to, well, spy on pretty much everyone. You might get a clue to the intent of the PATRIOT Act by its very name. Did you know PATRIOT stands for "Providing Appropriate Tools Required to Intercept and Obstruct Terrorism?"

In short, the act allows law enforcement and intelligence agencies to monitor phone, email and other communications if linked to terrorism investigations. And there are provisions allowing the government to expand oversight and monitoring of financial system activity. You get the idea.

Critics of the PATRIOT Act point to abuse and loss of privacy. Like many things, it sounds great on the surface. Who wouldn't want the government to be able to chase terrorists? But critics also believe the devil is in the details. Without sufficient judicial oversight, abuse is far too easy.

A guy and former NSA contractor, Edward Snowden, kinda blew the lid off things back in 2013 by leaking thousands of classified documents. This document dump showed the public that the spying and "listening in" activity wasn't limited to active terrorism investigations. The NSA was routinely collecting phone and internet data from ordinary citizens. Oops.

Was Snowden a hero or a zero? Did he blow the lid off government abuse of power, or did he recklessly endanger the government's ability to keep the country secure? That's for you to decide; we're just relaying the story.

And the story is, the action rekindled the PATRIOT Act debate.

The Patriot Act has since been tweaked, changed, and challenged in court, but the underlying discussion remains. Technology marched forward, so there are new ways to communicate and new ways for the government to eavesdrop.

A quarter century after 9/11, we're still asking, "How do you protect both the nation and the freedoms that define it?"

One of the stranger ripple effects of the PATRIOT Act involved library records. Section 215 of the law gave the FBI authority to demand "any tangible thing" for investigations, including the books people checked out at their local library. Librarians across the country rebelled, some posting cheeky signs warning patrons: "The FBI may be monitoring what you read." In fact, the American Library Association became one of the loudest voices against the Act, arguing that privacy at the library was part of American freedom. It even inspired a wave of "read-in" protests where people defiantly checked out books with provocative titles.

The Bio-Battle

In early 2020, Americans were doing their normal American things when a new word began to surface: coronavirus.

It began as some strange and unknown thing happening in China, but thanks to modern air and sea travel, it quickly became a worldwide event. By March, it was widely known as COVID-19 and struck fear into millions. The fear part was likely compounded by this being an "enemy" one couldn't see, feel or touch. You might or might not get it, and it might or might not kill you. Humans generally aren't comfortable with that kind of scenario.

Daily reports from the media and anecdotal stories from the social channels contributed to the panic. Hospitals were full. People were dying. There appeared to be a chronic shortage of medical supplies and equipment, like ventilators.

Then the lockdowns started. People were advised, and in some cases, ordered, to remain at home. Businesses shut down. Schools closed. The normal supply chains were disrupted, and it became impossible to find a roll of toilet paper.

The government messaging quickly became one of "flatten the curve," meaning, "Hey, if we all stay inside and avoid spreading this thing, we can slow down the pandemic in a couple of weeks." What was supposed to be a two-week flattening of the curve exercise became more like months, and in some cases, longer.

Some states imposed strict lockdowns, while others resisted prolonged restrictions. Mask mandates and new vaccines ignited all sorts of controversy, and everyone became a virology expert thanks to social media, although I never could find evidence of Facebook awarding PhDs in the subject. Good times...

By mid-2021, most of the panic had subsided, and COVID became more like a bad flu, still potentially lethal to some but not as exotic and mysterious as the 1.0 version. Some people continued to have serious medical complications from it, while others shook it off after a week or so.

In the end, authorities reported over 1.2 million Americans died from COVID. Did they die from COVID or with COVID? The medical community struggled with how to accurately consider the fatalities. If a patient presented with high blood pressure, pneumonia, diabetes and COVID, and later died, what caused it? Welcome to the challenge of medical record keeping. It's likely impossible to reflect pinpoint accuracy in terms of a singular cause of death. Like all public debates, this one will likely never be resolved either. Most would agree, however, that COVID caused enough damage to the country and the world at large.

The COVID era left other changes as well. People became accustomed to working from home, and many businesses found they could continue to function with all or most of the work-force working virtually. Some studies indicate that up to 22%

of the workforce continues to work from home full or part-time. That's about 32 million Americans.

Chapter 28

The Geeks Shall Inherit the Earth

The future didn't arrive with flying cars or space-based apartment towers like in *The Jetsons*. It showed up with a screeching dial-up tone and a browser that took forever and a half to load a photo. But then Moore's Law caught up. That's the one where computer power doubles every 18 months while prices fall by half. That led the tech stampede: plenty of dot-com dreams and busts, and when the dust settled, the world had changed. Our lives are now run by pocket devices while we share our dinner plates and innermost confessions with the rest of the world via social media. And more recently, AI is the new electricity: quiet, everywhere, and a little unnerving. Let's explore the digital age in America.

From Pets.com to Profits.com

If you're old enough to remember the era when station wagons roamed the earth, then you know the internet we take for granted today started with warbles, chirps and CDs in cereal boxes.

Unimaginable in our current environment of supercomputer-like power in our pocket smartphones, America's transformation to the digital age began with dial-up message board access with a landline telephone using a $3,000 computer that really couldn't do much of anything.

At least if you were lucky enough to make a connection to that "server" in the "cloud," you could choose from a list of five or ten options to do something profound like leave a text-only message for someone else. To put things in perspective, one could theoretically transmit just the words in this section across the phone lines in about 4 seconds using the latest and greatest gear. Heady days for sure.

But some saw the future of where this painful online process could end up one day. And those with all the great ideas flocked to Silicon Valley with dreams of convincing venture capitalists they were going to change the world.

No one knew for sure what exactly the future would look like, but there were hazy pictures of everyone buying everything online, entertainment at your fingertips, endless music libraries delivered to your home and later your car and pocket. So, the business model was simple, if overly hyped. Put a dot-com at the end of a catchy company name, and investors flocked to your door.

That worked great for a while. Profits? Didn't matter. Build an audience, and the money will eventually materialize. But eventually someone had to pay the piper. As it turns out, even frothing-at-the-mouth high-tech investors want to get their money back at some point.

Pets.com wasn't the cause of some return to sanity, but it was a classic example of many similar situations. The company started with the most valuable internet name ever—Pets.com! And they sold...pet stuff! Who in their right mind wouldn't just type those eight characters into their browsers whenever they wanted something for their beloved pets? The company spent millions on advertising and promotion because, well, the revenue and profits would come eventually. But after $70 million in advertising, first-year sales were only a shade over $600,000.

As it turns out, huge bags of dog food aren't cheap to ship and deliver to one's home. And people like to browse the aisles for dog toys for their energetic pups. In fact, they even enjoy taking Fido to the store to shop for himself. Pets.com never did turn a profit and went belly up in November of 2000.

But the early hype created yet another bubble. Remember when we discussed the stock market of the 1920s?

And, like in the 1920s, then came the crash. Between 2000 and 2002, the bubble didn't burst; it exploded. The tech-company-heavy NASDAQ lost nearly 80 percent of its value. Countless startups collapsed in short order. If you were in the market for slightly used trendy office furniture, it was a great time to be a buyer. Apparently, the basic rules of business, like the need to make a profit, still applied, even on the internet.

In fairness, the internet did change almost everything about shopping; it just took time and effort to figure out sensible business models. Just ask Amazon.com. And Google. And eBay. And many others. In fact, many of the world's most valuable companies are now tech behemoths with assets of bits and bytes in the cloud rather than inventory, equipment and factories.

During the height of the dot-com bubble, office chairs and Aeron furniture became status symbols of startup culture. Herman Miller's Aeron chair, which sold for about $1,000 each, was so popular that some investors joked you could measure a startup's "seriousness" by how many they had in their loft office. When the bubble burst in 2000–2002, so many failed dot-coms dumped their pricey chairs at auction that the Aeron briefly became the cheapest high-end seat on the used-furniture market. Today, it's remembered as the "chair of the dot-com boom."

Surfing the Web, Then Living in It

In the early 1990s, only about 1% of the world's population was online. The other 99% weren't missing much. Here in America, by 1995, right about 10% of people were online, plugging into their phone lines, and not getting all that much in return. At the time, with those blazing-fast 56K modems, they could download a single, pretty lousy resolution image in a minute, more or less.

But things moved fast. By the end of the 90s, as we approached the end of humanity with the looming Y2K threat, broadband internet access through cable and DSL was on the move. It reached about half of US households by the year 2000, just in time for the much-feared Y2K Armageddon. As a comparison, downloading that same kinda lousy image now took about half a second. Getting a decent photo (for the time) might take two to three seconds.

Then things took off. That whole critical mass of internet infrastructure and broadband access put over 1 billion people online worldwide by 2005. A mere fifteen years later, that number had exploded to about 4.5 billion. In the United States, as I write this, internet access penetration is somewhere in the neighborhood of 92%.

And the capabilities have grown even faster than the access. In just 30 years, the speed of data transmission has increased a million-fold. This matters because higher speeds make possible the things we now take for granted, like videos, music, movies and broadcast television, not to mention all the important stuff like managing the world's financial transactions and conducting business. Can you even imagine putting together an InstaCart grocery order using a dial-up modem?

So, first, we made the internet pervasive and lightning fast, capable of delivering all the information we'd use in a lifetime in seconds. Then we put all that power in our pockets.

Before 2007, mobile phones were clunky tools for calls and hard-earned texts, assuming you consider tapping a number key three times to create a single letter tiresome. Apple's iPhone changed all that starting back in June 2007. Yeah, I know, there were other devices, like Blackberries, available years before that, but they were limited in comparison and focused on messaging more than general-purpose, internet-enabled apps. The iPhone brought the power of the internet and ease of use that ignited the portable application market. Games, finances, social media, dating apps, messaging, camera, video, music, entertainment and much, much more were now available to anyone who could afford a cell phone plan.

The spread was like wildfire. In 2010, about 20% of Americans owned a smartphone; by 2019, that number had grown to something like 80%. Globally speaking, there are now over 6.9 billion (as of 2023).

And the power in the pocket is off the charts.

Earlier, we talked about how America sent men to the moon. Stop and think about this for a second. Earth is hurtling through space at 66,000 mph. And spinning at about 1,000 mph. The moon is orbiting the Earth at some speed, once every 27 days. Oh, and all this while the whole solar system is whizzing through the void at 500,000 miles per hour. And a bunch of engineers, using math, but also some early computers, launched a seven-million-pound rocket through all those moving parts, landed a piece of it on the moon, then directed an even smaller piece back home.

And the computers? The Saturn V launch vehicle digital computer had a capacity of 104KB. The Apollo command module computer used one of 76KB. And the lunar module, responsible for landing and not crashing, had just 36KB of memory. So, about 216K total.

When you take a picture with your phone, it requires (if you don't compress the photo) somewhere between 2 MB and 6 MB. Putting that in the same measurement units as the Apollo computers, that's 2,000 KB to 6,000 KB. When compressed, your Instagram pic requires about 100 KB to 200 KB of storage.

Now, back to our moon rockets. That means the amount of storage that the Apollo folks had to work with to get guys to the moon and back was about the same as that of one or maybe two compressed pictures of your pet.

My iPhone has 512 GB of storage. In other words, my phone has the storage capacity of about 2.5 million Saturn V rockets. And my phone was a heck of a lot cheaper, as the Saturn V carried a price tag of about $8.7 billion in 2025 dollars.

But what about raw computing power? Just how much of that are you carrying around in your pocket? The "massive" Apollo Guidance Computer could run 0.043 million (43,000) instructions per second. An iPhone 15 or similar zips along with over 100,000 MIPS, or one hundred thousand million instructions per second. Again, the power of your phone is the equivalent of 2.3 million Saturn V rockets.

This digital revolution didn't just connect people; it completely re-engineered our daily lives. From ordering pizza to balancing the checkbook and doing the Wordle, most daily life management can be done with our phones.

But the trade-offs became apparent, too. Many have become slaves to the notifications, calls and beckoning of whatever apps are on their phones. Attention spans have suffered, and only the future will tell what effects, if any, we'll experience with a lifetime of use.

The very first iPhone demo in 2007 was a high-wire act. The prototype Steve Jobs used on stage at Macworld was so unstable that it could only perform one task at a time before crashing. Engineers had built what they called the "golden path." That was a carefully scripted sequence of actions (like showing a webpage, then music, then a call) that Jobs had to follow exactly, or the phone would freeze. Behind the scenes, they even had multiple backup iPhones ready on the podium. The demo wowed the world, but it was held together with duct tape and prayers.

Y2K: When the World Didn't Quite End

We have to get geeky for just a minute. I know we just finished talking about the incredible power of today's technology, but it wasn't always that way. In the early days of computers, let's say before the year 2000, storage and processing power weren't infinite. When software engineers wrote programs to do everything from changing red lights to managing bank transfers to controlling air travel, every bit of computer storage mattered.

When you needed to store a year as part of a transaction of any kind, you usually just abbreviate in the data and code instructions the two-digit shortcut. For example, 1963 would be stored as "63." And so on.

But as the calendar inched toward January 1, 2000, someone figured out the bill was due for all these (necessary at the time) shortcuts.

The looming Y2K problem was simply this. What happens to all these programs and the daily activities run by them when the calendar goes from 1999 to 2000? In computer-ese, that's going from 99 to 00. And the machines would understand that "00" as 1900, not 2000.

Panic set in as no one really knew what would happen. Would planes fall out of the sky? Would financial systems melt down in confusion? Would red lights stop working properly? What about critical medical systems and records? And power grids? How about nuclear missiles and national defense systems? The list of potential problems was endless.

There was only one real solution: rewrite all the potentially at-risk computer code—fast. The federal government spent some $100 billion to identify the highest points of risk and fix them.

New Year's Eve of 1999 was a bit tentative as no one really knew what to expect. Was everything critically important fixed? Would your refrigerator go into open revolt at midnight?

The Pentagon was ready with nuclear bunker contingency plans. The White House ran a Y2K command center. President Bill Clinton tried to assure the nation in an "only partly joking" manner.

But you know humans. As at other times in the history of the United States, people kinda freaked out here and there. There were runs on basic supplies like bottled water and canned food. Survival-ists stocked up on gas, ammo and food. Some figured this was the biblical apocalypse.

Good news. We're still here. The country (and world as a whole) did not implode and fall into the Sun. There were some sporadic problems with websites, and there were reports of some casino slot machines in Delaware locking up. One nuclear power plant in Japan did have a radiation monitoring system fail, but nothing dangerous.

One computer scientist summed it up nicely: "Y2K wasn't a disaster because people treated it like it would be." That's kind of profound when you think about it.

Not everyone was convinced the Y2K "fix" would work. Some Americans went full-on prepper mode, and sales of survival gear and bunkers spiked in 1999. One Indiana man reportedly spent over $50,000 building a concrete shelter stocked with food, water, and even a goat for fresh milk. He emerged on January 1st to discover the world was humming along just fine.

Meanwhile, in Times Square, New York City's famous ball drop was Y2K-proofed with a backup generator and extra technicians on hand just in case the lights went out at midnight. They didn't.

The Gilded Age Jr.

We've gone from smokestacks, railroads and factories to warehouses full of microchips quietly humming along, creating magic. One might argue we're living in the "Gilded Age Jr." with the Carnegies and Rockefellers now replaced by Zuckerbergs and Musks.

While there are plenty of ultra-rich billionaires and billionaire families associated with "boring and traditional" businesses like fast food and Walmart stores, many of today's uber-wealthy class are first-generation tech titans who latched onto (or in some cases stole) a nifty idea and turned it into a thriving tech business. They are the inventors, disruptors, and sometimes opportunists who reshaped not only American business but also how Americans live, shop, and think.

Steve Jobs and Bill Gates have similar origin stories, although they later grew to be bitter corporate rivals.

Jobs sold his VW minibus, and partner Steve Wozniak sold his HP calculator to fund a new company, Apple Computer, in the family's garage. Their first product, the Apple I, was a DIY hobby kit most people built inside a wooden case. A year later, they released a commercially viable computer, the Apple II, and the company was off to the races.

After Jobs was booted from his own company in the 1980s, he returned in the late 1990s to revive an on-the-ropes business from near-bankruptcy. His relentless and obsessive focus on sleek design first and foremost, combined with user experience, eventually put some sort of Apple device in every pocket or home. The mission wasn't selling devices; it was fundamentally changing how we listen to music and communicate.

Bill Gates and friend Paul Allen got their start founding Microsoft by selling a BASIC programming language interpreter (that didn't yet exist) for the then-new Altair 8800 computer. About six years later, the company "Micro-Soft" made the big move, smartly insisting on licensing an operating system product, MS-DOS, to IBM instead of selling it outright for a then-amazing sum to the young software engineers. With personal computers beginning to land on every desk, that one move propelled the company into the stratosphere. The rest is history.

And then there's Elon Musk. Today, we think of Tesla, Starlink, the Boring Company and Neuralink. But a long, long time ago, way back in 1996, his business ventures began with a city directory service called Zip2. He and his brother founded the company, and when it was later sold to Compaq, Musk pocketed about $22 million. Then he got into the changing world of finance with a company that later blended into PayPal. That exit netted him about $175 million.

In 2004 and 2006, he invested some of the PayPal proceeds into SpaceX and Tesla, aiming to revolutionize spaceflight and automotive transportation. Those ventures propelled him onto the lists of mega billionaires, and his other corporate ventures didn't hurt either.

Earlier, we kind of ripped into the Pets.com business model, but some online retail businesses have done just fine. While Amazon.com seemingly was following the "who needs to make a profit" highway in the earlier years, it did eventually become financially successful. Founded at the height of the dot-com boom in 1995, it took almost eight years for the company to turn an annual profit.

While founder Jeff Bezos always had the plan to sell everything, the company deliberately started with books because there were so many unique titles that it was a natural fit for an online business. No local bookstore could ever hope to stock all, or even most of the available books. The product choice allowed Amazon to build the business while figuring out its logistics competitive advantage. Around the year 2000, the company began to rapidly expand into other product categories. Now they're seemingly in charge of planet Earth.

These people have become the Rockefellers and Carnegies of our day. There's rarely a lack of controversy surrounding some, and usually all, of them. They're admired. And criticized. And envied.

Depending on what day it is, Musk, Bezos, Zuckerberg and Gates each have an overall "average" net worth of about a quarter of a trillion dollars if you average the three. And Bill Gates is the poor one, valued at "just" $110 billion or so, so the others usually exceed the $250 billion number.

Jeff Bezos originally wanted to name Amazon "Cadabra" (as in "abracadabra"). But when his lawyer misheard it as "cadaver," Bezos quickly pivoted. He settled on "Amazon" because it started with "A" (important for early alphabetical web listings) and because the Amazon River was the largest in the world— fitting for his vision of the "world's largest bookstore." The name switch may have saved him from a very different kind of brand identity. Oh, and now that the company has expanded to everything, you'll notice the arrow in the logo extends from "A" to "Z." Get it? Everything from A to Z?

Scroll, Post, Repeat: The Social Media Revolution

It's tough to call the social media revolution a positive change when we see things like the following in our daily lives:

- Every third person driving down the road has their face buried in a phone. While driving a 4,000-pound missile down the highway at 70mph.
- You go out to a nice restaurant, and half the tables have one or more people doing nothing but reading who knows what on their phones. Seems lonely, and kind of rude, doesn't it?

- At most any social gathering, some number of people are present physically, but not mentally, because they're doing something important on their smartphone, like checking Facebook or playing Candy Crush.

While some revolutions result in freedom of expression and the ability for people to finally break free of oppression and live freely in public, the social media revolution had an arguably opposite effect. It caused Americans to move into the shadows and into themselves rather than out into the open, at least physically, if not virtually.

In fact, the social media revolution is when Americans (and the rest of the world) began narrating their entire lives. Not face-to-face, but from the distance created by a sending phone, the cloud and a receiving phone.

The "social media revolution" began in earnest with Facebook, founded in 2004. It started as a simple campus directory, picture-based, of course, and ultimately became the new, but virtual town square, complete with freedom of speech arguments. With communication now virtually unlimited and free to nearly everyone on planet Earth, human interactions have shifted from face-to-face to text and video chats for everyone, all the time.

Close on the heels of the longer sharing format of Facebook was Twitter, now officially called X. Founded in 2006 with the crazy idea of limiting posts to just 140 characters or less, it proved addictive to say the least. One now had to think hard to be able to overshare their life details in such a short format. With its limited "friendship required first" model, it allowed instant communication from everyone to everyone. Politicians loved being able to dodge the traditional media "filter" and speak directly to their constituents. Celebrities loved embarrassing themselves by posting inappropriate things during lapses in judgment. Ordinary folks loved being able to hear from people they could never hope to meet directly.

Then came the pictures. Instagram arrived in 2010, adding the power of photos. They say an Instagram is worth 1,000 words. Or something. Now, everyone was a virtual artist, trying hard to make their ordinary lives appear idyllic and postcard-worthy.

More recently, and on the heels of the YouTube video revolution, came TikTok. The short video format of this Chinese-born app, combined with a powerful algorithm that really did seem to know what you would like to see next, exploded onto the scene, especially among younger generations. Influencers weren't born on TikTok; they'd arrived before, but TikTok made the job title a career aspiration for many, many people. How-tos, life hacks, ideas, commentary, fashion, you name it, the content is there.

So take your pick. Does the social media revolution represent the downfall of all humanity? Or has it been a godsend, opening communication and social doors that could never exist without it?

The very first "viral" social media post predates TikTok dances and Instagram sunsets. In 2009, a passenger on US Airways Flight 1549 tweeted a photo of the plane floating in the Hudson River just minutes after Captain "Sully" Sullenberger's emergency landing. That single post was shared worldwide before most news crews even reached the scene. It was one of the first times social media truly outpaced traditional news, proving that an ordinary person with a phone could break a global story in real time.

Retweets, Rumors, and Reality

The early promises of social media were compelling. Everyone would have a voice. No more barriers preventing the "little guy's" voice from being heard. No more filters through the traditional media. Social media was to be the great equalizer.

In many ways, these promises came true. The world had never been so connected. Individuals never had the theoretical opportunity to reach millions. And also, in many ways, humans resorted to the same old bad behavior to negate some of the liberties made possible via social media.

There's an old saying that a lie travels halfway around the world before the truth has an opportunity to get its pants on. And that is doubly true for social media. Unlike a verbal, face-to-face falsehood, social media allows a lie to reach millions simultaneously. And if one dresses it up in something sexy or provocative, using pictures, catchy text, video, and a topic that already has everyone's emotional attachment, it'll spread like wildfire without a second look. It's just too much fun or too interesting not to hit that "share" button.

The result? False information often spreads faster than the truth because it's designed to be more sensational. Whether the source is part of an organized campaign by a foreign adversary trying to achieve some agenda here in the U.S., a troll farm trying to sell something or scam someone, or just some person who gets thrills from all the clicks and responses, the "junk" often doesn't get filtered from the real.

What does it look like in practical terms?

One study indicates that somewhere less than 1% of social media users generate the majority of false posts overall. However, the nature of these posts facilitates their spread disproportionately, thereby impacting many more readers than the number of creators would indicate. That's for posts and articles in general.

As for politics, the numbers are arguably much higher. Other studies indicate that up to 23% of political posts are somewhat untrue. And therein lies the reason for the great American debate on oversight of social media. Again, it's the age-old discussion: what's the line between liberty and safety?

Are these estimates true? Who knows. Most political "facts" are really more like political "opinions," and the views of the individual determine what is "fact" and what is "false."

Not many would argue that there's plenty of garbage and falsehood to go around on social media. It's way more fun to read and share entertaining stuff than to stop and consider whether the content might or might not be true. The bad news is that the stunning growth of artificial intelligence-based content generation capability makes it easier than ever for bad actors and trolls to create textual, photographic, and video content that simply does not exist in the real world.

In 2018, during wildfires in California, viral posts on Facebook and Twitter claimed that firefighters were setting the fires on purpose or that the blazes were started by secret government energy weapons. None of it was true, but the rumors spread so quickly that officials had to pause their emergency updates to debunk the false claims. Fire chiefs warned that the misinformation wasn't just confusing, it was actively dangerous, since it distracted people from evacuation orders and strained trust in emergency responders when time was critical.

Artificial Intelligence: The Next Great Disruptor

This is a chapter that can't be completed. As I write this, the artificial intelligence (AI) revolution is in its infancy, but growing fast. Really fast. Literally every day we hear about a new groundbreaking capability that will change how we live, work and play.

American history is filled with technological advances and their resulting impact on our society. The cotton gin, steam engines, trains and rail lines, affordable automobiles and mass-produced products, computers, the internet, and so on.

But this one has the potential to make all the others combined look like a minor case of the hiccups.

The twenty-first century saw AI leap from pure science fiction to pervasive reality. HAL, from 2001: *A Space Odyssey*, is pretty much here. We can talk to AI. We can have AI perform a growing array of tasks on our behalf. We can have AI answer all of our emails. Lawyers are presenting AI-created briefs in the courtroom. Doctors are using AI to diagnose and read X-rays. We've come a long, long way from a massive IBM computer and a chess program defeating Garry Kasparov in 1997.

The pace is stunning and scary. A 2023 survey found that one-third of U.S. workers were already using AI on the job. Much of that use is for writing code, performing research and creating graphics.

As with the dot-com gold rush of the 1990s, Silicon Valley companies like OpenAI, Google, and Anthropic are leading the charge, seizing sky-high valuations in the hundreds of billions of dollars. To beat the crowd to market, they're doing million and even billion-dollar contracts with key employees. It's that big. Sounds a bit like yet another bubble?

Where will it take us? No one really knows. Even if AI capabilities freeze in place right now, it will have a massively disruptive effect on the job market. Already, hiring of traditional coders has fallen dramatically, with some 10,000 jobs being cut in recent months. AI will certainly impact prospects for entry-level coding graduates who don't have tangible AI skills.

While Americans debate whether AI will destroy millions of jobs or simply change how the workforce "works," the impacts remain to be seen. If the past is any guide, we'll adapt, and AI will find its place as a tool to make humans more productive. Who knows, maybe it'll result in economic efficiencies that allow us more leisure time.

One interesting perspective is this. Studies have indicated that 90% of all data in existence was created in just the last two years. We can't make sense of all that information with our limited brains, but perhaps AI can put it to good use under human direction. Another data point might support this point of view. In 2024, the fastest-growing job category was "AI prompt specialist." If you're an AI rookie, that refers to someone who knows the tricks of how to talk to an AI to encourage it to produce the desired results.

The first "AI" to grab the attention of everyday Americans wasn't ChatGPT; it was IBM's Deep Blue beating world chess champion Garry Kasparov in 1997. That moment shocked people who assumed creative, intuitive games like chess were uniquely human territory. But here's the kicker: Kasparov actually won the first game of the match, and after Deep Blue's eventual victory, he accused IBM of cheating by having humans secretly feed moves to the computer. IBM denied it, retired Deep Blue immediately, and never allowed a rematch, thereby cementing the machine's place in history as the chess-playing AI that defeated the best humanity could put forward.

Chapter 29

Space, the Next Frontier. Again.

One of the high points of American history and achievement was the space program of the 1960s. The nation united over the idea of "infinity and beyond" and man's conquest of the next frontier—space.

While routine now, the idea of sending humans into the great void and eventually spreading humanity to other planets was an incredible idea at the time.

After a multi-decade lull, we're back. With satellites launching into orbit every several days and active development of Moon and

Mars-capable rocket platforms, the future looks interplanetary indeed.

Houston, we have lift off!

From Sputnik to Starlink

For most of the 20th century, launching a satellite into space was a rare, live-television-worthy event. The Soviet Union put up Sputnik in 1957, and for decades afterward, satellites were obscenely costly, bulky, and counted in the hundreds, not thousands. But in the 21st century, America has been quietly leading a space race that looks more like the dot-com boom, but in zero-G instead of Silicon Valley.

That's because the space program has changed. Once under exclusive control by NASA, with contracts for hardware and services doled out to private companies, space has gone commercial. SpaceX, Blue Origin, Virgin Galactic and a good ten or so others are focusing on different missions in the overall domain of space. Hey, capitalism is the American way!

Some are aiming at space tourism, like part of Blue Origin's mission and Virgin Galactic. Others, like SpaceX, are in the high-volume space trucking business, with some exploration thrown in.

The big gorilla right now is SpaceX, owner of the Starlink satellite network. Starlink is the space-based global communication network offering service to anywhere the sky is above. When the network is complete, that obviously means everywhere.

Starlink is not just one, or even a handful of satellites; it's thousands. As of mid-2025, Starlink has more than 6,500 satellites in orbit. Consider this. In the year 2000, there were about 600 satellites floating around Earth. In less than a decade, Starlink multiplied that count tenfold.

The pace is incredible, especially by 20th-century standards. SpaceX is averaging 15 launches per month. It's become as routine as the every-other-day Dallas, Texas, to Sydney, Australia flight. Each launch of a SpaceX Falcon 9 rocket delivers a string of 40 to 60 Starlink satellites. If you look up the schedules, you can see strings of "pearls" which are really freshly launched satellites zooming across the night sky, no telescope required.

The frequency of launches and high volume of deliveries per launch translate to somewhere between 200 and 300 new satellites every month. The ultimate goal (for now) is to have 12,000, and later 30,000 satellites in service.

Other companies are catching up fast. Amazon's "Project Kuiper" has approval for 3,200 satellites, aiming to provide broadband internet like Starlink. Other smaller companies are doing innovative things to continue to bring the cost of lobbing things into space down, like 3-D printing reusable rockets.

One big difference is the real reusability of the major components. While the Space Shuttle Program had reusable parts, like rocket booster bodies, it was no small feat to recover the leftovers and refurbish them for another flight. In the SpaceX model, the booster rockets land themselves on a barge, or more recently, have started to return to a big catcher's mitt mechanism at the spaceport. Parallel parking rockets is serious technology indeed.

Thanks to these innovations in reusability, the cost of sending a satellite into orbit has dropped dramatically. Not long ago, satellite producers faced a per-pound cost of tens of thousands of dollars. Now, the rate is just $2,000 per pound. And it will get cheaper and cheaper as we go.

In the span of just one generation, satellite launches went from being rare events of national pride to something more like space-based cell towers. No big deal when a new one goes up.

Starlink satellites are so numerous that they've actually changed what people see in the night sky. When SpaceX first started launching them in 2019, astronomers were shocked to find that long "trains" of bright satellites were streaking across telescope images. In fact, a single Starlink launch could ruin an entire night of observations at some observatories. Since then, SpaceX has added sunshades and adjusted satellite orientations to make them dimmer—but astronomers still warn that the sheer number of satellites could permanently alter how we view the stars from Earth.

Space (Traffic) Jam

While the planned networks of tens of thousands of satellites sound like a Boston traffic jam, it's important to remember there's a lot of room up there, and space between satellites and other orbital debris is generous.

However, that doesn't mean there aren't risks and concerns. With thousands of fast-moving objects circling the planet, space traffic management has become a real issue.

How fast? Low Earth orbit satellites like Starlink zip along at 17,000 miles per hour. The really high geostationary satellites are still moving a bit under 7,000 mph. So, while few and far between in "spacious" space, if one tiny thing hits something else at 17,000 miles per hour, it's a very big deal.

We're already at the point where traffic management is required. For example, astronauts aboard the International Space Station now perform avoidance maneuvers to dodge space junk.

In addition to the satellites themselves is the leftover trash, like the space version of McDonald's cups tossed on I-95. Every rocket launch leaves behind stuff like upper stages, fairings, and bolts. Sometimes, satellites break and stop listening to commands from Earth, turning them into useless debris, but those parts are still moving at 17,000 miles per hour.

Here's the problem. Any collisions between even tiny objects can send debris flying at tens of thousands of miles per hour, creating even more tiny objects flying off in unpredictable directions, also moving at 17,000 miles per hour. Something as small as a paint chip moving at that kind of velocity can punch a crater in a spacecraft window. Now imagine what bits of metal can do.

Scientists call the potential nightmare the Kessler Syndrome, named after NASA scientist Donald Kessler. Back in 1978, he was pondering the potential problems of too much space debris. What would happen if one object hit another? The potential ramifications are frightening.

Too much stuff in orbit could trigger a chain reaction. If one satellite collides with another, the fragments become new missiles, possibly smashing into more satellites, which create more projectiles. The problem is compounded by the fact that there is no air resistance to slow this debris down; it just keeps flying around until it hits even more stuff.

In Kessler's theory, this cascading effect could produce a dense cloud of space junk around Earth. If there's enough of that, the cloud could make certain orbits unusable for decades or even centuries. That could mean no more launches at all, as departing rockets would risk being hit by even a small piece of space junk.

As of now, there are 36,000 tracked objects in orbit that are larger than a baseball and more than 130 million pieces of smaller debris. That number is more of an estimate, but whatever the actual count, it's significant. The U.S. Space Command tracks these objects and works to predict possible collisions. This allows satellite controllers to make small, routine adjustments to flight paths to avoid catastrophes. In fact, that International Space Station maneuver is done several times per year to dodge debris.

When might this happen? Well, on a small scale, it already has. Back in 2009, an old and inoperable Russian satellite crashed into an active Iridium communications satellite. That collision created 2,000 pieces of trackable new space debris. So, the skies are already crowded, at least in the lower orbital zones.

Fortunately, it's not a predestined problem for the space industry. Options exist for proactive space cleanup, removing older and obsolete satellites from the skies, cleaning up debris, and so on. And new satellites could be programmed with a planned "death date" to deorbit them when they're no longer useful. Whatever the solutions, the space industry needs to get on the ball. Some experts warn of reaching a critical density in as little as 20 or 30 years, assuming we don't start cleaning up soon.

The United States, as the most active space player, is both the largest contributor and potentially the most vulnerable in the worst-case scenario. NASA is experimenting with cleanup missions, including robotic "space tugs" and giant nets or harpoons to drag debris down into the atmosphere.

The very first documented case of space junk hitting Earth didn't even cause a dent. In 1969, a piece of metal debris from a Soviet spacecraft reentered the atmosphere and landed in rural Cuba, smashing into a farm and killing a cow. The Cuban government actually filed an official claim against the Soviet Union for damages. That event is believed to be the first "space junk liability" case in history. Today, under international treaties, the launching nation is still legally responsible for any damage its hardware causes once it comes back down.

The Moon: Not Just for Visits Anymore

On December 8, 1968, NASA launched Apollo 8 toward the moon to complete a lunar orbit mission. Now, almost 58 years later, NASA and other international space organizations like the European Space Agency, Japan Aerospace Exploration Agency and the Canadians will execute a series of missions to set up shop for the long term on the moon. The first manned one, scheduled for early 2026, calls for the Massive Space Launch System to fling four astronauts almost 9,000 km past the moon, the farthest man has ever been from Earth.

Like Apollo 8, the *Artemis* II crew won't land, but just orbit to shake down the systems and procedures before returning to Earth.

NASA's flagship program is named *Artemis*, for Apollo's mythological sister. The goal is ambitious: land astronauts on the moon again by the late 2020s, establish a semi-permanent presence, and use the moon as a springboard to Mars. Simple stuff, right? After all, we've already been there, but this time we have newer rockets and way more powerful computers.

Artemis I, the astronaut-less test flight, successfully orbited the moon in late 2022, proving the massive Space Launch System (SLS) rocket and Orion spacecraft can do the job.

Sometime around mid-2027, *Artemis* III hopes to complete a crewed landing on the moon, one man and one woman, somewhere near the South Pole. They are scheduled to remain on the surface for a week before beginning the trip home.

The following year, the *Artemis* IV mission will deliver and assemble additional modules to the Lunar Gateway. This is a modular "space station" to establish a more permanent presence in lunar orbit. Multiple *Artemis* missions will deliver sections for assembly once they are there.

Next up is the *Artemis* V flight, which will continue the buildout of the Lunar Gateway. Last in the initially planned sequence is *Artemis* VI to complete the Lunar Gateway Project. Ultimately, that will serve as a platform for extended lunar presence and a launching pad for future Mars missions.

Unlike the 60s space program, NASA will collaborate with other nations' space programs to establish an international presence on the moon. Also, the effort will rely heavily on private industry. SpaceX is building landers based on a lunar version of Starship, Blue Origin is participating, and the Canadians are building robotic arms for the Lunar Gateway. It all sounds a lot like the International Space Station effort, doesn't it?

The key difference from the first round of lunar landings is that this new effort focuses on building long-term infrastructure on the moon. With its far-lower-than-Earth gravity, it makes an excellent platform for staging longer missions to planets like Mars. With longer-term living accommodations in place, we can start to think about extracting raw materials like water from the lunar ice and creating fuel on the spot.

The Artemis program isn't just about planting new bootprints; it's about making space travel more sustainable. One of the coolest targets is lunar ice. Scientists have confirmed that ice exists in permanently shadowed craters near the Moon's South Pole, where sunlight never reaches. Why does that matter? Because ice isn't just for drinking, it can be split into hydrogen and oxygen, making rocket fuel. In other words, the Moon could serve as a cosmic "gas station." If Artemis astronauts can learn to mine and process that ice, it may be the key to making deep space exploration, including Mars missions, practical.

Next Stop: The Red Planet

Frequently visible with the naked eye, the red planet has captured human attention for centuries. While we've sent robots, probes and even a helicopter-like drone there, no humans have yet set foot on the Martian surface.

However, much preparation has already taken place for a future Mars mission. As far back as the Gemini programs of the 60s, humans have been experimenting and learning how to live in space for extended periods. More recently, the International Space Station, Skylab and Russian Mir have taught their own valuable lessons.

NASA has always believed in practice runs that build and prove equipment and procedures in small, incremental steps. As far back as 1965, the agency launched the *Mariner* 4 mission, which flew by the planet. A valuable first step! We can get there!

Like the manned programs closer to Earth, the next step was to orbit Mars, and *Mariner* 9 did that in 1971. While circling, the mission mapped most of the planet, revealing plenty of Earth-like features, including dried-up riverbeds, volcanoes, and canyons. No Martians spotted, however.

Time to land. That was accomplished by the *Viking* landers in 1976. *Viking* 1 and 2 captured high-resolution photos and ran experiments searching for life. The results were tantalizing but inconclusive, leaving scientists arguing for decades over hints of biological activity.

More recently, in the 1990s and 2000s, NASA's *Pathfinder* missions landed a machine capable of moving around once there. It even brought a little friend, the Sojourner Rover. After that, the *Spirit* and *Opportunity* rovers touched down. The *Opportunity* Rover was only designed to last at least 90 days, but it kept going and going and going for 15 long years until it took the Martian dirt nap.

The unmanned landers continued with *Curiosity* and *Perseverance*, which completed more sophisticated analysis, looking for evidence of past or present life. *Curiosity* did find evidence of ancient water sources and organic molecules, but still no live Martians. *Perseverance* was the one that brought the *Ingenuity* helicopter, the first "aircraft" to fly on another planet.

A human mission to Mars has been on NASA's wish list since the early days. Apollo astronauts even completed some training for the Martian environment in hopes that a Mars program was in the cards after the completion of Apollo. Unfortunately, the timing for a Mars program always seemed to be "20 years from now."

Now, it's up to the *Artemis* Program.

The moon landings and Lunar Gateway projects will set the stage for a Mars expedition. Many of the objectives for the lunar missions are prerequisites for a Mars project. For example, things like long-term radiation shielding, improved long-distance propulsion technologies, and the biggie: extracting fuel from Mars once we get there. It'll be a heck of a lot easier to make it feasible if we don't have to carry all the gas for the trip home.

Most likely, if all goes to plan, sometime in the 2030s, we'll send some stuff in advance, so when live astronauts arrive, they'll already have a place to live and some essential infrastructure in place, like that gas station.

One possibility for the trip is the SpaceX Starship rocket. You've seen them in testing already. Yes, quite a few are blowing up, but the SpaceX folks are getting there with a Starship capable of carrying 100 tons of cargo all the way to the red planet. Others, like Lockheed Martin and Blue Origin, are working on habitats and Mars landers.

There's plenty of work yet to do, but things are moving. We'll see how the *Artemis* program moves along—that should be a good indicator of the Mars schedule.

In some ways, America is coming full circle. Early in this story, we talked about those who ventured into the unknown from Siberia, then from Europe, and then Westward across the continent. Next, we're headed outward into the great void.

The "Martian marathon" is real. NASA's Opportunity rover, which was only supposed to last 90 days, kept chugging along for 15 years and in 2015 became the first vehicle to complete a full marathon on another planet—26.2 miles. NASA engineers even celebrated with a "Martian Marathon" poster and medals back on Earth. Its final message in 2018, after a dust storm coated its solar panels, broke hearts everywhere: "My battery is low and it's getting dark." Scientists later clarified that it was a poetic translation of its last data, but the sentiment was so moving that it went viral worldwide.

Chapter 30

What's Next?

If you've made it this far, congratulations! You've just raced through a few centuries of American chaos, brilliance, blunders, and breakthroughs. From colonists arguing over tea, to presidents, legislatures, and courts wrestling with power, to inventors and dreamers who managed to bend reality into something new, America's story has all the components of real life: adventure, daring, comedy, heartbreak, tragedy and accomplishment.

The "American experiment" was never about reaching a clean conclusion wrapped with a bow and a Hallmark card. It was about asking questions nobody else thought to ask: Can ordinary people govern themselves? Can a nation remain intact while endlessly reinventing itself? Can you invent jazz, cheeseburgers, and the internet in the same country and maintain sanity?

The answer so far has been a messy, but resounding "yes." Of course, there's plenty of fine print. Every era brought new challenges and contradictions. Yet, Americans continue to plow forward in search of the next chapter. The American experiment has always been characterized by a restless curiosity and a stubborn belief that tomorrow can always be better than today.

And the story isn't finished. New chapters are being written every day in labs, classrooms, businesses, ballot boxes, and maybe even on Mars. The American spirit is still what it has always been: bold, noisy, flawed, creative, determined, and surprisingly good at pulling rabbits out of hats when it matters most.

Where does it go next? Of course, we'll always continue the great experiment right here on Terra Firma. But our future is also called outward into the stars, and with America's entrepreneurial drive and "nothing is impossible" spirit, it's a reality not too distant in our future.

The truth is, American history isn't finished. It's a living, ongoing experiment. And you're part of it. Don't worry, you can do it. You just survived centuries of American history.

Now get out there and continue pushing forward into the great American experiment!

About the Author

Tom has published about 10 books and a couple of thousand articles over the past decade or so while working as a magazine editor. He's the creator of Practical Guides—fun and lighter-side approaches to learning new things.

He finished college and his Master's of Business Administration degree about a hundred years ago. Before shifting gears and wading into the writing business, he spent a couple of decades in high-tech corporate marketing. Then he opened a restaurant, which was a really bad idea. He doesn't recommend it to anyone.

Tom is a voracious reader, having melted three Kindles so far, topically alternating between history, humor and well-written crime and suspense novels. Yeah, they're a great way to unwind.

You can find the latest at his website, and there's always a free eBook there for the taking, along with social media links if you'd like to connect.

tom-mchale.com

Also by Tom McHale

The Practical Guide to the United States Constitution

The Practical Guide to Becoming the Least Boring Person in the Room

The Practical Guide to Concealed Carry

The Practical Guide to Guns and Shooting, Handgun Edition

The Practical Guide to Reloading Ammunition

The Practical Guide to Gun Holsters for Concealed Carry

www.ingramcontent.com/pod-product-compliance
Lightning Source LLC
Chambersburg PA
CBHW060052150626
46556CB00017BA/35